MAKING IT IN HIGH HEELS 4:
WOMEN OF PHILANTHROPY AND CHARITY

Cover design: Lara Vanderheide
Interior design: Lara Vanderheide
Editor: Nicolette Hernandez

Distribution:
NewLeaf Distribution
401 Thorton Rd.
Lithia Springs, GA 30122-1557

ISBN: 9781927005439

Printed and bound in The United States of America

TABLE OF CONTENTS

Alicia Pereira, *Finding My Perfect Fit*   6
Caroline Jones, *The Heart is Smart*   12
Chilina Kennedy, *Finding Light in a Dark World*   20
Erika Eleniak, *Cum Veritas Libertas, The Truth Will Set You Free*   28
Hailey Briggs, *Being the Change I Wish to See in the World*   36
Heather Senst, *Not Feeling Successful? That's Your Problem*   45
Julia Mogus, *No Bounds*   55
Kathy Bazinet, *Paying It Forward*   64
Kimberly Underwood, *Change Up!*   72
Nara Abrams, *Imagine a Cure: a Lasting Legacy*   77
Brenda Richard, *My Passion to Succeed...From Dust to Diamonds*   83
Rachel Moore, *LOVE to LIVE*   92
Charmaine Edwards, *Stumbling upon S.W.A.G*   101
Claire Kerr-Zlobin, *Navigating the Void That Leads to an Authentic Life*   109
Denise Garrido, *An Indomitable Spirit*   118
Fabiana Bacchini, *Changing the world: It starts with me*   128
Kate Steen, *Be the Change*   139
Leigh Naturkach, *How Feminism Changed My Life*   162
Kristina Evanov, *Beauty For Ashes*   174
Megan Shaw, *Mind Over Matter: #mindoveralz*   189
Meghan Sherwin, *Creating Safer Streets for Our Children*   195
Melanie McGregor, *Every Experience is a New Opportunity*   201
Shaunessy Sinnett   214
Natasha Hope Morano, *The Girl who didn't wear High Heels*   224

Alicia Pereira
Finding My Perfect Fit

I think from a young age, I've always been searching for my perfect fit. I grew up the youngest kid of an entrepreneur and banking industry professional, whose greatest achievement as first generation immigrants, were their 3 kids.

Aaron: a handsome guy's guy, who we all knew would achieve greatness as we got older. He's now a doctor.

Andrea: a gorgeous brainiac, who from a young age showed how smart and talented she was with finances, numbers and planning, it's no wonder she is as successful as she is today.

And then, there's me, Alicia.

I was always the loudmouth of the group. Taking up everyone's sharing time at the dinner table, and *always* getting in trouble for being up to no good.

For as long as I can remember, I excelled at the social game, but not necessarily the game that everyone else was playing. While my brother and sister were studying, I would find creative new ways of making "cheat notes" appear on pens, jeans, hands and even calculators...it was dedication and quickly became exhausting.

The amount of time I focused on not studying was time I'm sure I could have spent on actually studying and achieving the same mark. I remember before my high school geography exam, I slept with my textbook under my pillow in hopes I would dream through each page in the textbook and memorize all of its content.

That was by far the worst exam of my life. I remember at one point I resorted to drawing funny pictures besides the blank answers, because I figured maybe my professor would give me marks for making her laugh. Turned out not to be the case. I passed the course, by the skin of my nose.

One evening at the dinner table, my parents were talking about college and university. Back then *(and it wasn't too long ago)* there was kind of stigma that only smart people went to university and "less dedicated" people went to college. My parents had mentioned that they were so excited for their kids to all have something they could only dream of at our ages, further education.

They went down the line talking about how important school was and trying our best. When they got to me, I remember them saying, "Now remember Alicia, just because your brother and sister are going to university doesn't mean that you have to. College is not a bad thing. University just *isn't* for everyone."

My parents are super loving and have always supported all of their kids, while amazingly treating us equally. So it's not like I lived with the parents from Matilda or the aunt and uncle from Harry Potter!

But my parents were totally right. I remember understanding exactly what they meant at the time. School just wasn't what I excelled at. I was more a sports and hands-on learning type-of-gal.

One thing that I excelled at in school was English, specifically writing. I loved writing! I could be transformed into my own reality and make myself the hero, villain or even the athlete who scores the winning goal of the championship game. Being able to create a powerful story with my mind or tell someone's story through my interpretation, always made me feel like a puppet-master. I always loved when people would read my writing and tell me how they interpreted it. I wasn't just good at it...I was great.

During high school was when I started figuring out what I wanted to do in life. Or so I thought. A few years ago I read an astonishing fact that said my generation *(which is only about 10 years older than your generation)* would change careers a minimum of three times. Three times! My mom has happily worked at the same company for more than 30 years. So how the heck can I change not just jobs, but careers three times?! *Fun fact: I'm 27 and currently on my second career.*

Writing came pretty natural to me, so I started to look into places that would help me foster that talent. I found Journalism. I began writing for my local community magazine, *The Canorient Contact* and quickly became the youngest Editor they ever had. At just 16-years-old, I was editing (with the help of an amazing team) a magazine that was seen by hundreds of people. It was a great way for me to foster my talent and help me build on my passion for all things writing.

I remember thinking about telling my parents what I wanted to do, and internally questioning that maybe they would want me to do something else. I wasn't sure that my South Asian parents would approve of a job that for the most part, didn't come with health benefits and unless I started off as an anchor, even Anderson Cooper didn't start off as an anchor – it didn't pay the best.

I painted a picture in my head, my mom would cry (because she always does) and my dad would tell me that although they would support whatever I wanted to do, he didn't come to Canada to provide a world full of endless opportunity for his kids, just to have his "carefree" daughter become a Journalist.

I'm so glad looking back that I have an open relationship with my parents. I am honest with them and they are just as honest with me. So when I told them about wanting to be a Journalist they literally said, "You'd be great, so what's your next step?"

Looking back, I wasn't surprised, but I am glad I went to them for support.

It always feels better when you have the support of people who love you. And if you are reading this and you don't, there are a lot of places that you can find it. Remember it takes courage to follow your dreams. People who don't follow what they set out to do generally are too afraid of failing. What you have to remember is that everyone who is successful has essentially failed dozens of times. The more successful they are, likely means the more failure they've been through. I was lucky to have an amazing support system with family, friends, and mentors in the writing community that I could rely on for honest feedback. Look for those people and reach out to them. I have loads of students that contact me all the time for feedback, advice and help; and I am always happy to help.

Remember I mentioned that I am now on my second career? Well Journalism didn't work out the way I wanted. It wasn't that it was too hard, and it wasn't that it was too easy. It's just that it wasn't for me. Those are things that you will find out along the way. Who knows, maybe I will go back to the wonderful world of news, but right now I am enjoying what I am doing.

That's the purpose of life: to live each day, having more fun than the day before. Trust me, whenever one door closes, another two swing open so hard that it draws you into a whole new world, and you can't remember anything before it.

Currently, I work in Communications for a charity close to my heart, World Vision. I am able to travel the world bringing stories from underprivileged communities to Canadians. I love helping others. You grow a lot and find out who you are through meeting and interacting with people that you've never met before. There is a sense of unparalleled gratitude you get from talking to a mother about her hopes and dreams for her child. It reminded me of my mother who grew up living in poverty, my grandmother hoped for a better future for her kids, and my mom is amazing. So if I could help even one child grow up to be the type of mom mine is, then I've made the world a better place.

It is also important to give back to those who are not as fortunate. Remember that as you grow into successful adults. One of the things I am fortunate enough to do is speak to students about new media, social media, public relations, charities and how they all interact with each other in today's modern, fast-paced world. Recently, I was a guest speaker at a University PR class and I was asked by one of the students *if I could talk to my 15-year-old self, what would I say?*

I had to think about it. You see, I wouldn't tell myself to do things differently, because everything - every heartache, every fight, every failed test, every feeling of insecurity - I felt back then has led me to right now, and let me tell you, right now kicks ass! Life is beautiful; we are living in a world full of opportunity. But, I know sometimes in high school I doubted that I would find a career and a purpose in life greater than me.

I started telling the students that I would tell myself to keep doing what I was doing. I would tell myself to keep being me. Here's what I would tell my 15-year-old self:

Dear High School Self,

I'm proud of the person you are right now. What you are doing is important, school, sports, friends, family ... they are all key to your future. I want to tell you a few things from the future. You need to get out of the box and be open to exploring life and the world. It's very important – seeing how others live their life and appreciate what they have will make you a better daughter, sister, friend, cousin and in ten short years...even a wife. The luckiest one in the world!

Make sure to look out for others and follow your gut. When you think you don't fit in, remember how loved you are by so many people. When people tell you not to jump at new opportunities, just do it. You are an explorer by nature; so don't let anyone hold you back.
I'm not going to tell you too much, because you have a fun life and are about to embark on the most important years.
Don't waste your time on getting caught up in the everyday drama of high school where everything seems like it's the end of the world. Because it's not, the world is a lot bigger and you will soon find your footing.
Stay on track with school, it's important; no one can take away your education. If you find others that don't fit in and others make fun of or criticize, comfort them and stick up for them. It may not be the cool thing to do, but as a leader, others will follow you – make sure to tell them that it gets better.
Finally, if you can, write a book about vampires, werewolves or hobbits, it totally becomes a faze in Hollywood.
Live life and have fun – your life only gets better, you volunteer overseas in university and it changes your life completely. You are able to see how people live thousands of miles away from you. It lights up something in you and starts you off on a new career path, one that you never saw coming.

Above all, you meet the man of your dreams and get married in your mid-20s. You haven't met him yet, so have fun and don't waste your time. Love is such a treasure, and marriage really is the best! It's the greatest feeling to see yourself through the eyes of a person that adores everything about you. Treat it with care, be open to it and be sure to love loud & proud ☺

I hope you find the beauty in life and in others. Peace, happiness and always make room to follow your dreams!

Cheers,
Alicia

CAROLINE JONES
SINGER, SONGWRITER & FOUNDER OF THE HEART IS SMART INITIATIVE
THE HEART IS SMART

Children embody creativity that defines human nature. A child's imagination is full of wonder. As a little girl, I spent hours drawing pictures, painting with watercolors, and writing stories, plays and poems. When I began singing lessons at the age of nine, I immediately recognized music as the alchemist for all the creative mediums I loved: words, colors, textures, and emotions. Lyrics and melodies began to take the shape of songs soon after. I recall feeling the same passion and creative inspiration that fuels me now it did as a little girl: indescribable excitement and awe for the ideas that arose from my imagination. As a child, I never thought to second-guess or criticize my ideas. My fearlessness as a child didn't block any inspirations that came to mind. And without having the self-consciousness of an adult, it allowed my ideas to flow freely. Children possess innate *courage*, a word that stems from the Latin root *cor*, meaning heart.

Uplifting, inspiring, and providing a medium of expression through music is my passion and life's purpose. I founded The Heart is Smart Initiative (which is a nationwide school tour), its music curriculum and the movement of young dreamers within. I have built my career as a singer/songwriter touring hundreds of schools across the country – elementary through colleges, public and private – performing my acoustic, storytelling-based show, and conducting master classes in vocal performance, songwriting, and modern entrepreneurship.

Music serves as my portal to wholehearted, joyful living, compounded through service to others. The Heart is Smart program developed from my desire to connect and give voice to young people who shared my vision for a more inspired, self-empowered, and creative generation. As The Heart is Smart movement expands, I frequently find myself in a leadership role to many young men and women full of questions: How do I write songs? How can I begin building a career based on my own vision? How do I find the courage to follow *my* dream instead of succumbing to the expectations of others? How do I express my emotions intelligently, creatively, and constructively? I am continually amazed at the number of young, eager hearts that are opened and impassioned through music on The Heart is Smart Tour. In a recent e-mail following a performance, Cashay, a high school senior at Golden Arts & College Prep Academy in Columbus Ohio, wrote,

The words of your songs and advice [on happiness] really resonated with me. This morning, I was feeling really down and insecure about myself, and after I [left] your concert, I felt so comfortable with myself and back to normal, loving my impurities and imperfections again. Your songs are very inspiring, and I'm glad you're [touring] schools, trying to make an impact on kids. You inspire me and make me feel like my voice can be heard. It makes me really want to take charge and strive to inspire others as you have inspired me.

The cornerstone of my intimate, acoustic performance is authentic storytelling – evocation of pure and deep feeling across the spectrum of emotions. Great art, particularly music, gives voice to our within, which is sacred and universal. Great art resonates and touches the human heart, and for this reason human collectives have composed, played, listened to and gravitated towards music since time immemorial. In the mystical ancient art of alchemy, base metals transform into gold. Similarly, music softens the base metals of isolation and fear, uncovering the golden potential for good in the human heart.

The invitation "let's play" sums up my intention each time I step onstage. Every heart beating in the audience desires to feel connected, and to resonate with who they really are through music. This unity represents the highest purpose of music, one that I approach with humility and gratitude. At its best, the concert experience is a transformational one, one in which both the audience members and the performer leave with a sense of passion, peace, and lightheartedness.

I have thought a great deal about the art of performance as an act of service. I have spent much of my life studying gifted performers who create through song an environment of great love and harmony (no pun intended). I have observed that great performers practice the ability to serve as a vessel for the kind of authenticity and evocation of emotion that compels the audience to listen, feel and connect. To bring play – childlike passion and wonder – into a performance is an art born from experience, self-awareness and mastery of craft. To perform without interference of negative emotion requires a strong foundation of technique, a depth of professionalism acquired through experience and a strong trust in oneself, *regardless of an audience's reaction*. In his book, *Free Play,* Stephen Nachmanovitch references the German term *funktionslust,* "the pleasure of doing."

A performer must couple the joy of expression with a sincere intention to uplift and inspire the audience. This level of pure expression requires a certain level of detachment tempered by razor-sharp perception of the audience's state. The audience gives the *gift,* the *privilege,* the *honor* of their attention to the performer. This pact carries enormous responsibility and potential for transformation.

To hold the sacred offering of the conscious attention of others *without allowing it to obstruct the purity of expression in performance* is the measure of greatness. Only the best performers master this art. I seek to accomplish this balance between total awareness of the audience's level of engagement and complete surrender to the music. If the performer has too keen an awareness of the audience's perception of her or her performance then she is following, not leading, and reacting, not inspiring. The art of performance is a *very* fine balance.

"Spirit of the Earth," one of the original songs in my show, pays homage to the generation of students who will create the new world. The first verse states:

> We will raise our voice as one
> At the setting of the sun
> We will dance until the dawn
> Tell the story how we want

I share with the students that if music changed my world, it can change the worlds of others. As a unified collective, our beliefs and actions are extremely powerful and hold enormous potential for good. After I performed "Spirit of the Earth" at Plank Junior High in Oswego, Illinois, a sixth grade boy shared, "I don't know about the whole world, but you sure changed Plank's world today."

The hallmark of my radio show, Art & Soul, is collaboration and storytelling. The show, which airs on Sirius XM's *The Coffee House*, delves inside the **art** of songwriting to the **soul** of the song, hence the name Art & Soul. Sirius XM serves as a platform on which to share my musical values: each show features a guest singer/songwriter with whom I swap stories and songs in the spirit of a Nashville guitar pull or songwriter's round. The guest and I share the stories behind our songs, duet on each other's songs and discuss the messages and intentions behind our artistry. The spirit of collaboration that fuels Art & Soul, in turn inspired The Heart is Smart Project.

The Heart is Smart Project, my newest venture, is a college tour and collaborative album featuring student arrangers, composers, instrumentalists, singers, and recording engineers at music colleges and conservatories nationwide. At each stop on The Heart is Smart College Tour, I stage recording sessions of my songs with student choirs, string sections, orchestras, jazz ensembles, rock bands – you name it.

The Heart is Smart Project provides college students the opportunity

1. To connect, collaborate and record my music with me
2. To attain professional credit
3. To experience a recording environment
4. To take part in the grassroots movement of young talent who will one day lead the new music industry

I will coalesce the recordings we capture on tour into an album whose sales will benefit each school's music scholarship programs, as well as the student arrangers. The most exciting part is that the album is entirely *student driven*: arranged, performed, recorded and produced by super talented and passionate college students who seek to build a career in music.

I believe that in the future, education will focus on nurturing the inherent creativity of children. I believe that education will emphasize each heart's uniqueness, goodness, and gifts. The human ability to focus through thought and cultivate awareness of emotion distinguishes us from all other earthly creatures. Each person has the potential for and ability to tap into the infinite stream of ideas that have inspired and guided humans for millennia. It is my sincerest intention to foster this within each of the students I encounter.

However, as Stephen Nachmanovitch writes in *Free Play*, many people have conditioned emotional habits that prevent access to the wellspring of inspiration available. The Inner Obstacles, as Nachmanovitch refers to them, consist of self-doubt, fear of rejection, dependence on rules, impatience and "rigid expectations." He expands,

"What we have to express is already with us, *is* us, so the work of creativity is not a matter of making the material come, but of unblocking the obstacles to its natural flow."

The creative "material" that Nachmanovitch refers to originates from reflection and receptivity rather than force. The spectrum of emotions experienced over the course of one's life provides endless potential for inspiration and creative expression. Life's twists and turns result in learned lessons, help us to understand more deeply, and create anew. These "essential accidents," add richness and depth to the palette of feelings a performer can paint with (Nachmanovitch, 89). Obstacles also contribute to personal and artistic growth provided that a foundation has been laid of "faith in the rightness of our aim...in the integrity and mystery of our own evolution." (149)

I know firsthand the potential for growth and fruition hiding in life's challenges. For a few of my teenage years, my natural creative wonder was obscured by insecurity and perfectionism. I allowed the opinions and expectations of others to guide my choices, rather than listening to the inner voice that had guided me towards inspiration and creative fulfillment since childhood. I believed that if I lived up to the model of perfection defined by others, I would win approval and attain happiness. I checked all the boxes in the traditional definition of success, but in doing so, I lost my connection to my heart. The well of inspiration that had manifested in my songs, stories, poems and plays seemed to have dried up. In his masterpiece *The Alchemist,* Paulo Coehlo writes, "Don't give into your fears. If you do, you won't be able to talk to your heart."

Negative emotion manifests to alert, "This is not the path to happiness." Fear and insecurity obscure our true goodness. Each of us comes into this world with a gift and purpose, a means of contribution, creation and service. Our emotions let us know how aligned we are with this destiny. I did not fully understand the language of emotion during my teenage years, but I *did* know that I had a creative gift. I felt that I had something to give, but I feared that if I trusted my heart, it would lead me away from fulfilling the expectations of others. Eventually, though, its call became stronger than my fear. I got tired of feeling numb and fake. I got tired of feeling rigid and tense. Author Anais Nin wrote, "The day came when the risk to remain tight in a bud was more painful than the risk it took to blossom."

The time comes when you prioritize your connection to your heart over winning the elusive approval of others. The time comes when you would rather be happy than perfect. The time comes when *you* define success for *you*. Every great man and woman has learned and practiced this lesson. Every great genius, sage, and artist has been a trailblazer, an innovator, a brazen dreamer. In 1997, Apple Inc. released a commercial featuring the slogan "Think Different":

Here's to the crazy ones. The rebels. The troublemakers. The ones who see things differently. They invent. They imagine. They heal. They explore. They create. They inspire. They push the human race forward. Maybe they have to be crazy. How else can you stare at an empty canvas and see a work of art? Or sit in silence and hear a song that's never been written? The people who are crazy enough to think they can change the world, are the ones who do.

As an up and coming artist in this day and age, I am freer than ever before -- freer in terms of the musical tools available to me as well as in terms of the sharing and distributing the music I make. Advancement of technology in the past twenty years has diminished the power of the gatekeepers in music. Each person now has the freedom to decide to listen to any song, any time, anywhere. The tastemakers are no longer men in business suits, but young hearts eager for a feeling found in song.

It is beautiful to me that so much richness and diversity of genres, instruments, styles and people around the world are inspired and uplifted by the making of and listening to music. The floodgates have burst *wide* open, and many people in the music business are panicking. This climate of fear and greed stifles creativity. I, for one, am rejoicing. To remain an artist of integrity, purpose and conviction, while remaining open to inspiration amidst this multiplicity and variety is the new-age challenge/opportunity. It's one that I think will be the new criteria for artists in the future.

The fine balance that I always trust my gut, heart, or inner voice to guide me towards is to make music with *soul* first and foremost. I know that people are as hungry as ever to be uplifted, inspired, and *compelled by feeling* to listen. I know this because *I am*. This *connection* is the market – not money, not sales, but shared values rooted in the emotion of music, from which true influence stems. I am so grateful to my musical heroes – Willie Nelson, Jewel, Mahalia Jackson, Dolly Parton, Jason Mraz, Robert Johnson, Zac Brown – for paving a path of artistic integrity that I may continue to pave.

As a young person who is blessed to be living her dream, I will share that achieving your dreams requires that you first be happy and authentic where you are. "There is no way to happiness," wrote Buddhist monk, teacher and author, Thich Nhat Hanh. "Happiness is the way."

Learn the language of emotion that your heart speaks. Commit to the practice of lining up your emotions, thoughts and beliefs, with your vision for who you want to be and what you seek to create. Greatness begins with the groundwork. Action and opportunity will follow. The path will become obvious to you. Like love at first sight, you'll know it when you see it. You'll know it when you feel it. Practice new beliefs. There is a call in my heart that will make itself known to me. There is greatness in my heart waiting to be unlocked.

You will come to know your limiting beliefs by how they feel: negative, anxious, painful, sad, and dark. Once you begin listening to your heart, your limiting beliefs become more obvious to you. The heart has an intelligence of its own, separate from the intelligence of the mind. The heart cannot reason, memorize facts or solve math problems. The realm of the heart is *feeling*. Emotion is the language of the heart, as are colors and brushes to a painter. Through the language of emotion, your heart guides you to make the best choices. The language is simple: negative emotions arise when you are temporarily disconnected from your heart. Happiness is a simple result to the connection to your heart.

An important acknowledgement: happiness is *not* selfish. It is your birthright. It is the basis of true love and compassion. The happier you are, the more you will feel inspired to reach out with true kindness to others. Embody authenticity and you will inspire others to do the same. You cannot help but uplift and serve others when you embody happiness.

Albert Einstein wrote, "The most important decision we make is whether we believe we live in a friendly or a hostile universe."

That fundamental belief will continue to be evident to you. You create your life based on your beliefs. "What you are comes to you," wrote American transcendentalist philosopher Ralph Waldo Emerson.

Practice the beliefs that you want to perpetuate. Practice beliefs that align with the truth of your heart: inspire passion, enthusiasm, kindness and creativity. Pretty soon, you will see the contrasting negative emotions as helpful tools instead of personal flaws.

It means the world to me that music can inspire the heart of another, as it inspires, impassions and enlivens mine. I live to follow my musical passion. It touches and amazes me that in doing so, I may inspire and serve others. In his book *The Golden Compass*, Philip Pullman writes that life's highest purpose is *connection*. Each person represents an amalgam of stories and dreams shaped and colored by life experience. I will close here with a lyric from my song "Sooner or Later":

Tonight we dance on the wings of tomorrow
Tonight elation is stronger than sorrow
Sleep, sleep, my darling,
When you awaken
Clear is your conscience
Day will be breaking
Your heart is stained glass
Painted by the past
But the future's so bright.

Chilina Kennedy
Finding Light in a Dark World

When I was a little girl I wanted two things – to perform as much as I could, and to help animals in need. I am now 36 years old and I have been a professional singer, actor and dancer for over 16 years. I've toured the United States, starred on Broadway, and recorded albums. Performing has been my career and I've been passionately devoted to it since I was a child. I have "made it in high heels" and have been extremely fortunate to be able to say that I have achieved many of my dreams. However, despite the success I've had, my desire to give back has always been present, especially to the most vulnerable beings on our planet.

I am the only child of a retired Brigadier General in the Canadian military and a feminist, ex-hippie mom. We moved around constantly when I was growing up – including several Canadian cities, the UK and Australia. Moving around in this way exposed me to many experiences and allowed me to become immersed in other cultures learning native languages, ways of life, and different customs.

My parents made sure I travelled while we lived abroad and I had the opportunity to see parts of Asia, the Middle East, Europe and the Pacific Islands all before the age of 18. I saw the world as it was, not just as it seemed to appear from the windows of expensive hotel rooms or military bases. I was exposed to some of the worst poverty in the world and terrible abuse toward human beings and animals. This exposure was instrumental in my lifelong desire to become an activist.

But before I launch into my early activist years, I must first share how I followed my creative path as a performer. When I was a baby, my parents would put headphones on me and play all sorts of music from Beethoven to Woodstock. My mother claims that when she was pregnant with me and she played her guitar, I would move to rest my back against the guitar's vibrations. Clearly, performing was in my future, but I didn't find my desire to act until I was a teenager.

My high school was holding auditions for *Anne of Green Gables*. I was in grade 10 and very excited to be considered for a chorus part, so you can imagine my shock and joy when they decided to cast me as Anne, herself. This role started a massive momentum towards a performing arts career that would eventually take me across North America and to Broadway.

As fate would have it, my career had come full circle when I was offered the part of Anne in *Anne of Green Gables* at the Charlottetown Festival, right after graduation. I was over-the-moon with excitement because this had been a dream of mine, since I did the production of Anne in high school. I had put it on my list of lifetime professional goals. I had taken a trip to Prince Edward Island with my father and my best friend to watch one of my favorite actresses play Anne. As I was watching from the audience, I knew right then and there, I just had to play Anne.

My dream finally came true. I was going to be playing Anne herself where the show had originated, run for 35 years, and on the island where Lucy Maud had called her home! Amidst all the attention and the excitement, (seeing a larger than life-size picture of myself as Anne on the side of the Confederation Centre that everyone in Charlottetown could see), I nearly lost myself in the ego of it all.

Until I suddenly woke up one morning feeling a little full of myself, but empty in a way I couldn't explain. I was missing something very important in my life and I felt a desire to do something different than what I was doing at work. I needed to shift the focus away from myself and onto something or someone else. That is when I discovered the PEI Humane Society.

One morning I drove out to the shelter, which is beside a beautiful, picturesque pasture filled with cows. I filled out some paperwork and began volunteering every week as a "dog walker". I did far more than walk and play with dogs. I bathed kittens overrun with fleas. I washed dishes. I cuddled with newborn puppies and comforted distraught dogs taken in from bad homes and careless caretakers. I hadn't quite understood the impact this volunteering would have on me, or the lesson I would learn from it, until one day when I was changing the paper on the kennel floor of a new arrival. I laughed out loud and tears came to my eyes when I saw the face staring back at me from the urine stained newspaper. It was myself as Anne. No other lesson could have given me the gift of humility quite like that one, especially when I needed it most. And no other work has been as fulfilling to me as anonymously helping other beings, without any attachment to personal gain.

Throughout my formative years and young adulthood, though I was deeply committed to my passion for the arts, I never lost my desire to be an activist. Sometimes it got put on the backburner, but it always resurfaced again.

I remember the first letter I wrote to the newspaper. I was nine years old and enraged with smokers who littered the streets with their cigarette butts, so I wrote to the paper and told them about it. I asked the polluters to clean up their act and truly believed they would listen to a nine-year-old. At that age, I had a deep respect for the environment, even though it was the eighties and no one had really heard of "environmentalism" yet.

I also felt very passionate about world peace and wrote secret prayers that I buried in the ground, hoping that somehow this would have a lasting positive effect on major issues such as global hunger or the problems in the Middle East.

It was again around the age of nine that I first saw images of laboratory rats and rabbits that had been hideously disfigured and tortured for the purposes of testing human products. I had heard about something called vivisection at school and did research to find out more about it. I came across television documentaries, books and articles that gave me plenty of information on the animal cruelty that goes on in laboratories for medical and cosmetic testing.

I saw guinea pigs with holes burned through them, where you could see their intestines - they were still alive and sitting in cages. I learned that not only small animals and rodents were being used for these purposes, I read in a newspaper that thousands of dogs were being killed every year for the purposes of testing toothpaste. Vivisection and animal testing is something I have never been able to come to terms with and it upset me tremendously as a child, especially because we were being taught that it's okay to use animals in this way if it benefits the human race.

I was passionate about a wide variety of issues and as I got older. They became more and more numerous, and I became more and more heated about them.

During my travels, I saw first-hand what poverty in East Asia looked like and the human and animal rights abuse that happened regularly. My family was not prepared for what we'd see as we travelled from Bangkok to Phuket to Hong Kong. I saw children begging on the streets of Bangkok, who did not have any limbs to feed themselves or the will to do more than simply stare at us. My mother was warned to take off the rings on her fingers, as they could potentially be cut-off by street thieves. The people we saw were desperate, and their living conditions were abysmal – communities beside highways made out of tin and cardboard. I started to put together the complex circumstances that drive human beings to abuse other human beings and animals – they are most often desperate and lost in a vicious cycle of fear, violence and poverty. I began to develop much more compassion for people and not just for animals. I realized that to heal our planet, we must have compassion for every life and every species.

On my trip to Thailand, I saw a chained elephant standing alone on a concrete pad all day long. Elephants are particularly intelligent, highly-socialized beings with incredible memories. This elephant was by himself, taken from his family and forced to stand there hour after hour on display as if he were an inanimate object, all for the amusement of tourists. My heart ached for this poor, depressed creature and I wondered how anyone could possibly walk by him without taking some action to ease his pain, especially since elephants are so highly regarded and prized in many parts of the world. In that moment, I was embarrassed to be a rich tourist and ashamed of my ignorant and unfeeling human race. I could not believe that people could be so careless and apathetic. The images and experiences I had in Thailand and around the world affected me greatly. I wish that all people could see these things firsthand so they might be moved to action.

Unfortunately, as noble as my intentions were from childhood to my teenage years, I never felt I made more than a small ripple in the ocean of change that is needed to make the world a kinder place. I had too many passions, too many causes. My energy was too spread out. Once I was back in my North American comfort zone, back in the safety of my own small community, my memory of the elephant, the maimed children, and the lab rats became dulled and distant. Once I was back on stage, I realized that I loved my performing life too much to give it up in order to pursue activism full-time. I ended up feeling defeated and depressed. It was easy to believe that it is impossible for one person to make a difference. This was my mistake.

I have a not-so-secret secret: every little bit makes a difference. Truly. No matter how small an act, it is always worth doing. I wish I had known this when I was younger - I might have made more of an effort, no matter how insignificant it may have seemed to me at the time. Luckily, I learned that lesson by watching others and becoming inspired by their actions. As I got past my teenage years, I became less concerned with my arrogant desire to change the world or fix it. Instead, I started doing what I could when I could find time to do it. I became much more humble about my responsibility toward others and realized that if I truly want to "change" the world, I must start with myself.

My early 20s was spent on tour with the hit musical *Mamma Mia!* For two and a half years, I traveled across the US, to every major city except New York. We stopped in many places twice, including L.A., San Francisco and Boston. I was making more money than I knew what to do with for someone so young and with so little professional experience.

By this time in my life I was heavily involved in environmental, political, and health issues. I was learning about the horrors of factory farming, and so I started contributing to a *Mamma Mia!* company weekly newsletter, urging people to make more responsible choices. I was very disheartened by the lack of recycling happening in the US at that time. None of the theatres recycled and neither did our company housing. So I decided to set up a recycling system at the theatres as well as a drop-off program for the actors. Once a week, company members could bring their bagged recyclables to the theatre and I would take care of it. Each day off, the musical director (who was also a passionate environmentalist) and I would drag huge bags of recycling on the subway to a recycling depot. We would drop it off and then go for breakfast together. This was an arduous task and sometimes really gross, but I just couldn't live with myself if I didn't do something about the needless waste going on right under my nose – in my workplace and in our homes.

I also took over a Broadway musical tradition called "Lotto Blotto". Lotto Blotto is a weekly 50/50 raffle and the proceeds go to charity. Sounds simple and easy, but I was shocked at how much money we raised. I was always surprised by the generosity of our cast and crew, especially when, every week, not a single winner of the draw ever took home his or her half of the money, but donated it back to whatever cause we were donating. I, of course, had the privilege of choosing the charities to which we were donating and this is where my wide variety of passionate causes finally proved useful. We donated to homeless shelters, women's groups, schools (funds directed to underprivileged children), and animal shelters. We got to know how we could make a difference to the lives of the people and animals that inhabited the cities in which we were performing. And it felt great to be doing it. Instead of coming into town and just doing our show, we were actually making a difference and giving back to our communities.

Over the course of my life so far, I have learned that the most vulnerable beings on our planet are the ones that have very few laws that protect them. Their value is determined by what they can offer us in the way of financial gain, with very little value being placed on them simply existing and contributing to the balance of life on our planet. These vulnerable beings include children, animals, the elderly, and single mothers. I made this conclusion by carefully observing where most abuses occur and to whom. I believe we can judge a society by the way we treat our most vulnerable members and when I learned how much suffering occurs every day, in our country alone, I began to understand my own human race in a very different way. I began using the term "human-centric", meaning that human beings tend to place their own interests above all else and human life above all other living beings.

One example of "human-centricism" is the way we treat animals in conventional factory farming practices. I was speaking to a fellow actress one day and the subject of meat came up. She said to me, "Cows were put on this earth so we could eat them," which is exactly the kind of attitude that makes me believe that we are "human-centric." This attitude makes us tolerate the deplorable conditions in which we keep animals that are destined for the dinner table. As a result of conversations like that one, I became a vegetarian for a few years and later began eating only humanely raised meat. I started researching everything to do with animal cruelty, boycotting offending companies and donating to various animal welfare charities.

I learned that pigs have the intelligence equivalent to seven-year-old child and that they are very social creatures. In factory farms they are confined in tiny metal crates for their entire lives until they are transported in harsh conditions, such as extreme heat and bitter cold, to their slaughter. We close our eyes to these atrocities because we are still under the ignorant, old-fashioned assumptions that animals do not feel, they are not intelligent, and their worth is only determined by their market price. Do they not have value just by being alive? Don't we all?

I suppose that until we begin to value our own human lives in every part of the world, it might be difficult for human beings to value other forms of life. But we can try. It is never too late to make a change or to live more compassionately. We always have hope if people care enough to change their actions. Only by changing our own patterns can we truly change the world.

Now, my writing piece is not meant to be a pat on the back to my amazing volunteering efforts. In fact, to my shame, I have always felt that I could have done so much more. This is simply an account of my personal journey with the hope that through reading it, you might feel that it is never too late or too early to start volunteering, or working for change, and that no amount of effort is too little. There is always something to be done and whether it's helping humans, animals or the environment, it's always worthwhile to make the effort, if not for the cause itself, then for the balance it will surely add to your life. And we can do this while still having our careers, realizing our dreams and making it in the most fabulous pair of high heels.

I was taught the ripple effect in high school and it has stuck with me ever since. Without trying to sound simplistic or idealistic, I truly believe that one person can and does make a difference. We have no idea how our actions will inspire others and change the world. It is arrogant of me to try to change anyone. But I believe that there are forces in the universe that we cannot possibly comprehend and they are at work every moment of every day.

The best teachers lead through example. When we spend our precious energy healing ourselves and the planet, when we act with love and compassion, and when we stop our negative patterns, we forever alter the fabric of our collective energy. My most beloved quote is one that is hanging in my favorite locally owned and fair traded coffee house in Stratford, said by Margaret Mead:

Never doubt that a small group of thoughtful, committed citizens can change the world. Indeed, it is the only thing that ever has.

Erika Eleniak
Cum Veritas Libertas
The Truth Will Set You Free

What is "The Truth?" It's taken me 45 years to find the key and unlock the Secret Door and to discover what lies on the other side... Myself. My Truth. Not the self that others labeled me as or even I thought I was- the Baywatch Girl, "That Blonde Actress", someone's girlfriend, etc.

But I found ME. The Me I was meant to be.

My name is Erika Eleniak. I am a devoted seeker of all things Spiritual. Perhaps the title "Spiritual Alchemist" fits best. I am Mother to the Light of my Life, Indyanna - I am a teacher, a writer, and an actress. I've been known as an actress the longest and have been blessed to have a 34-year career in the entertainment industry. I am beyond grateful for the incredible journey it's taken me on. It was quite the windy and rocky road.

One thing you should know about me is that I do everything backwards. I'm not the most graceful learner either, but I'm definitely a survivor. The thing is, I wasn't really alive until the birth of my daughter in 2006. So, I guess that makes me 9 years old to date.

I feel I've lived five lifetimes in my 45 years of living, so choosing 1 or 2 stories to tell you is very challenging. Especially, since I can very confidently tell you that I, (we as human beings) EVOLVE. Every event and period of time absolutely creates who we are and who we become.

I began acting when I was 10 years old. We didn't have a lot of money when I was growing up. I went to public schools in Van Nuys, California. My neighborhood was pretty tough, but I loved my childhood and my friends. We were our own special gang.

Being in the film industry, I felt like I "stuck out like a sore thumb." At times, this was really hard for me. Especially during the times I had to be walked to school because there were girls who wanted to beat me up. They called me stuck up. I didn't want to stand out. I didn't want to be different. Yet, at the same time, I knew there was something inside of me that liked doing what I was doing - that creative imagination inside of me, always wanting to play. I was afraid. If only I knew then, what I know now... So much gained through my Spiritual Discoveries.

I remember when I was twelve years old, I played a small part in the film *E.T., The Extra Terrestrial*. One day, two kids approached me and asked me for my autograph. I was *so* freaked out, I ran upstairs to our apartment and cried! I didn't want to be different!

Truth be told, I was different. And so are you. Yet, we are all the same. How does that make sense? Cut us open and were all the same on the inside, right? Yet, with over 7 billion people on this planet, there is only ONE you. There will only ever be one you. That blows my mind! Doesn't this just point to the fact that YOU, (we) are all pretty cool?!

But as a kid, (and for many years to follow) I allowed peer pressure and fear- fear of being different, fear of standing out and looking stupid, fear of failing which stopped me from taking advantage of amazing opportunities in my life (both personally and professionally). Have you ever heard the saying about fear? The one that defines it this way:

F- alse   E- xpectations   A- ppearing   R- eal.

This is so true! 99% of the time, we create our fears ourselves. We fantasize and visualize what we're afraid of over and over in our heads, rehearsing them again and again, until we've scared ourselves to death! This keeps us stuck like deer in headlights, we're so afraid to move. It's awful.

I once had the opportunity to audition with a very famous actor, reading with him for an also very famous director, but I was so scared that I said no! I had a ton of auditions for huge film projects that I didn't go on because I was so afraid of embarrassing myself and looking stupid. I let fear choose for me too often. We all feel it, but we don't have to let it rule us- we can overcome it by putting one foot in front of the other, keeping us moving forward.

But no matter what the circumstances, there was still something inside of me that never allowed me to quit. I knew I was meant to do great and cool things, to shine- I just didn't know how to identify that part of myself back then. But I do now! It's a part of ourselves that "just knows" what's right for us - the spirit within us. It's ours- our strength, our courage, and our guide. I did know that as long as I persevered, the opportunities would always come, but we do have to "suit up and show up". And being *different*? Funny, you know the old saying in fashion that "Brown is the new black?"
Well, I say, "Different is the new normal."

What is *normal* anyway? Being different is awesome. Our differences are what make us so successful! When we celebrate our uniqueness and the things about us that <u>we</u> think are cool, that attitude is not only what lights us up, but it's also contagious! It will also light up everyone around you, too.

And as far as the way we look? There are so many beautiful people in the world with gorgeous faces and bodies that are so shallow, you can see right through them! They're like a piece of cardboard with no light inside. Like me, I definitely "dulled my shine" and dimmed my light by hiding the real me. Owning the things that make us stand out- our uniqueness, sometimes takes courage to do. But when we do own that part of us, we actually blossom and become a great gift by contributing our light to this world.

Now, while I could easily go off and tell 12 more horrible stories because I let fear make most of my decisions for me, I would be focusing on the drama instead of the point: the essence of fear, is self-doubt. And when we have self-doubt and fear and allow those feelings to overrule our decisions- we lose. In my early career, I didn't necessarily have a game plan or goals I wanted to accomplish for myself. But I listened to what I was feeling in my heart "most of the time."

The times I did follow my heart, the results were incredible. Sometimes, the fear-based decisions I made were awful, but that's okay too. That's life. I've discovered that it's what we do in response to the choices we make, which matters most. I am a much more goal-oriented person today, and I feel like my goals can really help me stay on track, but they do not define me! Life likes to throw us curve balls and we need the flexibility to be able to roll with them. I know that when I ask Spirit for guidance and am still enough to listen, I'm good. You know that old saying "I'll believe it, when I see it?!" Well, I heard it said better this way, "I'll see it, when I believe it".

What kind of a life do you dream of having?

We cannot sit around and wait for our desired experiences to find us - they won't. We have to first dream them, envision them, feel them and then take action. That's it! That is how we plant the seeds of our Dreams. Then, we let go and we watch them grow...

What seeds will you plant? An inspiring and fun thing I love doing to get motivated is to create a "Dream Board." I take a poster board or even a corkboard, and go crazy with the things I love and intend for myself. I tack on photos, magazine clippings, and drawings, the sky's the limit. Hang it up with positive quotes where you can see it many times throughout your day.

There is so much focus in Hollywood on the body and for girls and women of today. This has played a huge part in our trying to achieve unrealistic and unhealthy ideals of "perfection" for ourselves. I found it exhausting and consuming, emotionally at times. I was really a "yo-yo"! I would diet, exercise, binge, and would do it over and over again. It can really rob us of our peace and joy.

I recently had my breast implants removed after having them in my body for over 22 years. The doctor said I was very fortunate because one of them was on the verge of rupturing, as there was a small leak beginning.

I was a natural size C, but at the age of 22, I was so insecure about the shape of my breasts, that I had implants put in. What a disaster. I woke up on the operating table, which was done in an office. Looking back, I realize how dangerous and crazy it was! Accidentally, a nerve was stitched and I was in excruciating pain for a very long time. I got an infection and had cysts develop around the area for years. It was a hot mess. It was so freeing to make the decision to be ME. The me I was born to be.

I take solace in knowing that we are the co-creators of our experiences in life. We get to choose. It took me a long time to realize this but today, I choose to be Free. Free to be ME.

I have freed myself from the "Hamster wheel of insanity." I've jumped off that ride. Yes, I love cheeseburgers and fries, in fact, I consider myself a "cheeseburger connoisseur." Am I a size "0"? Nope. But I'm healthy, strong and curvy. Yes, I exercise at least 3 times a week. I hike. I run. I get outside and hang out in nature. I eat healthy during the week- fruits, veggies, beans, lean meats, eggs, some whole grains, and oatmeal. And come Saturday? Look out! FREE DAY. I eat whatever I want! Balance.

I love food. I love life. We are meant to enjoy both. Yes, BOTH. And sometimes, my Saturday "free to eat what I want day" turns into Sunday, as well. It's okay! I relax because I know what I feel like when I don't choose Balance: Crap. So, I choose wisely. The key is in remembering that <u>we have the power to choose</u> *how* we want to live. How we want to feel. I am not a doctor and while I cannot give any nutritional or medical advice, I can share with you what works best for me. After all, life is delicious!! Let's eat it up, with a spoon!

My Uncle Eddie Carroll was an amazing actor. He was also the voice of Jiminy Cricket since 1973. He did a brilliant one-man-show impersonating Jack Benny, which even impressed Jack Benny's Family. His advice to me was: Take three actions DAILY toward the goal or area of interest that you want to accomplish. Period.

Everyday, create momentum in your dreams by taking three actions that will support it. Is it making a phone call or sending out an email? Or maybe do some research on the Internet or in the library? Find role models who are successful in what you love to do and research how they did it, etc. By taking any 3 actions a day, you are moving forward and you will be amazed at what starts to happen for you! Doors will open, one after another.

One action that I have taken in supporting my healthy self is stop "dumbing myself down." I did this constantly! I said what I thought other people would want to hear or expected me to say. Have you ever done this? I didn't want anyone to think I was conceited or that I thought of myself as better than anyone else, so I would find ways to put myself down.

I would make fun of myself or take a compliment someone gave me and turned it around so it wouldn't sound true. If someone said I looked nice, my reply was always, "Why I really don't!"

Or if I did a great job, I'd have to say why it wasn't so great. Argh! We don't ever have to do that! Instead, we can be proud of who we are and grateful for the talents, abilities, or beauty, we`ve been given.

GRATEFUL is the key. Don't be embarrassed by your Talents and Gifts! They are your Blessings. In fact, we are given our gifts to SHARE. We are being quite selfish by hiding them away from others. And when you're sharing, your gifts may inspire someone else. THAT`S the ticket! That's what life is all about. When we shine our light and someone else gets inspired to shine hers. It doesn't get any better than that. Can you picture a dark concert stadium? It starts with one flickering light, then another, then another, until the whole stadium is lit up. Beautiful. It starts with you. Believe it! I do with ALL my heart. I am so grateful today for all my challenges in the past and the trials I've overcome. I now know and FEEL what strength and courage I have and what I'm really made of. Also, how truly loved and supported we are. So now, I say YES to my life and this incredible journey. I feel like it's just beginning...

My Daughter, Indyanna was born 9 years ago, and she has been my truest and biggest inspiration to be all that I was created to be. I know that my purpose is to SHINE for her-so she can learn what her abilities, talents, and gifts are so she can SHINE her light. She'll shine for you. She'll shine for the Universe. This is our contribution to Spirit. Using all that we have been given to contribute something here on earth before we move on. It is so fantastic and wonderful to me that though I feel like I have lived 5 Lifetimes in my 45 years, I honestly feel like I just got here. Life is like that. Awe-inspiring, isn't it?

I love where I am today. I'm 45 and feel like every single thing, person, place and event in my life has shaped me to become who I am now. My biggest dream come true was having my daughter. Now that she's here, my purpose is to raise her to be of service - to give back to my family and friends who have ALWAYS been there for me.

I do my best to be available for every soul I meet who may possibly need my help, in some way. I say the prayer, "Thank You For Using Me Today" everyday. I also teach Unity Principles to kids on Sundays. I am a student myself at Unity Church, getting my Spiritual Enrichment Education, so that I can get my Teaching License. What's my next big dream? It's to pay what I've learned forward as a speaker. It's a lot of "Church Talk," right? But I am not religious. I just love Spirituality. I have a non- denominational and unconditional Love for the presence I believe guides and loves us unconditionally, right back.

One of the most valuable gifts I've received comes in the form of being still and listening. For me, it's a routine of waking up at 5am when my home is quiet. I settle in my big cozy chair with a blanket and my dog, Jack, at my feet. I go within and listen. It takes me a while to let the "monkey mind" or chatter in my head become still, but once I do, I'm able to connect with God- in the Field of Infinite Possibilities. It's in the quiet that I find answers I need.

We have been given a very beautiful gift and that is our own life. It's precious. It's difficult, messy, mysterious and incredibly blissful. The key to having a very joyful and purposeful life I believe, is remembering that in each moment of every new day, we get to choose. We don't always get to choose our circumstances - true. But we always get to choose whether we react or respond to them. We choose whether we let circumstances *define us* or choose to *move toward* better circumstances, one baby step at a time.

Please don't sit on the sidelines of your life! Life is not for spectators! It's for participators! So if there is something you've always wanted to learn or try (as long as it's healthy, legal and safe for you) DO IT!! If you find you don't love it - success! You can cross it off your list and add it to your repertoire of experiences to share. And if you do love it? Voila! You may just be answering a calling from your Heart. That is a whisper from Spirit. Happy Adventures.

Today, I am a huge believer in paying forward all the Blessings and good that we receive in our lives. I am currently an acting teacher at the Antonio Sabato Jr. Acting Academy to up and coming actors. I help them hone their craft, which will hopefully result in long-lasting and fulfilling careers. I also teach acting as a means of therapy to teen residents at the Evolve treatment center. I help the kids there discover creative ways to express themselves in a healthy way. We work on various exercises using improvisation, scene work, monologues, writing and even music to explore different avenues of expression. The beauty of our group sessions lies in the moments when I can see the light come in, and they have a moment where they feel proud of what they've done. Every week, I leave them with an inspirational quote that's printed on index cards. My goal is to help them feel confident in themselves and to understand how powerful their light is. This is why I believe I am here - to shine my light and help others shine theirs.

Thank you so much for letting me share my experience, Spiritual Truth and a little piece of my story with you. *May you remember who you are and how beautiful your light is, always.*

HAILEY BRIGGS

GOVERNOR GENERAL CARING CANADIAN AWARD RECIPIENT
BEING THE CHANGE I WISH TO SEE IN THE WORLD

Hi, I'm Hailey, I am 15 years old and live with my mom and sister. I'm on a competitive rock climbing team, enjoy world traveling, and am passionate about changing the world. Now that we've broken the ice, and you know a little about who I am, I'll share my story with you. A few years ago I made an ambitious decision. I stepped out of my comfort zone instead of taking the easy way out and made a difference.

I have always considered myself lucky to grow up in a family that is very open and honest with each other. I'm so close with my mom and sister that we call ourselves, *The Three Musketeers*. Growing up, we always talked about and have been aware of the issues that plague our world. For as long as I can remember, I've always understood how lucky I am to have been born in Canada. I've always known that there are other families out there who have to survive on less than a dollar a day, or that there are 58 million children who aren't able to go to school.

With this in mind, we sponsored a girl in Cameroon, Africa, sent packages to a family in Cuba, and my personal favourite, carried out spontaneous acts of kindness for friends and strangers. One of my fondest memories was when we noticed a very friendly woman at the gas station near our house. Every time we would walk in to pay, she would greet us with a big smile. She was always positive and friendly, no matter the day, so we decided that she deserved some kind of thank you. We bought her a fancy box of chocolates and attached a note to tell her how much we appreciated her kindness. When my sister and I gave it to her, she was thrilled. I loved knowing that after all the times she had put a smile on my face, I could finally return the favour. Knowing that we were doing something good for others made me feel like I was making a difference in other people's lives and encouraged me to continue. By doing all of these things, it gave me a deeper love, gratitude and appreciation for my life and gifted me with the opportunity to discover my passion for helping others.

When I was 12, my dad offered to take me to an event featuring Marc Kielburger, one of the co-founders of a charity called *Free the Children (FTC)*. FTC is a charitable organization that has the mission of breaking the cycle of poverty through education.

Me to We, an organization started alongside FTC works to inspire youth across the world to stand up and take action for what they believe. Me to We hosts annual events all over North America called, *We Day*, where a stadium full of hard working youth gather and are excited about being the change. They inspire them through public speaking, information on global issues, and a lot of fun activities.

FTC and Me to We's main goal is to inspire the new generation that they have the power and capability to change the world for the better. FTC had been a charity I had fundraised for at school, so I was familiar with the topic and interested in learning more. My dad taking me to this event ended up being one of most significant turning points in my life. My eyes were glued to Marc the entire time, listening avidly to everything he was saying. He talked about FTC's main goals, and really got into some of the deeper issues that families around the world have to experience, such as child soldiers and sweat shops. I remember towards the end looking around at all the other kids texting on their phones and thinking to myself, "There are so many things that are so much more important than the latest drama at school."

When Marc spoke of young children my age not having the opportunity to go to school, I was devastated. I have always loved school, so it seemed so unfair to me that children didn't have a choice to attend. Education determines your future! If you don't go to school, you won't get a good job, and that can mean the difference between escaping the cycle of poverty or having to sell your children into child labour. If these kids didn't have an opportunity to change their own lives, then I wanted to take advantage of being born in Canada, and use my resources to give them a chance. Another huge part of what interested me was a 12-year-old boy, the same age as me at the time, started the charity. I thought to myself, "If this kid could do something this big, why can't I?"

I was instantly drawn to what Marc had to say and knew that somehow I wanted to be a part of Free the Children's movement. So, after hearing Marc speak I wanted to learn more about the global issues and what I could do about it. Lucky for me, Me to We has a summer camp called *Take Action Academy* where you can do just that. It was a bit on the expensive side, but I begged my parents to go and even paid for some of it myself.

Finally when summer came around, I packed my bags and set off to a week that completely changed my life. Camp was everything I had hoped for and more! We really got inspired about how we could change the world through workshops, blind dinners, volunteer days, and of course a guest speaker who told us all about his tragic days of being a child soldier.

You want to know the secret to changing the world? Just do it (I promise I'm not advertising for Nike or anything). It is so easy to come up with a million excuses as to why you can't, and that's literally all that can stop you. I mean yeah, it does take a bit of effort, but is it not worth it? Of course it is!

Think about it this way, what are your goals? What is your dream job that someday you would like to pursue? There are probably a bunch of ideas popping up in your head right now of "Oh yeah, I want to be a doctor" or "One day I want to travel the world."

Now picture yourself in a different scenario, where you live in a developing country, working day and night with little food or rest. You have never gone to school, never plan to, and in terms of your hopes and dreams, you don't have any. There is a huge chance that you'll be stuck doing the same job until you pass away leaving it for your children to do. I wanted to give these children a chance to have their own dreams.

The whole week at camp, we worked hard on our action plans and what we were going to accomplish after we left. We brainstormed with each other and had amazing facilitators who helped us come up with smart and attainable goals. One thing we really focused on was a formula on how to create change. First, you take an issue or cause that you are very passionate about, combine it with your interests and what you love to do, and you are changing the world.

I chose to focus on the lack of education in the world, so I could help provide children with opportunities to change their own lives. The typical goal was to raise food items or sell bracelets for a local charity, but being the high-spirited and very ambitious child I was and still am, I decided to go bigger than that.

Coming home from camp I excitedly explained to my mother that I wanted to raise the full amount of $8,500 to build a school in Kenya. This $8,500 would be the total amount for the supplies and labour needed to build and finish a school-room in Kenya. Everyone I told about my goal was highly supportive, but by the looks on their faces, I could tell there was a bit of doubt in them, as to if I could actually pull this off. This only made me want to do it more.

I really had no big plan as to how I was going to reach my goal, in terms of knowing exactly what and when I was going to do something. But in my opinion, you don't need to have one, as long as you stay driven and come up with new ideas as you go. I started small with a garage sale, but I knew that I'd have to run A LOT of them if that's how I wanted to raise the money.

I sought out new ideas and advice from as many people I could, until finally I talked to an older girl from camp and she gave me the perfect idea. She had made a website where people could go on, read her story and donate to her project. This was the perfect thing for me because it combined a cause I felt strongly about and two of the things I loved most, reading and writing. I designed and made the website and blogged weekly about my experiences. It was a great way to get out there and receive donations from people I wouldn't have met otherwise. I also enjoyed the whole process of editing the website and finding videos to post on it.

The next step in my journey was probably the most difficult part for me and continues to challenge me to this day. I was given the opportunity to write and give a speech in front of about 60 people. To you this might not seem like a lot, but to 13- year-old me, it was one of my biggest fears. Another part of it was that I was and still am (to most people's surprise) extremely shy. So much that when I got up to speak in front of those 60 people, I completely froze and could not speak. I would open my mouth to start, staring directly down at my paper, and nothing would come out. Fortunately for me, I had a close family friend who had supported me through my goal, standing right next to me, calming me down with encouraging words. It took me a minute to start, but when I had, my passion for what I was doing shone through and took over. The group was highly supportive and all very proud of me. Afterward, I collected donations and made over $1,000! I was proud of myself!

Before the speech I had actually considered turning down the opportunity because of my discomfort. I decided to go through with it only because I told myself that no one has ever made a difference in this world without having to step out into the unknown. You think it was easy for Gandhi to lead a movement to free his country of British rule? You think Rosa Parks didn't have to step out of her comfort zone when she refused to give up her seat to a white man on the bus? These were all questions, I would ask myself when I considered backing down. This speech was the first taste I had of really being shoved out of what was comfortable for me and although it was terrifying, in a way it was also exhilarating.

I continued on my journey with the project I called *8500 for Kenya*, holding 3 more garage sales (2 of which I danced on the corner in goofy costumes waving signs), continuing my website posts, and becoming more and more confident in myself as I progressed.

Another opportunity for me to share my story through public speaking came up toward the end of my project. I was offered a large donation of $2,500 from the Wilfrid Laurier University. The only catch was that I had to give a short speech at their Annual Horn of Africa Conference. This conference was an opportunity to raise awareness for the issues occurring in Africa at that time, and that year they decided to start giving out donations annually to a cause working to solve these issues. So, as you can imagine, this was a huge honour for me. Out of all the charities out there, they chose a 13-year-old girl with a passionate heart and a huge goal.

This would only be the second time I had ever spoken in front of a crowd, and it was to a bunch of intelligent adults. As you can probably imagine, I found this quite intimidating. I was scared, but how could I turn down an opportunity like this? So, once again, I got thinking. I wrote a speech and practiced every night until I knew it like the back of my hand. I ended up doing very well, impressing the group and myself for what I accomplished.

A short time after, I finally completed my 8500 for Kenya project in only 14 months. It just happened to be a coincidence I finished my first project two days before Me to We's We Day event. After the super-inspiring day of speeches, music and receiving a personal shout out to celebrate reaching my goal, I was pumped. Even more so when I got a message from my baseball coach (who had been highly supportive with 8500 for Kenya) telling me that his 2 daughters, my good friends, wanted to get involved too and suggested we start a group.

So here I was agreeing to a second project only two days after the completion of my first. My sister joined this one, so we were a group of four girls, two of us at 14 years old and the other two, 11. We got together and decided that because of a recent drought in Africa, we wanted to raise $5,000 to build a well in Kenya. We called ourselves *The Water Warriors.*

Our first task as The Water Warriors was to make our own website where we made an educational video, posted blogs, which would generate most of our donations. We hosted a Family Movie Night event where we had food, prizes, games and of course, a hilarious cartoon movie. Everyone had a blast, us included, and the event raised just over $1,300. We finished our goal in only nine months.

The next part of my life journey was probably the experience that inspired and had the greatest impact on me. I had the amazing opportunity to travel overseas on a Me to We trip to Kenya, Africa. After I completed my 8500 for Kenya project, my mom offered to take me to Kenya to see the school that was being built and to meet the kids who would attend.

Let me just say that this country holds a very special place deep in my heart. When we were not busy at the build site making a dormitory for the high school, we were out and about learning as much about the Kenyan culture and life as we could. We went on water walks where we walked alongside the mamas carrying heavy jugs of water, visited the local market, learned about their everyday lives, and went to multiple school communities to meet and play with the children. I loved visiting the schools to meet the kids, because in some way or another everyone would break out in song and dance. Arriving at a school the kids would sing and perform for us while we were there, while we were leaving, and everything turned into the glorious smiles and voices of the Kenyan children. We would be driving through the community and children would run in from all directions yelling, "Jambo, Jambo" (hello, in Swahili). The people were always so friendly and welcoming to us, no matter where we were.

Coming home from my trip, the most common question I would be asked was, "What was your favourite part?"

This is probably similar to answering who you love more, your mom or your dad. Ok, maybe not quite, but you get what I mean. It's tough to answer. If I had to choose, it would be the people and the happiness that just radiates off of everyone I met.

We were on a walk to meet with the community men's group, when some children came running over to us. The kids each had a stick and a little plastic wheel off a wagon. They were running back and forth pushing the wheel around with the stick and just had the biggest smiles on their faces. They were having the time of their lives! That's when it hit me. I have so many luxuries, and here are these kids running around with something I would have considered junk, but were having the most fun I've ever seen.

The Kenyan people live through poverty every day, but they are the happiest people that I have ever met. They take what little they have and make the absolute most of it. The people I spent time with, the people I got to know, are not the people I would see in World Vision commercials. They are not what I would imagine people living through poverty would look like. My Kenyan friends see the beauty in every single thing that they have, and to me, that is a valuable lesson we could all learn.

Coming home from Kenya and finishing off my Water Warriors project was definitely not the end of my adventures. Stopping my fundraising was not considered an option. Following the completion of my second project, we expanded the group and started my third. We are a group of 10 youth under the age of 16 and we call ourselves, *Youth for*

Kenya. Currently, this is what I'm spending my time and efforts on, and so far it's going great!

We have a goal to raise $10,000 by the end of 2014; $2,000 of it already has gone to sponsor a girl to go to school in Kenya, and the remainder is to go towards providing health care in Kenya. So far, we have hosted one event, which raised over $2,000 in donations, and have a lot planned in the upcoming months.

Call me crazy, but as I lead this group, I also run a fundraising project at my school with 4 others to build a school in Kenya, and I also helped organize the sponsorship of a girl to attend Kisaruni, an All-Girls Secondary School in Kenya. What can I say, I'm a girl who dreams big.

Some of you might wonder where I plan to go after this and to be perfectly honest, I don't really have a clue. I have a goal to raise $50,000 by the end of 2016, and so far I've raised approximately $30,000 combining all of my projects. My other goal is to continue my public speaking, something, I have grown to not completely dislike and hope one day to become a national speaker. All of this may seem very intimidating, but trust me, before writing all of this down, I had never actually considered what I was doing to be that big of a deal.

Looking back on what I've been through, I realize just how much it has affected who I am today. Every little part of my journey that may have seemed insignificant to me at the time has molded me into the passionate person I am. These projects and experiences have helped me grow as a person, shaped my values, and most importantly given me something to fight for. I am a huge advocator of doing what makes you happy, fighting for what you believe in, and following your dreams. My story is only an example. My dream to change the world. What I'm saying does not only apply to fundraising, it applies to chasing your dreams and passions. Without love, happiness, and passion what's there to live for? It's never too late to start.

Here are some of my tips on how to achieve greatness:

- Take action for what you believe in!
- Write down your goals and what you would like to achieve and post them somewhere you'll see it every day (bedroom, bathroom mirror, etc.)
- Continue to educate yourself on your passions and interests
- Inspire yourself everyday! Go to events, read inspirational material, videos, etc.
- Surround yourself with people who are only going to lift you higher
- Excuses can be buried into the ground where they will forever be forgotten. You don't need those.
- Just do it and never give up!

When you find something you are passionate about, all that hard work is worth it.

Heather Senst
Not Feeling Successful? That's Your Problem

I had arrived from the US, married to the man of my dreams. Leaving a great career in Los Angeles for Toronto was at the time choosing personal over professional. A choice I would still make today. I didn't know a soul and had no history. Looking for a job in a city like Toronto, where everyone seemed to know each other or had gone to either Queens or Western was a bit daunting. I sat down and began to pour over the Toronto 411 and latest issues of Playback (Canada's broadcast and production journal) looking for work in Television. I would challenge myself to secure at least two meetings a week that led to at least one more.

My husband could cover the bills, but that wasn't our deal. I wanted to make it in this country and work was part of my identity. Besides I wouldn't see him anyway! He worked too hard! I worked under the table, until I could obtain working status.

Unaware as I was, but eager to work, I took a job under the table until my landed status came through a year later. I was told when searching for a job, regardless of the fact I moved from working in TV's metropolis, I needed to understand "CANCON." Well CANCON (Canadian broadcasting rules and regulations) really only took a bit of time to figure out and soon I was working my first job in television. It was intense, dominated by a talented, yet dictatorial leader whose language was as fierce as was his temper. I was intensely unhappy, but looking back I have to say I learned a lot and met some truly great people whom still worked for me 13 years later.

After about nine months into the job I was working, I landed one of the top creative jobs in broadcast media, Creative Director, and yet I still didn't feel like I had "made it." My mind still felt very much like I was fifteen and just starting to figure things out. I felt like a fraud. When will I get found out? Ironically the first two people I was to report to were said to be "difficult to work with" and yet I flourished.

Over the course of 14 years, I created a large and powerful team from scratch, won hundreds of awards AND I became a Vice President. A title that I was told by our President could never happen, the company wasn't big on expanding their roster of titles even though "creativity" was a large part of our DNA. Curiously, I was asked by Human Resources, and others why becoming a vice president was so important to me; "Titles shouldn't define who you are." Bull S@#!

Unfortunately or fortunately, it not only defines you, but increases your salary. I will say however, that you should always act "presidential." Be a leader, do things outside your job description, set and execute a vision and goals-regardless of title and then when you do get the title, you're ready and no one is surprised.

I refused to take no as an answer to my quest for my title and continued to push at every opportunity until it became a reality. I refused to be the women who gave up the corner office because that's just what we do. Being a VP wasn't always my goal, but as the department expanded and we took on more and more responsibilities, I took it as my responsibility to make it happen, for me, for the company, and most especially for my team.

And do you know what the owner of the company said when I asked him jokingly why he hadn't congratulated me? He said, "You know Heather, I didn't congratulate you because I assumed you were already a Vice President!"

Imagine that. Curiously though, finally reaching my goal of becoming a Vice President, Creative Director left me oddly unsatisfied. Could the drive been better than destination? Or was the drive so exhausting that the destination left me flat?

Why did I feel like I wasn't successful? Well, it's likely the "grit" that drives me. I'm not saying it's necessarily something you should emulate, but likely through my experiences there's something to learn.

Even as a young kid, I knew I HAD to do something special with my life. I still don't think I've found it. And honestly, I'm on a constant search. People who know me may not believe it, but inside I was a pretty shy person. It takes a lot of effort and internal pressure for me to "rule the room," but I'm also competitive and have high expectations of myself. I did whatever I could to overcome my fears of "not being the best" as in my mind, the meek will only "inherit" the earth.

Sadly, it wasn't about enjoying the moment, but looking for the next big "win."

Truthfully, this used to take the "fun" out of things due to the pressure I put upon myself. How enviable it was to see people responding incorrectly to questions and being "okay" with it! To play fun and not necessarily to win. To try and fail without feeling like they failed. To have the voices in their head speak to them in positive messages instead of negative.

Starting out, I think I did what most people think they do or will do, and that was work my ass off. I would work harder, longer, smarter. Constantly pushing myself to learn and do just about anything to get the job done and be noticed for my efforts. People say they are willing to work hard, but I've gotta tell you, after over 20 years of management, it ain't true. The cream still rises to the top as they say. I could write a book EXACTLY on how to become successful and yet most people wouldn't do it. Trust me. There's no secret sauce. It doesn't matter your IQ your EQ or whatever. It takes complete perseverance, determination and sacrifice. It's not a matter of time, but a lifetime.

It means being the example, getting to know your peers and manager. Forget this notion of "work life balance." It doesn't exist when you are starting out. It means drinks with the boss, dinners that go too late with the client, and depending on your circumstances, missed soccer games. Is it TRULY what you want?

For as long as I remember my insecurity and ego kept pushing me forward and allowed me to take on many a battle to get ahead. I was the one texting from the labour room, and back in the office the very next day after my premature twins were born! No bragging rights, just the opposite. I'm trying to point out my insecurity that someone else might step in and to do my job as well as me. My family just accepted that that was me and went along with my "work ethic." Once the kids were born, I definitely tried to "do it all," but truth be told, work was my child as well. Thankfully, I had a husband who was equally driven and appreciated what I did and we could financially pay for help at home. I had literally "won the lottery," and yet I continued to work like I had something to prove.

Looking back and after loads of introspection and reading, I realized I was probably a pretty horrible boss at the time who was still trying to "climb the ladder." I was a contrarian, judgemental, likely not willing to give the recognition or respect people really deserve in the boardroom, nor offered mentorship I could have. Leading a creative environment you need to be, no you MUST be, accepting of risk. Only I likely instituted a culture of fear: fear of failing and fear of failing me.

I've had to stop and question whether I'd feel this way if I were a man. I guess I can never know - but what I will say is that I've worked for many a great man and frankly a few great women. It would take another book to explore why this is. I have amazing friendships with women. I couldn't imagine my life without them, but as for the work front, well I hope I was able to mentor a few, male or female.

I was still making genuine progress in my career, but certainly not many friends. Afterwards I found out from our CEO that he used to call me the "Ice Queen!" Not exactly a term of endearment. It seems fairly obvious to me that what he was trying to say was in the past, he looked at me as cold, unfeeling, unapproachable and stiff. A term he whole-heartedly would say does not describe me today.

It took that experience and a few other similar "punches to the gut," like a human resources 180, or "confidential" feedback documents from my staff and peers that hurt like hell as to what was there in black and white. As much as I'd like to rationalize it all away, I couldn't. I had to realize what I had no idea about, but what others clearly saw. Rather than ignore the evidence or strike it off as jealousy or un-American (look, I could have gone there!) I chose to reflect upon it, study my heart and mind, and look for the truth. And wow, did it stare back at me.

I was a "black or white" thinker in a creative environment, someone who couldn't really picture what it would be like to walk in someone else's shoes. Frankly, I was someone I didn't want to be anymore.

So I did what some say is next to impossible. I changed. I saw it all very clearly. I had to change, I knew what I had to do and I wanted to start it yesterday. I called my behaviour as "Old Heather and New Heather." It's kind of like Coke and well, let's hope more successful than, "New Coke!"

The reception to "New Heather" was swift and successful. I'm certain my boss took a deep sigh of relief, although my team's performance was always exceptional, now I was approachable. And the work got even better.

It was a real challenge at first because I thought all those characteristics I exhibited were part of my success. If I let go, even a tiny amount, will I begin to tread as opposed to swim? Little did I know, I likely would have been more successful, and my team and family much happier had I done this work earlier in my life. But alas, I can't beat myself up over that fact. Looking at life with a glass half full means at least I still had time to change my course. Some people never do or when they do, it's too late.

I've got to tell you ever since I embraced this change, I have never looked back and rarely go home with a knot in my stomach, like I so frequently did in the past. For the past six years, based on outside research conducted on our company, I was told my department had the "highest fulfillment" rate of any department in the company. To me, this is proof that the changes I personally undertook were having an extremely positive impact on my team.

Without going too "Oprah" on you, it's almost too personal to try and describe the changes I made within myself and therein for my team. But I became aware, present, understanding, truly caring -not about myself, but about everyone else. Was it timing? Was it time? I'd like to think had I made these changes earlier, things would have been even better.

True conflict is something I almost never engage in anymore because I have shelved my ego and address challenges with the belief that people rarely knowingly enter a situation trying to be rude or antagonistic. They genuinely have a different point of view, one I try to truly understand. And by first listening (a skill few actually practice), talking, while respecting people have differing backgrounds, thoughts and opinions, there's almost never need for argument. My "shyness" and reticence to do certain things is almost all gone. I no longer feel the need to be "the best." I just want to be authentic, supportive and kind. If you are doing the right thing, and I believe we all know what that is, you have no need to worry.

Giving people credit for what they do, publicly recognizing their talent and hard work, supporting a peer when things get heated, being kind, basically doing the "right thing," well it fulfills me like you couldn't imagine. Seeing people succeed and knowing you had a small part of it, it's one of the best feelings in the world. And the fun part is that as a result, people just want to keep doing better and better and they want to include you more and more.

I can proudly say one of my producers is making award winning films in Iceland, another a top Creative Director at Fox Sports in LA, and an Art Director is now calling the shots at Maple Leaf Sports and on and on. But the true successes are the ones that now are leading where they were once too afraid to lead: the one that left to be with his family after his sister passed away, the one who was finally able to have a child and has chosen her priority confidently and with grace, the one who lost her job after 20 years and has the confidence and reputation to rebuild. I'm there for every one of them.

The story doesn't stop here. So far it's not necessarily "happily ever after." I got laid off. My "work family" was dismantled. I tried my best to place people where the company could continue to work best, as well as where they would be most fulfilled. All those years, all that time. All gone.

Sadly a huge part of my identity was suddenly stripped away. What do I put in the line where it says, "business phone number?" How do I respond to that annoying, "And what do YOU do?"

The phone stops ringing, my opinion is no longer needed, the only emails clogging my phone are from Groupon, and I feel odd asking for money from my husband each day. You think in life "the best person" keeps the job, but in my case it was pre-determined that I was to be replaced. But where was the "kiss"?

After 14 years of building a hugely successful team, it is completely torn apart. Some laid off, some asked to stay, all transplanted to different places and different cultures. Me, I'm "mom" to twins that are another example of my grit and "take no prisoners" attitude. I came from the generation that thought we had all the time in the world to have kids and chose to put our careers first. BIG mistake.

It took me over five years of ups, downs, heartache, serious meds, needles (including shooting up in some sketchy places like the back of cabs and HBO office bathrooms), alternative methods, science and a whole boat load of money (which I am extremely fortunate that my husband and I could afford), to have them. Born at about three-and-a half pounds each, six weeks in the NICU and one needing two surgeries, I had my family. Ahh, but there was another miracle in the works for us, from a higher power than Cornell Medical Center and The Royal Bank, as shortly after I was pregnant with my third.

People would often say, "Wow a mom of three, you must be busy!" To which I would feel the need to somehow add, "Yes, and I work full time as well."

What I didn't add is that I sit on boards, committees, authored a children's book and do volunteer work –I like, no I NEED to be busy. So you can see the pressure I feel internally and externally now. I'm often asked, "So what are you going to do next? I can't imagine YOU staying at home for long."

So if that's what I do choose, who am I letting down?

My friends say I'm the busiest "non working" person they know. I sit on several boards, several committees and over involve myself in my kids' lives. I don't like to see an empty calendar.

If I do go back to the "working world" at this point, I don't think I have the heart to work as hard as I did. I don't think I could give so much of myself or my family's time, unless it's something entrepreneurial.

I was asked to write this chapter for "Making It in High Heels" and I'm feeling sheepish. Have I made it? For now, I've exchanged my two-piece suits for two-piece Lu Lu Lemons and my high heels for trainers. I'm not sure how I feel about it. I've worked in TV for over 20 years. So far my full-time mom job is tougher than any deadline I've ever had. But do I have the right stuff? How will I measure success- the number of toilet seats down and grades up?

My real passion for now is simply to give back. I've had my turn at the wheel. So what can I do to help young girls filled with anxiety over school and social issues? Or how do I help women trying to make it in a creative industry that's sadly compressing, and more often than not run by not-so-creative men? And lastly, what can I do to support the things most important to me in my community? I've had success in life, but it never came without some degree of struggle.

I've realized my pure joy comes from making others happy. I'm proud to say I stay in touch with most, if not, all of my previous employees, and I would like to think they could call me at anytime for any reason. We were a family.

You want a job? Forget Playback and HR departments. Find out EVERYTHING you can about the industry you are most interested in. Go to the parties, the industry events, find out about one person—their interests - get yourself in front of that one person. Network until you do. None of the major cities in Canada are too big that you can't connect with that person. They like golfing? Well guess what? So do you! (Seriously, if you don't golf, start taking lessons) Why do you like their company? Their industry? If you don't have an answer, then guess what? Someone else does. It's not enough anymore to send in a resume and show up.

I would interview people for television jobs and when I asked them, "So what about our channels could you improve upon?"

And time and time again, I'd get the answer, "It's hard to say because I don't have cable."

If you don't have cable, why would you want to work in TV? If you can't afford it, then at least go watch it at a friend's so you can be prepared to answer any questions. Sounds simple, right? Then, why do candidates time and time again come to interviews without even researching the web sites?

I'd speak at universities and after ask if anyone had any questions. Guess what? Plenty of times not one person would. Here I was, coming to them, at the time representing a large potential employer and no one would follow up with a question or even ask if they could contact me after. This was their opportunity to impress and not one person took me up on it.

How many of us have a mentor? I sadly went through my life with not one person to help guide my decisions. I can tell you unequivocally that this is a huge mistake women make. We feel like we should be able to go it alone. If I had had someone, a teacher, a coach, anyone there to provide leadership in my career…well, all I can say is I wish I had. Period.

I'm not criticizing schools, but I have seen A LOT of resumes…can anyone write anymore? Who's looking at their demo reels? Who's coaching these kids? There seems to be a gap.

Another great thing to do is to find a non-profit organization you feel really passionate about and try to get on one of their committees or even the board. It will give you board experience; allow you to further network, and best of all give back to your community. It will provide you with a tremendous amount of satisfaction, more than watching the latest episode of "The Bachelor" I assure you.

I'm sure if you're reading this, you've read "Lean In" and books like it. It's especially tough for us gals. At some point, if you want a family, you have to "lean back," unless of course your husband owned a multi-million dollar software company. I've heard more than one speaker tell women to opt out and leave room for the rest, if family is your goal. WOWZA. You're a manager, law is you get a year of maternity leave, you get two resumes on your desk, equally qualified, one a man, one a woman, both about 30 years old. Who do you hire? The answer should not be that easy.

I'm happy to share my story and more of it at any time in the hopes it offers any help to anyone. Being faced with endless possibility can be freeing, but sadly for many it's just plain freezing. I would love to help motivate young women and girls to accept the reigns and confidently steer their own course in life. It's in each and every one of us to avoid some of the hard lessons, the shameful moments that can occur when we don't. I can tell you I'm going to enter this new phase of my life with a "take no prisoners" attitude. Stay tuned...

JULIA MOGUS
NO BOUNDS

Stories. Tales. Imagination. Adventure. Fiction. Non-Fiction. Books.

For as long as I can remember, books have always played such an important role in my life. Looking back, I wonder if it had anything to do with growing up with no cable television, or spending time at our local library every week; I guess books were always there for me.   When I close my eyes, I can smell the distinctive scent of those crisp new pages in a book, almost like the smells you remember from your favourite bakery.

Many nights my mom or dad would read me a story, tuck me in bed, kiss me goodnight and then close the lights and door behind them. That was the moment I would cautiously pull out my flashlight, open my book, and dig myself deep in the covers to read a new and exciting adventure. Yet, life wasn't always as perfect as it may have seemed, and with every good story, there was always a good beginning. Here is my tale.

Growing up, I believed that the world was kind and fair and if you tried hard and did your best, then that was what truly mattered. I was wrong.

My mom and dad were always kind and hard working, believing in giving opportunities to their children to explore many different things. I began figure skating at the age of three and within a few years I was competing in local events. I trained hard and enjoyed the challenge of trying new feats, pushing my body to new limits. As the years went by, I continued to work hard at school, training vigorously at skating practice, and reading whenever the opportunity presented itself. I thought maybe I wanted to be a competitive figure skater who might someday compete in the Olympics. I thought maybe I wanted to be a teacher, pharmacist, or even a ballerina. Truthfully, I didn't know what I really wanted to do with my life. I was only nine.

It was the summer of 2009 and my figure skating coach had approached my parents, telling them they had to enroll me in a competitive training camp if I was to compete and do well at the provincial level. I was excited because I loved skating and enjoyed the thrill of learning new jumps, spins, and skills. By the eighth grade, I was training close to 6 days a week with several different specialized coaches, and missing school twice a week.

Life seemed good, and somehow I was able to effectively manage my time, so I was never behind in my studies. In the car ride to my practices and competitions, I was able to squeeze in tons of reading and learned the fine art to avoid car-sickness. I read about all kinds of famous people who devoted their lives in making our world a better place. I fell in love with the *Harry Potter* series by J.K. Rowling and even imagined myself one day going to school in a faraway place not much different than *Hogwarts School of Witchcraft and Wizardry*. Reading did that for me. It gave me a window to escape whenever I wanted to, and the ability to travel to places I would have never imagined.

Growing up, my family believed in the value of a good education and that was something I saw great value in, even at such a young age. My teachers were always so supportive and kind, and had confidence in my ability to manage my time effectively between skating and school. My grades were good; despite the time my skating had taken me away from school. My parents worked hard to help me explore my desire to skate and compete; making huge financial commitments without ever making mention. They also taught me about balance; how important it was to make sure I made time to finish my homework, spend time with my friends and to never stop reading. Things seemed really good and I was happy. But that didn't last very long.

I competed at the Provincial level and was selected for the Future Star program with COS Skate Canada. Like most girls, I was thrilled to be considered worthy of such an opportunity. I worked hard, and truthfully believed your personal best was all that mattered. My parents always told me to do your best and not worry about being the best. I really believed in them, until I witnessed the brutality of unkind words from some parents to their children when they didn't win a medal, or from coaches who felt they needed to condemn their skaters who executed a less than perfect performance. Yet, the harshest reality came to me when my coach told me I wasn't good enough, not committed enough, and not smart enough to be a competitive elite figure skater. In the end, it didn't matter if I did my best. Unfortunately, my parents were wrong.

By the age of 10, I had already volunteered numerous hours as a program assistant with Skate Canada, teaching children, teens and those with special needs how to skate. Whenever a young skater was scared or upset and felt alone on the ice, I was there to comfort them and sometimes make them smile or laugh. I enjoyed helping the children I taught, and found great satisfaction in knowing I was somehow making their experiences on the ice fun and enjoyable. I continued to train hard and compete in many local and provincial level competitions, but as I continued to grow, which presented greater challenges on the ice, combined with my coach's negative treatment; the skating world changed and it just wasn't what it used to be. It was no longer fun and enjoyable.

I again found solace in reading. It gave me a window to see the world in so many different ways. I began to learn about things in life or places around the world I had never seen before. Having no cable TV at home meant I could read books *before* they were made into movies. Reading was like opening a door to a whole new world. I was in control of what world I wanted to be in. When I felt sad, I knew I could open that door anytime and fill my heart with much happiness and joy. My coach was wrong. I was smart enough to find that door I needed and to know her words meant nothing to me.

In the years that followed, I continued to train, volunteer and do well in school. I was an honour student and spent my free time in between on-ice and off-ice training on the benches outside the rink, finishing my homework or reading a book. I had such a thirst for knowledge and sometimes felt isolated from my fellow skating teammates.

My sister Emma, also a competitive figure skater, was someone who understood my personal journey, and together we sat on those benches, finishing our school-work, while eating our thermos prepared dinners our mom would always pack.

One day a fellow skater walked by my sister and I, and said we were losers and nerds. It was only words, but it felt like a bucket of cold water had hit our faces. She was a great skater and I couldn't understand what we were doing wrong to warrant such a mean comment. We weren't losers. And if using our free time to read books, or catch up on our school-work made her believe we were, than we were proud to be nerds!

Spring was a great time because it meant my mom, sister and I would be able to go to local garage sales in search of great books. Sometimes books were as low as a quarter a piece! My Emma and I loved buying books, and we became quite good at bargaining for a cheap price. We found gently used hardcover children and teen books and sometimes even brand new books.

Saturday mornings were our special time. We would wake up at 7am and hit some great yard sales before heading out to volunteer for 4 or 5 hours in the rink. We found a lot of the same great books we cherished and sometimes in the afternoon when we finished volunteering, we would make our way to second hand stores in search of more. Emma and I just kept buying many great books and we promised ourselves that we would give these books to kids who might not otherwise have a chance to own good books. We didn't know who or where to send these books, we just knew they were as valuable as gold, and would someday bring a child as much joy and love as they have brought us.

We did some searching online and found a study from the University of Nevada that said having as little as 20 books in the home propelled a child to go further in school and it didn't matter if they were rich or poor. And so we continued to buy and collect, and it was around that time that my sister became a page with the Ontario Legislative Page program. We learned about our first and former Ontario Lieutenant Governor's Aboriginal book drive. We were so thrilled to finally find a home for all the books we had bought and stored, and patiently waited for the book drive to open so we could donate our treasures.

In October of 2011, my sister and I walked away from the skating world after months of questionable conduct from our coach. Emma had just recovered from a broken toe and an open fracture injury only months before, and triumphed in a personal best in the pre-novice short and long program. I had just competed in a novice short and long program and too felt proud of my accomplishments; despite the lack of validation from our coach after months of hard training.

It wasn't until my sister competed in her long program that our skating world came crashing down. Emma was verbally assaulted with much criticism, negativity, and then forcibly pulled down in front of her fellow teammates, skaters, coaches, and spectators, all while a video camera was rolling. Witnessing the pain in the tears that flowed from my sister's eyes and the heartbreak of a sport we loved so much, we knew we deserved better. And we knew that our mom was right. It didn't matter if we were the best in a sport we loved, we gave our best and that was all that mattered.

There would be no medal or justification to ever replace human compassion, dignity and respect. There are no acts of bullying, even from those in a position of power, to warrant our compliance in thinking it was okay to be belittled and made to feel worthless. The children we taught on the ice those many Saturdays over the years showed us that it's okay to fall down on your own because no matter what, you will always get up. And so we did we get up. We walked away with our pride and confidence in knowing that no one will ever push us down again.

Months had passed and news came in an email to my sister and I that the Lieutenant Governor's Aboriginal book drives had been cancelled two years prior and with no plans to resume. After buying and collecting books during the years before, my sister and I had close to 400 books. We knew we needed to get these books up north, even it meant putting them in the back of our mom's minivan and driving for two days. At home, my sister and I continued to do much research on Aboriginal communities, and where our Lieutenant Governor had sent the books.

We learned about the 49 First Nations communities in northern Ontario, known as the Nishnawbe Aski Nation, and how children and teens living in these remote communities have little to no access to good books. First Nations children were on average 4 to 5 years behind in literacy skills. Students on the reserves receive about 20 to 30 percent less funding than non-Aboriginal students living off the reserves. I thought how could this be possible? In school, we were never taught about the inequalities facing our Aboriginal people or what life was like on the reserves today. We had no idea that the Nishnawbe Aski Nation comprises two thirds of Ontario and is 90 % isolated with 28 communities only accessible by plane. We felt like we knew nothing about them and so we began our mission to learn and do everything we could to help our fellow brothers and sisters in the north.

Books were something we always had, and for the most part of my life just took for granted. It never occurred to my sister and I that there were practically no public libraries on the reserves and schools were equipped with old and outdated reading material. One day as my sister and I sat on our beds, we wondered why some children are given so much and others so little. We wondered how unfair it was that we had access to thousands of books in our school, our community libraries and at home; yet, kids in our own backyard, living on the reserves in northern Ontario didn't. Emma and I knew about the lack of education resources in third world countries and the impoverished communities around the world... we didn't have a clue this was happening in our beautiful country.

I felt in my heart an overwhelming sense of empowerment because I knew my sister and I were not losers. I knew I could share something my sister and I deeply cherished with other children and teens in this world. We called ourselves, "Teens on a MISSION." At that moment, as we sat on our beds, we made a pledge to bring the gift of reading to First Nations children and teens living in remote northern communities of the Nishnawbe Aski Nation.

In the summer of 2012, we contacted the National Post newspaper telling them we had 400 books valued at over $3,000, which we would like to ship to the children and teens of the Nishnawbe Aski Nation. We had a mission and we needed the support of others, if our mission was to succeed. It was at that time that a local Town Councillor, Pam Damoff, saw our vision and helped us to secure a location at a local mall to collect more books.

By the end of the summer, we had collected over 6,000 books and raised awareness of our plight throughout southern Ontario. Born out of a love of reading, my sister and I sent off our very first shipment of 6,000 books to all 49 First Nations reserves in northern Ontario that summer. We successfully negotiated a generous discount of 90% off from a First Nations owned airline, Wasaya Airways LP, and sold candy kabobs and collected in-kind donations to raise much needed funds to pay our shipping invoices. Books were flown by planes, boat planes, and on chartered flights to schools up north. It felt so good to know our friends would be enjoying many of the great books my sister and I have always cherished.

Books With No Bounds was born from the heart and soul of two crazy bookies (a.k.a. book lovers) with a vision to send good books, improve literacy skills and education for Aboriginal children and teens living in remote communities. We embarked on our journey with a few hundred books that we were determined to throw in the back of our parents' mini-van, chanting amongst ourselves, "Nishnawbe Aski Nation or BUST." We were going to get these books up north, no matter what. In the months to follow, we sent our first shipment, we met with local politicians, schools and First Nations leaders and soon found ourselves on a journey out of the pages of our own adventure book. Hundreds of letters, photos, cards and paintings began to pour in; thanking us for the good books we had sent, and at times, kindly asking to please send more. We wrote letters back, but just couldn't keep up.

A young girl living in Fort Severn wrote us a letter than resonated in our hearts for a long time. She told us about her community, how they have been waiting for a new school to be built and if we could come and visit. Her name was Dana and she spoke of the beauty of the wildlife in her community and how much she enjoyed Halloween. She said she went to school made up of 5 portables and was going to receive a new school in 2013. We knew we had to meet the girl behind the letter, and so in May of 2013 we travelled on 4 planes, arriving 10 hours later in the most remote and isolated community in Ontario, Fort Severn.

When we stepped off the plane it felt almost surreal. Nothing had seemed familiar and although we were in Ontario, we felt like we were on the other side of the world. It was so beautiful, yet hauntingly quiet. There were no paved roads, and for miles we saw abandoned fuel tanks, dirt roads with pockets of water, littered with forgotten plastics and other litter. We saw children playing on the broken fence and handling a gas can, most likely found on the side of the road. Their faces were beautiful, yet their clothing was covered in dirt and sometimes a few sizes too big. A young boy, not much older than 7, rode past on a bike he could barely touch the ground to stop. And then the most incredible thing had happened.

A young girl approached us, and pulled a small folded and worn out paper from her coat pocket. As she slowly unfolded the paper, she looked up at us and asked if we were the girls in this photo who had sent the books. I turned to Emma, and we smiled with tears streaming down our faces and looked at each other in disbelief. We looked at the girl and said, "Yes, that's us!"

She smiled and hugged us and said thank you for sending the books. This young girl had carried in her pocket a photo bookmark my sister and I had sent 7 months earlier. We knew in that moment, the importance of what we were doing, and we knew we couldn't stop.

In our mission to send books to children and teens, we began to attract the attention of media and found we had a voice and a story to share with the world. The Ontario Regional Chief, Stan Beardy, once told us that these children do not need a little bit of books - they need a lot of books. In the months to follow, after returning from Fort Severn, we were approached by orphanages and school programs in Uganda and Ghana, Africa, asking if we could please send them books. After shipping books to our friends in West Africa, we again found ourselves in a remote community in Kenya, Africa, this past summer, helping to build a school and plant and harvest crops through a scholarship with *Free The Children's* Me to We program.

We returned home even more determined to help children around the world. By spring of 2014, we had sent 40,000 books, thousands of crafts and school supplies, computer tablets, computers and more to communities in Canada, Uganda, Ghana, and the Philippines. We have built a library of books for a women's shelter in Fort Albany and a Health Centre in Sioux Lookout. Teachers and Principals from the reserves have sent us notes saying how much their students appreciate the books. We had even received a letter from one of the communities that reading test scores have gone up as a result of the books we had sent throughout the year.

If it takes a village to raise a child, than it must take a village to raise a reader. The books we send are from the shelves of so many children, teens and families in our own communities. They are from the support of many wonderful authors, publishers and organizations like, First Book Canada. The high cost of shipping has been raised by generous in-kind donations through fundraising initiatives in schools, community clubs, and businesses.
Our village and global community has played a huge part in making our dream possible.

A good friend and mentor, Pam Damoff, once told us the answer is always "no" unless you ask. And for every "no" we received, we worked *that much harder* to receive a "yes".

There are truly no bounds to what you can do and who you can be. And despite the things that have caused us pain in the past, we have grown stronger and more determined to cast smiles on the faces of children around the world. We never doubted the power of will and determination in making this world a better place.

When I begin to feel like something is impossible, I remember the faces of those kids who fell down when they first learn to skate. I remember the faces that believed they were never going to get up and stand tall on those skates. I knew they only needed a gentle nudge to make it on their own. I know that no matter how many times we all fall down in life, we must always try and get up.

KATHY BAZINET
PAYING IT FORWARD

My burning desire to make a difference in this world started very young. I was nine years old the first time I saw my younger brother being bullied. At recess, a group of girls informed me my brother was being roughed up over in the junior section of the schoolyard. I ran as fast as I could and sure enough, there he was in the middle of a circle of fifth graders, each pushing him to the next while calling him names. I was so much smaller than the older boys, but without a thought I ran straight into the centre and gave them a piece of my mind. Still to this day I am not sure if it was the look of fierce protection in my eyes that scared them off, or if it was simply the shock of it all. Either way, I grabbed my brother and ran off untouched. The look of fear, sadness and shame was not on the face of those boys, but rather on the face of my tiny sibling. That moment was burned into my memory. If only the older boys knew what it felt like for my brother, I was sure they would never do such a thing again. It became my mission to live a life seeking and creating opportunities for understanding that could lead to change.

Let me take a brief moment to introduce myself. My name is Kathy and I consider myself to be living a life that is truly blessed; not perfect, not always easy, but one that I am successfully living each day to the fullest. I am passionate about my two amazing daughters, my own personal development and growth, my loved ones, and that each day I contribute in some way to making this world a better place.

I believe this world truly is a beautiful place and each of us has the ability to make it even more so. And when we do it together, the synergy is where the magic happens. For me a big part of the magic is in giving back.

I spend my work days inspired and aspiring to change lives. I have worked over eleven years as part of the self-help services for the Canadian Mental Health Association. Each day, I hear of people's deep and profound struggles. Through the peer support services I design, these struggles can be transformed into hope for better days and a passion for wellness. When I am face to face with someone in his or her darkest moments, I see that person as whole, complete, and full of potential. I do not want people to see me, my brother, or anyone else, as broken, as someone needing to be fixed or changed, so I treat others as I wish to be treated. In doing so, I honour both the other person and myself. I leave most of my work days knowing that I have made a difference in this world.

In the summer of 2013, my father, daughter and I went to Kenya to provide hands on support to one of their communities. Our humanitarian work included building a dormitory for an all-girls high school, farming and water walks in the Maasai Mara region. I have come to know that the more I give, the more I receive. The feeling one gets when a small child takes your hand, with smiling eyes, as she thanks you for helping build a school for her, is priceless.

For me giving back is about walking alongside others, providing a hand up whenever possible, and honouring the path each soul must walk on this earth; in the efforts to do so without judgment or even the thought that I know what's best for another. It is, however, my privilege to reach out to others and lend a helping hand whenever possible. By giving back, I receive so much more. It creates a feel-good feeling that stirs my soul and makes my days all the richer. When you experience the difference you have made in someone's life, it changes you forever.

When we arrived home from our Africa trip, I was motivated to do more. I sent out an email to the others we met while on our travels and initiated a challenge for us as a group to raise $10,000. This would be enough to sponsor one young Kenyan girl to attend the high school that just a week before we had poured our own sweat and blood in helping construct. To my surprise, the majority of those involved were also moved to action, and within one week we raised $14,000.

In Kenya, if you are fortunate enough to go to high school, the Kenyan government pays for your university schooling. The young girl we sponsored wishes to complete both high school and university, to better her life, the life of her family and her community. As we give to her, she will pay it forward in many ways.

Let me go back a bit and share the greatest influence for my life direction. My brother has a rare condition called Sotto Syndrome, a medical and developmental disability.

Witnessing his physical, medical and emotional struggles shaped my life from a very young age, and led not only to my career choices, but how I would fundamentally live my life. That day on the playground, watching my brother get bullied, was the defining moment when I dedicated my life to helping others. My brother had enough struggles just simply surviving. I on the other was the lucky one and in my mind it became my privilege and responsibility to make a positive difference in the lives of others.

Knowing I wanted to make a difference in this world was not enough. In eighth grade, my class assignment was to write and deliver a speech; mine was titled, "Sometimes When You Laugh It Hurts". Yep, you guessed it. My speech spoke of that dreadful day when my brother was bullied in the schoolyard. And sadly, I had countless other heart wrenching examples to share. My speech focused on the importance of understanding how damaging our words can be on others and the importance of getting to know people in order to understand their journey.

From an early age my belief was that understanding creates empathy and that was something this world needed more of. I envisioned a world where we would see each other as brothers and sisters. Where we would reach out to help each other rather than fight. A world where we could celebrate and embrace our differences. Some would say I was (and still am) naive and as John Lennon says a "dreamer", but when I delivered my speech, others listened!

I won first place in my class. I was invited to speak at the regional level competition, where I placed third. I was able to push past my own perceived barrier of a learning disability, being shy, and an introvert. Through conviction I expressed my passion for my beliefs.

Even though I was just one person, I could still make a difference. When you are passionate about something and take action, people will listen. Throughout my school years, I found the more I gave back, the more I helped others, the more I found out who I was and started to love myself.

Now that I have children of my own, my main motivation is to be a role model for my two daughters. I have volunteered on their school council, led large fundraisers on behalf of their schools and given my time to a number of their sports teams. We as a family continually dedicate our time and effort to support others. We have sponsored a young girl in Cameroon, Africa for over ten years now and for the last five we have financially contributed to a family in Cuba. We have gone door-to-door collecting for the *Heart and Stroke Society* as well as participated in a number of run/walk fundraisers. We participate yearly in environmental restoration projects including neighbourhood clean-up projects.

When my girls were just 13 and 11, they took on their first of four, *Free the Children* campaigns in a coordinated effort to help eliminate child slavery. In just three years they raised over $25,000 and this past summer my eldest won a scholarship to travel to India to do humanitarian work.

I give back because it's a way for me to show my gratitude for the blessings I have in my life and to give thanks in honour of those who have given me a helping hand. When I help others, I in-turn help myself become more of the person I desire to be.

There was a time in my life when I lost my way. I found myself working long, hard hours to pay for a house, own a car, family vacations, etc. I strived to be Superwoman, almost single-handedly organizing a large school fun fair, volunteering for countless kid-related organizations, running from sports activity to sports activity, and essentially taking on so much that sleeping became less and less of an option. I was promoted at work, moving into a high-pressure role, and simultaneously trying to be the best daughter, sister, friend, I could be. I lived my life based on what other people expected of me, what society said I should do, and what I thought was "right". I gave everything I had within me until I was exhausted, depleted, and had nothing left to give myself. I went from living to existing.

In the late fall of 2008, I was diagnosed with Multiple Sclerosis. I was thirty-eight years old, an executive director of a non-profit organization, a single mother of two very beautiful, active, and spirited girls, and was constantly on the go. I could easily have been crowned "Independent Woman of the Year," so this diagnosis was a blow beyond anything I ever experienced.

I immediately decided to take some time off work to create a care plan for myself. Where to begin? I always enjoyed adventures and pushing myself beyond my comfort zone. I needed something that would shake my world, help me see my life differently, and something so bold it would move me from seeing my future as doomed. I called my friend and said, "Have you ever considered skydiving?"

A few days later, I found myself in the door of an airplane at 14,000 feet above the earth, ready to take a leap of faith. "I trust in this moment! I free myself of needing to be so independent. I release myself to really, I mean really, live!"

As we left the plane, I was in complete awe. I forgot to smile pretty for the camera guy. I forgot I was falling at 120 miles an hour. I forgot I was afraid of what tomorrow might bring. Instead, I could not take my eyes off the ground, in awe, in appreciation, in a state of pure joy. I trusted my instructor to take care of me. I trusted myself to do my required tasks, and I trusted the experience. That was the ultimate sensation of freedom!

Eighteen months later, my neurologist cleared me. Miraculously, "somehow my brain was cured." How did I do this? I focused back on me. I took a long hard look at my life and remembered why I did the work I did, remembered why I decided to have two beautiful children, remembered what I loved about my life and I reprioritized my days. I took time off work to focus on healing my body, mind and soul. I worked with several alternative care doctors in addition to the traditional medical stream. I corrected my eating habits and I started an exercise routine. I focused on wellness, which included a balance of giving and receiving, living mindfully and a commitment to strive to live each day in a state of inspiration.

I have come to appreciate the balance of giving and receiving. I also believe there are six key ingredients that can lead us to success:

1. Passion

I recognize that knowing my life purpose and my goals are a life-long, changing process. Pay attention to what stirs your soul, what makes you smile, what motivates you. These are your passions, and these are the things worth going after. Some practical ways to gain this awareness are to volunteer your time and read a lot of books. Volunteering is a great opportunity to explore first-hand different experiences. Reading different books such as biographies, self-help, and history will help you broaden your understanding of the world you live in and the possibilities become endless. Watch videos from the Tedx series, an online resource of "Ideas Worth Sharing." Explore, travel and play – enjoy all that is around you.

2. Knowing what you stand for

Later in my life, I came to understand how important our values are in guiding our life choices. I have come to understand there are two driving values: our supportive values and our pain values (unsupportive). We have a choice in life to be guided by love or to be guided by fear. There are times when both serve us well. It is important to know which is guiding us and to consider if this guidance is supportive or unsupportive. When I look at my two amazing daughters I cannot even begin to imagine the pain a mother must feel as her child is taken from her and forced into child slavery (this fear is one of my pain values). As I support my children in their campaigns to bring awareness and raise funds for *Free the Children*, I hope in some small way we are helping to reduce the pain that another feels at the hands of this global issue. My values and my family's values guide our time, money, and efforts to find and support organizations that are aligned with those values. The more you know yourself on a deeper level, the more empowered you become in creating and guiding your own life.

3. Hard work and drive

Not everything in life will come easy. Not everything worth doing will feel good. But moving beyond the obstacle, pushing past our fears and embracing the challenge in order to fulfill our life passions is so worth it.

It was not easy knowing that I could not always protect my brother and the bullying would continue, despite my best efforts. It was not easy to listen to the stories of the young, innocent children who are forced into child slavery. It is not easy to sit with someone and listen to his/her pain and struggle as a result of his/her mental health issues. When it's not easy at times, that's when hard work and drive are needed most.

Some of my greatest moments have come at the heel of some of my darkest moments. My hard work and drive come from these dark places and a desire to be the change I wish to see in this world. Find the things in your life that motivate you and find ways to include them in your daily practices to stay focused on your path.

4. Discipline and daily habits

Each of us has the privilege and the responsibility to design our own lives. Our daily habits and decisions create the foundations for our future. Make a conscious choice to add daily practices that will move you in the direction you most desire. One of my daily practices is the review of my vision board –a collection of photos or inspirational sayings that depict what I desire for my future: goals for my family, fitness, finances and my own self-exploration. It's on my bedroom door so that it's the last thing I look at before going to sleep and the first thing I look at upon waking. It reminds me of where I am heading.

As Martin Luther King Jr. said, "Darkness cannot drive out darkness: only light can do that. Hate cannot drive out hate: only love can do that."

Each day I am motivated by finding the ways in which my love can make a positive impact on the world around me.

5. Fail and Fail Big

I know very well that failure and mistakes are supposed to be a good thing. It's a sign of action, trying, and effort.   True success can never be accomplished without experiencing failure. But also know how difficult it is to celebrate these moments. Thomas Edison failed close to 10,000 times before he invented the light bulb. But the key was that in his mind he really created 10,000 ways in which the light bulb did not work. I have come to realize time and time again that I learn just as much, if not more, from my mistakes as I ever have from my successes. It is the story we tell ourselves that determines if we have supportive thoughts or unsupportive thoughts. Embrace the value and even celebrate failure in your journey.

6. Role models

We all need role models, so select wisely, as these people will help shape your life. Although I was born after the deaths of both Martin Luther King Jr. and Gandhi, both have a significant influence in my life. I listen, read, and watch biographies, autobiographies, and speeches on these two highly influential change agents. For me, King and Gandhi represent my desire to be the change in this world despite the hard times, and to face the challenges despite the risk or consequences. Each is an example of one person's will to create change and make this world a better place, and in turn created a momentum for change that was unstoppable.

I understand the importance of the people I surround myself with, as the saying goes, each person is the average of our five closest friends in terms of money, success, and life satisfaction. Choose wisely.

There have been times in my life when I had my head down and found myself blindly following the rules and expectations. I have sat back and watched as the path formed in front of me because I did not seek to understand what it was I truly wanted for my life. But, there have also been other times my life that have truly been all mine: freeing, magnificent and filled with awe.

If today was my last day, I would not want to leave this world filled with regrets, sorrow and bitterness. I wake knowing that I am living the life I have designed, the life I want, and the life that is authentically mine. It's the little things that make all the difference. It is about building daily habits that change one's landscape. I want to look back on my life and feel joy in the memories, satisfied, delighted, and proud of who I am and what I have done in this precious, short life of mine. I love the life I have created for myself. I wish for each and every one of you the same. Dream and dream big. Then give it all you've got to make those dreams your life and enjoy the journey! I hope my story serves as a testament that YOU can be all you desire and that living the life you dream is indeed possible!

"We become what we want to be by consistently being what we want to become each day." Richard G. Scott

KIMBERLY UNDERWOOD
CHANGE UP!

When I was a little girl growing up in poverty, I never felt any different from the other "middle class" kids. To me, my life was "ordinary". Days without food didn't feel more or less different from the days when we had food.

I've always felt like my family was "rich". Our family vacations weren't lavish, like retreats to an exotic island or Disney World. We went on long road trips together to Prince Edward Island, Nova Scotia and New Brunswick. Along the way we would pitch a tent, fish for our dinner, and roast marshmallows while my mother would tell ghost stories. And I wouldn't have wanted it any other way.

In the '70s, my single mother had two little boys and was left without any kind of assistance. Young, inexperienced, and with a couple of jobs on the go, she had to make day-to-day decisions like whether or not to spend $10 on food or on clothing that week.

One day, my mother fell terribly ill. She was bedridden and unable to care for herself or my brothers. My eldest brother, at only 8, had to take on some of my mother's duties. It was during this time, my mother realized things needed to change. Wanting so badly to provide a better life for herself and her children, she approached Social Aid and was given two options:

1) Accept Welfare cheques until her children turned 18, or
2) Paid education

She chose to go to school in hopes to improve our lifestyle.

I look back at what my mother went through, and to see the transformed woman she is today, is truly remarkable and empowering. Her triumphs in her early life seemed almost impossible to overcome –especially alone. As early as I can remember, she has always taught me to create a world of my own - a world that I can only define. When you know who you are and where you stand no one can take that away from you. She is my biggest inspiration for starting *Change Up*.

Growing up, I very rarely had my own clothes. My clothes were always my brother's "hand me downs". I was teased a lot in school, and often struggled with my self-identity. I never really knew the importance of clothing until now.

We often take advantage of luxury when we have the opportunity. We all do it. We underestimate the true beauty and power of clothing. It shapes the way we feel about ourselves as it gives us confidence, which is also a precursor to our future.

When you buy something new, whether it's for work or a special event– how do you feel when you put it on?

Personally, I feel invigorated, motivated and most importantly, I feel confident.

As a child whose family once lived a life in poverty, I felt compelled to giveback to our community and to share our story with families going through a transitional phase in their lives. *Change Up* is about inspiring others and creating hope and opportunity through custom packaged clothing.

At an early age, I knew I wanted to help others. I wanted to create a charity that was meaningful to me and to my experiences. So in 2011, I founded Change Up Charity, and since then have partnered with Toronto's first women's shelter, Interval House as well as NAAAP (North American Association of Asian Professionals) in hopes that we can continue to spread the word and make a difference in our communities. Change Up has also provided a new service where we now work alongside counselors to deliver a great product to our partnered transitional homes.

Let's get started and begin with the basics! One of the toughest parts about starting a charity - is starting a charity! With little to no resources and a small amount of start-up capital, determining where and how you are going to spend that money is the most challenging.

The best way to implement a business is to take baby steps. Create a mission and a vision, make a step-by-step list of things you must do to execute this.

I began by registering my charity with the Ontario Government. Once I had an idea of what kind of charity I wanted to create and how I was going to do so, I learned how to design and create my own charity website through a website builder.

I personally donated $1000 towards the charity's initiative, which allowed me to create the "LOVE-T" for a T-shirt drive. I needed to find a way to market the charity to the community, while raising donations.

Since Change Up is a clothing charity, with every one T-shirt that was sold, one was donated. The proceeds went towards the sourcing of new clothing, "The shirt that gives back twice!" Once I created a buzz about Change Up, I began to cold call potential sponsors and in-kind donors that would help get the charity moving along.

My advice when calling potential sponsors or donors is to find an organization or individuals who believe in your mission and currently support a charity that is similar to yours i.e.: Supporting families living in poverty. Keep in mind that companies you are targeting are likely getting similar calls on a daily basis from similar organizations such as yours also looking for support. So be unique in your approach, rather than cold call, do some research and find out which department or person handles fundraisers and sponsorships, and then send out a customized package directly to the individual(s), making it feel less informal and more personal. Remember, kindness and sincerity takes you a long way. I had one of my members of the board make the follow up calls, and it seems to work in my favor, because a different approach or delivery can be refreshing. It is very important to have your board members and volunteers believe in your cause as it results in a positive outcome.

Don't be discouraged or offended when you hear, "No thanks!" because you'll hear that more often than not. It's usually based around two things: your charity doesn't align with their initiative, or the company could be closed for the year with their program donations, and you may have to try to apply the following year.

As a not for profit, finding ways to cut back on spending is key! Any "in-kind" help you can receive is your golden ticket, which means you're one step closer to making a difference. Every dollar counts, and every dollar you save will help you grow your initiative. Success is about making a difference, whether it's an individual, a family, or a community, you are helping shape a life in a positive way daily and that's what's important.

A fundraiser doesn't need to be big and lavish, rather small and intimate for your first time or every time for that matter. Make it what you want and be realistic about it. In kind donations are a great form of sponsorship. Say the company you have contacted has closed their charitable donations for the year, you can then kindly ask them if they would be willing to give an "in-kind donation," which can consist of a gift certificate (for a draw or raffle prize), some help with media content (to get your name out there), or to come to the event as a guest speaker to show their support for your cause.

Starting this charity has been very rewarding. I am blessed to have a great support system, which includes my family and friends. As the founder of Change Up, I have not only learned a great deal about the process of a start-up, such as rules and government regulations, but also about myself - my strengths and weaknesses, and of course my breaking points! Without my Board of Director Linda Lu, I don't know how I could have made our inaugural event in 2013 happen!

Every day brings new challenges such as, "Where will we get funding?"

"Where and how will we find our next set of sponsors?"

And that's the beauty of the whole experience; it's about pushing yourself and your boundaries to make it happen! What will motivate you are the people you will be helping and the lives that you will be changing. There were many days when I felt overwhelmed and wanted to cry into my pillow every night. I was stressed out, things were unorganized, plans kept changing and well, that happens.

But I didn't give up because I had to complete my goal: sell a certain amount of tickets to support my cause for the year. Even if I didn't sell a sponsorship package, each day I made it an effort to sell at least one ticket, because that one ticket allowed me to buy three outfits for a well deserving family, and that is what kept me motivated. In 2013, Change Up Charity raised $22,500.

So set a goal and be realistic about it. Remember that a charity is for the betterment of individuals and the community. Even if you raise $50 or $5,000, that's still more than what you had before you started. Don't ever lose faith in yourself. What you're doing is changing the world and it's a beautiful thing!

Starting your own charity, like any business, is a lot of work, but it's also rewarding. The first time I truly felt like I made a difference in someone's life was when I planned a family day with the women and children at Interval House. I couldn't help but notice this beautiful woman with the biggest smile on her face. She played with the bottom half of her sundress and said, "Does this look familiar to you?"

Immediately, I gave her a big hug. She wore that dress to show me her appreciation for what Change Up has done for herself and her family. I will never forget that moment. That's why I'll continue to fight for these women and children because they deserve to feel beautiful, happy and safe.

I want to take Change Up to a national level. I want to be able to support at least one women's shelter in every province in Canada within the next year or so. I plan to take Change Up out West to Los Angeles with a focus on children living in poverty who are bullied in school. It's a major issue that needs to be faced and Change Up can help alleviate some pressure by providing these children brand new clothing.

I feel it's my duty to shape a child's mind at the earliest stages of life. Children are the future, and coming together as a community to harness those early stages can make a big difference.

Sometimes along the way to fulfilling our destiny, we meet a few people who need a little help fulfilling their own. We all have to start somewhere, so let's get there together.

Nara Abrams
Imagine a Cure: a Lasting Legacy

One of my earliest memories was going for a walk with my grandfather. As we strolled down the street, a lawn sprinkler suddenly came on. With one swift motion he leaned over, scooped me up in his arms and held me close to keep me dry. I vividly remember his yellow wool Lacoste sweater on my cheek and the smell of his Nivea face cream. He was a strong, confident man and I felt that he would always be there to protect me. But just before my 6th birthday, my grandfather was diagnosed with an acute form of leukemia. A month and a half later he was gone at just sixty years of age. That was my first experience with death and my first exposure to cancer.

Growing up, I had an incredible family. My husband describes us as the "Cleavers," a 1960s idealized suburban TV family. My dad was a hard working businessman who loved his job and provided well for us. My mom had her own business and was often able to work from home, which gave her plenty of time to spend with my brother and I as we were growing up.

Mom was enthusiastic, fun-loving and never took herself too seriously. Most importantly, in all her dealings with people, she was a truly genuine person. If she was happy for you, you could read it in her smile. If there was sadness, she was compassionate and dependable in her support. Through her words and action, Mom had the unique ability to make the good times even better and the difficult times more bearable. That was the family environment in the nurturing little nest where I was raised.

As time went on, I did well in school, had lots of friends, was part of the high school swim team, graduated from university and got a great job in human resources. I met my husband on a blind date and two years later we were engaged. Just a few weeks before our wedding, I got a call from my mother - one I'll never forget.

I was told the call was just to say hello, but she didn't sound like herself. After questioning her (a lot) she reluctantly told me that her doctor thought she might have leukemia. I stopped in my tracks. I couldn't believe what she had just told me. My first and only experience with leukemia was with my grandfather. It was my understanding that people did not live with this illness.

I was devastated. Two people who loved me had been struck with the same disease, and I knew what had happened to the first one. I was deeply saddened at the unfairness of my mother's diagnosis. How could this have happened? Why her? What could I do? I had many questions and terrifying thoughts.

I decided that I wouldn't simply watch what happened next, but instead would get intimately involved. That included attending all of her doctor's appointments and hospital treatments. Our family was hopeful after her diagnosis was confirmed as a chronic rather than acute form of the disease. The doctor told her, "You will probably get run over by a truck before this gets you." This news did relieve the panicky feeling that something disastrous was imminent.

Mom knew she had an incurable disease that could become aggressive in six months, a year, or maybe not for five or ten years. Nobody knew for sure. However, every day she woke up to the inescapable fact that her body carried a time bomb with a fuse of unknown length. How did Mom cope with her illness? She followed Winston Churchill's advice during the Second World War, she kept calm and carried on. It was remarkable to see!

She still went to her art classes, the gym, shopping, traveled and enjoyed the theatre. She did not slow down until her body did.

She even continued working up until a few days before she passed away. She loved her career as a bookkeeper. She loved numbers and balancing bank accounts. She would stay up all night to make sure that every penny was accounted for. She was highly respected by her clients for her loyalty and dedication. She didn't work because she had to. She worked because she really enjoyed it.

Within a few years, things changed for the worse. Her disease progressed to the point that treatment was required. We assumed that she would lose her hair and would be nauseous and fatigued. Fortunately, her side effects were minimal and she responded to treatment.

When you're dealing with a loved one who has cancer, you quickly learn to celebrate successes, big or small. You're fighting something you have no control over. As a family member, I chose to be what my Mom called her "cheerleader." I made encouraging signs, charts, and photos and did everything I could to keep her motivated.

After her treatment ended, I thought we should celebrate. I envisioned a cocktail party at my house with 50 friends and family. It then occurred to me that I could do more - I hosted a gala event to raise awareness and money for leukemia research. Many people (including my parents) later told me they thought I was crazy to take on such a huge project. We called it "Imagine A Cure for Leukemia", and optimistically hoped to raise $50,000. But when all the money was counted, the event sailed well past our expectations. 600 people attended and we raised $80,000 after expenses.

Why did so many people choose to participate with their presence and give so selflessly with their wallets? It certainly wasn't because of any slick advertising or promotional campaign. People came out because the evening was billed as a tribute to my Mom. Many were personally aware of her story. One person told another and then another, and word of the event quickly spread throughout the community.

But there was even more to it than that. . .

Many people are stricken with some form of cancer, and many fight it bravely. There was something special about the way my mother carried herself that made her story so much more compelling. I spent a lot of time thinking about that, and here was my conclusion: Mom had a zest for life that was infectious. She was an optimist. She refused to burden others with her personal challenges. She didn't complain nor did she rail out against the unfairness of life. And she suppressed any discussion of her worries or fears, so that those around her would feel more comfortable. In a nutshell, she became a role model for how to deal with adversity of the worst kind with dignity, poise and grace.

A few years after Mom passed away, I bumped into a shop owner of a store that she loved. The woman expressed her condolences and said she was so sorry to hear about my Mom's passing and that she had no idea she was sick. My Mom did not want to be known as an unwell person for the better part of her illness. She felt very good and wanted people to think of her that way.

She gave leukemia a human face and touched people with a desire to act with a sense of urgency. Her story reached out and inspired hundreds of people. It resonated broadly because inspirational people give us hope, they provide encouragement, they bring values to life through the examples they set and they make us aware of what we're all capable of accomplishing. The wonderful gift of inspiration is what my mother gave to me, and to our family and friends.

Unfortunately, her leukemia proved to be a relentless disease. In a few years, it became harder to manage and she was experiencing uncomfortable, even painful symptoms. Watching her go through that was the hardest thing I have ever experienced. She remained committed to not letting her illness take over, and somehow found the strength to engage with her grandchildren and keep up with her client work. But the battle was not to be won. On October 11, 2007 at the age of 60, my beloved mother passed away.

In the aftermath, I wrestled with my conscience about continuing on with the charity. Supporting my mom had been the basis for starting it, and now that rationale was gone. However after a period of reflection, I was persuaded to keep going for three reasons:

1. I knew that Mom would have wanted it for the benefit of others.
2. I realized how strongly I felt that other families should not lose loved ones to leukemia and my contributions could help make that happen.
3. I felt that over time Imagine a Cure for Leukemia would link the memory of my mom to my young children.

There are some very special people I have met along the way. Some have survived their diagnosis and others have not. They all hold a very special place in my heart and are absolute inspirations to me. I think about what they have gone through, as well as the family members who are left to grieve their passing. I am not a medical expert, but I am a person with compassion. After having lost a loved one, I can relate to both the people who are faced with a diagnosis and to those who experienced a similar loss.

And while the charity was started to honour my mother's inspirational fight for survival it has continued ever since as a tribute to her character and spirit. By the end of 2013, after eight years of fundraising, Imagine a Cure for Leukemia had granted a total of $1 Million for promising leukemia research.

But the story doesn't end there. At the end of 2012, my ten-year-old daughter, Bayley, developed a fundraising idea of her own to support the charity. Her concept was to organize an event for kids, by kids themed around the summer camp activities that all kids love. With that as a framework, the program called, "Camp Imagine" was born.

Bayley was enthusiastic about bringing this idea to life and happily spread the word among all who would listen. She then formed a committee of seventeen friends and their parents to plan things out. The kids brainstormed ideas and wrote letters to request donations from retailers, friends and family. In this way, Bayley exposed other children to the notions of community service and providing help to people in need. There was a tremendous turnout for the event and it raised nearly $20,000 for leukemia research. In 2014, "Camp Imagine" will be expanded and repeated as a major fundraising activity.

And so the legacy of inspiration has trickled down from mother to daughter and from daughter to granddaughter. Mom would have been pleased!

I think back to one of our first fundraisers, when we received a large donation from an airline, two tickets to be raffled. I called Mom to tell her, and her reaction was something I'll never forget. She started shrieking with excitement! She was out for lunch with her friends and said, "I am so excited! I can't believe it, Nara got airline tickets for the Event!"

She was laughing, enthusiastic, and I could tell she was really proud of me. It wasn't a huge effort on my part to ask an organization for a donation. But for my mom, she knew exactly why I was doing it. I was doing it to help find a cure for leukemia. While she knew her future was not certain, I think she felt proud knowing that the money we raised (and will continue to raise) will help others like her.

BRENDA RICHARD
MY PASSION TO SUCCEED...
FROM DUST TO DIAMONDS

As a child, I remember lying on the grass, looking up at the blue sky and watching the clouds slowly roll by. I was carefree with not a worry in the world. We lived on the outskirts of town, on my grandfather's farm. It was exciting and peaceful. As children, we always had something to do no matter what the season. We had mini bikes and snowmobiles and we would use every inch of farmland when we ventured out on them.

Alas, life cannot always be so carefree. My life changed significantly following the birth of my second child. I began to experience full-blown panic attacks. Out of nowhere, my heart began to race intensely and my vision became blurry. My breathing was limited as I started gasping for air. My whole body was sweating and physically shaking in panic. I thought I was dying. I had only been home from the hospital for one day and I was not sure whether my condition was a result from just giving birth or something else. This was all new to me.

I went to see the doctor. I had developed a mental health condition called, Anxiety. In the past, I had always been in control of my life; this was not the time to fall apart. I had two children to care for, what was I going to do? I was given medication to help relieve the intensity of the attacks and over time it decreased, and my condition became more manageable.

It came time to return to work following my maternity leave and life seemed to be going well. I had a well-balanced life, both personal and career-wise. But, I began to feel a decrease in my moods. As time went on, I felt less able to concentrate at work and meet deadlines. I was unable to stay focused and I could no longer stay on top of my job; each day I arrived later and later to work. I felt very tired and could not get enough sleep. As the emotional pain grew deeper, my feelings of worthlessness increased. Stress levels began to accumulate, and my anxiety attacks increased. I found that even the smallest everyday tasks would just overwhelm and exhaust me. It was very hard to even function when it came to the everyday simple tasks. I just wanted to stay in bed.

My children were young. I pushed myself hard to ensure that my moods and behaviours did not affect my children. I can't say my husband was supportive. He did not understand my mental health condition, nor did he take the time to. In his mind, I was unproductive and lazy. He thought a quick trip to the doctor would fix me all up. I felt abandoned, lost, frustrated and judged without his support. I could not understand how he could not be empathetic. After hearing the same comments day after day, "You're lazy. Just get up and do it. There's nothing wrong with you."

You tend to question yourself as to whether or not he's right and that I might just be feeling sorry for myself.

At the time, others were not able to see any changes in my behaviours because I hid them from the world. I would not allow myself to show society how dysfunctional I was. I was in fear of losing my job or even worse, being locked up and taken away from my children. I was determined not to let that happen. I kept my emotional feelings and hurt inside and was very limited to who I shared them with.

I went to see my Family Physician. I needed to know why my life was so out of control and exhausting. This time the doctor diagnosed me with having a severe Depression and General Anxiety Disorder. I was unfamiliar with this illness and wasn't sure what I needed to do to make life better again. Prior to my illness, I knew in my heart that with self-determination I could overcome anything. This was how I had approached everything in life, but at that moment in time, I was weak and had absolutely no strength to fight.

As I look back, I remember how difficult it was for me to accept the fact that I had a mental health illness and needed to take medication. This affected both my self-worth and self-esteem. I knew I needed to take action before the company let me go for poor performance. I had no other choice than to give in, accept the fact that I had an illness and approach my manager to explain my situation to him. I felt frustrated, constrained and defeated. At the time, my manager was very understanding and sounded quite concerned about my health. He immediately arranged a leave of absence for me.

I was off work for an extended period of time. When I returned, I was surprised to find that my position was not held for me. It was my understanding that they had to hold it for me as long as I was on leave. Over the next eight months, I struggled to find work by applying for other positions within the company. This became a dead end and I approached my manager to discuss things further. During our conversation, I was offered a severance package. A severance that had to be signed and taken that day or I may not be offered anything else.

I immediately declined and began thinking about where I was going to go from there. I knew in my heart that this was unjust and that I could not withstand another dramatic loss. I had already felt stripped of my identity when I was diagnosed with a mental health illness and now I was losing my job. I asked myself, "How am I going to move forward?"

I felt backed into a corner. I consulted my Family Physician. I knew that I was still legally employed at this point, so I chose to take another leave of absence and applied for short-term disability. All the stress was not helping my mental health. I was declined. Time went by, I did not sign anything nor did I return to work, instead, I chose to take the loss of my job because I had no control over that, but I would not let them steal my dignity. I pursued a lawyer to see what my options were.

The lawyer informed me that this was a case of discrimination, a wrongful dismissal and that I had the option to place a lawsuit against the company. However, I could not benefit from both a lawsuit and a company severance; I could only have one or the other. Well, you know that self-determination I spoke of earlier, I was going to look for another opinion. I already felt worthless, undervalued and discouraged. I asked myself, "How many others have the company treated this way?"

Justice needed to be served. The stigma of mental health needed to have a voice. I took my anger and turned it into a positive passion. A passion to have my voice heard no matter what the outcome. Well I had one lawyer work on my severance; I had obtained another lawyer to pursue the lawsuit.

After many months of waiting, justice did prevail. I not only collected my company severance, but I also won the lawsuit. I realize I may not have put a dent in the company's bank account, but I came out with a personal victory of my own. I leaned back in a chair and sighed with relief. I did it! I did it for all those who could not find the strength to fight for themselves. It was not all about the money. It was about treating people with respect and not robbing them of their dignity. I will struggle with a mental health illness for the rest of my life. Why disregard people like us from being part of society? We can recover and manage a full and productive life. There is a lot of stigma around mental health and I know I am just a needle in a haystack, but I just felt a strong need to fight for justice.

The road to recovery is not easy and don't let anyone tell you otherwise. It's a gradual transformation that we go through. We may take five steps forward and feel like we are getting somewhere, only to fall two steps back the next day. Never give up hope and always believe that you can conquer and prevail in the end.

The most difficult part for me during my recovery was not having my family to relate to or understand my state of mind. I felt misunderstood and was very isolated. I found it difficult to reach out for support when no one around me could understand the emotional pain I was going through. This weighed heavily on my illness as I struggled alone and unaware of the resources that existed that I could have reached out. I thought I wasn't normal since I was not aware that others experienced similar mental health issues. No one around me knew where to direct me either.

After meeting with my Family Physician and having several conversations around my mental health, I was finally given a referral to see a psychologist. I jumped at the opportunity to speak to someone individually around my struggles. What was there to lose? Within a few weeks, I began seeing a psychologist and continued to do so for quite some time. She helped me sort through my life and bring a better understanding of it to me.

Over time, she showed me that there was nothing wrong with me. I was just going through a difficult time in my life and that mental illness was a common illness among many. No one was immune from it. She provided me with a sense of belonging by validating my thoughts and feelings. I began to feel somewhat human again, which made me realize that maybe it's okay to think and feel the way I did. My opinions did matter. I am part of this world. She continued to encourage me to accept and love myself for who I am. I will never forget the enormous impact she made in my life. I consider her an angel in disguise, given to me at the exact moment in life that I needed her most.

As I continued my journey, I strived to let go of a lot of my unhealthy behaviours and thoughts; unhealthy behaviours that I may have created in the past in order to protect myself and feel stable in an unstable environment. I challenged myself to change negative thoughts into positive ones. First, I needed to totally accept myself for who I was and love myself unconditionally in order to get to a place where I could understand others and not place judgement on them. Self-acceptance is the pre-requisition to change.

I felt strong enough to venture back out into the world again. I wanted to challenge myself to see if I was capable of returning to work. I approached the Canadian Mental Health Association and applied for a volunteer position on their Crisis and Distress lines. I worked 4 hours a week and provided peer support to individuals experiencing mental health and/or addiction issues. This encouraged my recovery and helped me realize that I was worthy and I did have a purpose in life; a purpose of helping and supporting others through my shared lived experience with mental health.

I began to feel in control of my life again. I went back to school to study Social Service Work. Some would look back and get quite upset thinking about their illness and the wasted years it brought them, but I didn't. I felt a strong need to take what I had learned from my hardship and turn it into a positive experience, where I could help others who experienced similar mental health issues. I wanted to empower individuals and be that little ray of hope in a time when they needed it the most. I wanted to support others when they made that courageous choice to choose life. I wanted others to dream about what the rest of their life could look like to them. I volunteered and shared my experience of mental health on the Crisis and Distress lines. But I wanted to do more. I wanted to further explore my skills, talents and passion.

I lost my best friend to suicide. I can vividly remember hearing the news. I was in shock and disbelieve as I fell to the floor crying. While gasping for air, I kept telling myself that this could not be happening. Questions began racing through my mind. The last time I saw her, there was no indication of distress. Life was good she told me.

To this day I question, "Why? Why didn't she open up to me?"

She knew I struggled with mental health because we spoke of it often in our conversations. I felt guilty. If only she had told me, I may have been able to help support her and prevent her from this tragedy.

This personal event in my life made me want to reach out more to those that struggle with mental health and/or addiction issues. I would at least want to be given an opportunity to make a difference in another person's life. The care, compassion, and understanding you give to someone can make a world of difference in their life as I experienced with my psychologist.

At the end of my school year, I was accepted to complete my student placement at an organization called, "Self Help Alliance". Self Help Alliance provides peer support to individuals experiencing a mental health and/or addiction issue. A peer is anyone you share a mutual experience with. It is the act of people sharing a mutual experience that gives each other encouragement, hope, assistance, guidance, and understanding that aids in recovery. Peer support is helping another person move on with his or her life, and seeing their situation and circumstances differently, with hope and self-determination.

Self Help Alliance provides one-to-one peer support, peer and recovery groups, advocacy and entrepreneurship assistance, and many community resources. This self-help model of recovery was a perfect fit for me, since I followed a very similar model through my own recovery. My passion is to share my lived experience with others experiencing mental health and/or addiction issues and support them while they travel down their own road to recovery.

Before my placement ended at Self Help Alliance, I was hired on to work as a facilitator. I was ecstatic. I had exceeded my highest expectations. I was going to do what comes naturally to me, helping others. I have been with the organization for three years and have seen many recovery story successes.

Many of the success stories I've witnessed are a result of a program I co-facilitated called, "Skills for Safer Living". This is a 20-week psycho-social/psycho-educational intervention for people with recurrent suicide attempts. I remember sitting in on my first group session and just feeling emotionally overwhelmed, absorbing the fact that I was hopefully going to be given my first opportunity to make a difference in another person's life. I felt both honoured and scared. Honoured to be a part of the participants' journey to recovery and scared that I was not going to be good enough in helping any of them.

As I glanced around the room, I could not totally understand why any of the individuals participating in this group would want to end their own lives. They were all beautiful people with no flaws that I could see. I did not observe any physical wounds or deformations that would state that these individuals were ill, or ill enough to want to end their own lives.

I have struggled with my own suicidal thoughts before, but I thought, these people deserved more in life. There were a few individuals that were not quite ready to open up to us and there were those who were at that point in their recovery that were willing. Throughout the 20 weeks we began bonding and building strong, trusting relationships with the group participants.

I have witnessed many participants beginning group with a strong desire to end their lives and then walk out of the group 20 weeks later with a whole new outlook on life. I have even heard a few of them say that they wanted to live rather than die. I have seen the enthusiasm in participants attend the on-going "Peers for Safer Living" support groups offered following the completion of the program. As I see happiness starting to bubble up inside of them, I can only smile and pray for their continued success in recovery.

A fellow co-worker once said that we are the hands that temporarily hold on to the hope for the program's participants, until they are strong enough to take it back. I feel this is a privilege to be trusted with such responsibility. It is heart-warming and humbling knowing that my words and actions have helped save a life. I am empathetically inspired when I have the opportunity to help others. I am motivated by the loss of my friend to support the vulnerable souls that experience the depths of mental health.

I feel I have found my true purpose in life. I run a grief peer support group, facilitate recovery groups and support individuals through one-on-ones. I continue to learn and develop everyday not only from workshops and training, but through the people I support. Recovery will always be part of my life and I will always feel the effects of my illness, but I will never let my illness define who I am as an individual. My hope is that others believe that recovery is possible.

I had an opportunity to sit on the Waterloo Region Suicide Prevention Council. For a year and a half, I was able to volunteer my time in promoting many community events around Suicide Prevention. Our mission is to reduce suicidal behaviour and its impact on individuals, families, and communities. We envision a community where all people are supported to develop their full potential, live to their life potential, and enjoy a positive quality of life. One of our largest fundraisers is our annual bowl-a-thon. Last year, $40,000 was raised for suicide prevention within our community. We hold many educational workshops, conferences and community events. Our hope is to bring suicide awareness to all within our community.

It is organizations like Self-Help Alliance and the Waterloo Region Suicide Prevention Council that drives my passion in life. I believe that if we each do a little, it can add up to a whole lot and a difference can be made in the world. As my passion leads me, I look forward to the adventures that wait for me on the horizon. I was ill and had many years where I did not feel worthy or a part of this world, now my recovery has allowed me to not only give back to the community, but to find my true purpose and meaning in life.

The newly learned skills and positive supports I have gained along the way will allow me to live to my fullest potential. What more could I ask for!

As Kelly Clarkson states in her song, *Dark Side*, "Like a diamond from black dust, it is hard to know what can become if you give up."

I wanted to know what I could become. Every day, I live my life to the fullest with an open mind and a heart full of enthusiasm. Every day a world full of joyous pleasures and surprises are presented to me. It is my awareness of these that reveals my true hidden potential. Potential that allows me to live a healthy, happy, well-balanced life. I believe that it takes a lot of courage to choose recovery, but recovery is possible.

Looking back, it could be easy to think I spent most of my journey alone. I did not have the benefit of support from my family or friends, and the professional networks I came in contact with were helpful, but limited. But then I know that I was never truly alone, the three most important people in my life whom have now passed have always been with me. My mom, Marilyn Dorscht (nee Oswald), my dad, William (Bill) Dorscht, and best friend, Kim Kube have all watched over me, inspired me to continue my recovery, and to follow my dreams. They all continue to drive my passion to succeed in life.

RACHEL MOORE
LOVE TO LIVE

Growing up in a very challenging environment, with parents who drank, smoked and used recreational drugs, my perception of "healthy" was tainted. No disrespect to my parents, or parents of an era who may have been raised with similar influences; however, after being exposed to other lifestyles, and conflict resolutions, I believe my "eyes of understanding" did not see beyond the limits that were placed upon me.

Less than one month after my 11th birthday, my mom was in an alcohol related car accident. Her life lingered in the balance for years and she lived as a quadriplegic in and out of hospitals until she passed away. I was 23 years old.

From the age of 11 to 17, I lived in nine different homes and felt very displaced. With feelings of abandonment, I walked the streets, used drugs and alcohol because I was feeling lost and welcomed the escape.

In dark days, I desperately sought help. I was feeling overwhelmed and welcomed any assistance that didn't end up in psychotropic meds. I sought out counselors and group therapy, but unfortunately I did not come across any therapies dedicated to grief, loss, and abandonment.

By the age of 21, I was a single mother of two. For many years, I was in an abusive relationship that through verbal, mental, emotional and physical abuse I was broken and became hopeless. After being physically assaulted by my partner, police were involved. Repeated incidents exposed me to women's services, which led me to see that I was being controlled and abused if I did not adhere to my partner's demands or expectations. As this revelation sunk deeper within, I attempted to leave the relationship several times. I had minimal support and this was a challenge. Abuse ensued.

Sometimes, I just didn't feel like running and hiding anymore. At times, I was afraid to be beaten. I had flashbacks of brutal attacks from my past and chose to cower. Until one day, I was just so tired of the abuse that I was prepared to die trying to get out rather than staying in the nightmare that had become my reality.

We simply were not healthy for each other and I was becoming abusive myself. I wanted more for my children, not a repeat of my childhood. I stood my ground (slipping here and there), which led to one final assault when I was pregnant with my son. My partner was then charged and incarcerated.

Through the years, I struggled raising my children, but strived to do my best. I read books about healing through forgiveness, parenting, health and wellness, and fundamental values. The values I learned possessed meaning and depth to life. Through stepping "out of the boat" by trying new things and ways of coping, I realized that once I changed my limited perception based truths to limitless possibilities, I was able to see beyond my challenges and work toward healing and happiness.

With the ebb and flow of learning, I found a rhythm that granted grace from God and developed the courage of a brave lion. The hopelessness started to dissipate. When I received a sense of release, from forgiveness, I experienced a very liberating sensation. I rejoiced to be free from the chains that kept me bound. I longed to share the same HOPE with others.

My heart's desire was to help anyone who was struggling because I understood not having direction, not having spiritual guidance, or someone to look to for support. I had been in a cycle of abuse and abandonment and was challenged in believing my self worth. I had a heart of compassion for those who I witnessed suffering. I believed that with support and love, I could help others through the same.

I dreamt for many years of opening up a healing center. A place where people could come and find healing through many forms, specializing in art therapy: music, drama, dance, painting, expressive sharing, group sessions, including gardening, cooking and understanding our emotional connection with food.

Coming from a sordid past, I had several friends who struggled with abusive partners, drugs and alcohol. Many of which needed help and a safe place to turn. An opportunity was presented, over 17 years ago, to open our family home to someone who needed someone to give them a hand, a word of encouragement, and place to rest and gain the stepping-stone to something greater. Since that day, my children and I have been privileged to simply love and provide hope in a season needed for families, troubled youth, and single moms.

I felt a profound connection with so many because I remembered where I once was, and the support and love I needed. By offering my help to others, (doing some of the things I wished had been done for me in my time of need) in a small way, I felt like I was giving back to me. I felt grateful for being able to help others, and I felt good for loving myself more each day because through loving others, I was able to love me.

Over time, I had to learn to set boundaries without enabling, without condoning, choosing acceptance and love for the people my family helped. Through the years, I have come to realize that people often resist change *because it's difficult*. They revert back to what's comfortable, even if it is abusive. In the initial stages, this was very difficult for me to witness. I felt as though I had failed.

I cried many times when the people I had grown so fond of returned to ways of living that they sought to change. I had to come to terms that I was simply just a vessel and a stepping-stone. I was a "facilitator" of sorts offering HOPE of a brighter tomorrow, without the expectations for how or when a person will choose to love himself or herself again. It's been challenging, but I believe I've improved since. In the past, I desperately needed boundaries, truth, wisdom and love. Now, having some experience and structure, I strive to share the same unconditional, unadulterated, and untainted love that I once needed with others.

A few years ago, I suffered with a migraine that lasted for days. I lost track of time. I could barely get up off the bathroom floor. I was determined to find out what was really going on with me. I was "sick and tired" of being sick and tired. I went to my family practitioner and had some tests run. I had had ongoing issues for many years and the results returned the same, "inconclusive" as to the root cause, and was handed a prescription.

Thank God, in the same week, I was introduced to a nutritionist and a naturopath. When I went to see the nutritionist, I was skeptical and I did not disclose any symptoms. I asked her to run the tests and to reveal the findings. In the first few minutes, the Certified Nutritional Practitioner (CNP) had started to name signs and symptoms based on the findings. I was shocked. I was interested to hear more of what she was talking about as she described so many of my signs and symptoms without me speaking a word. These were NOT general. They were VERY specific.

I walked out of that office feeling hopeful. I was dedicated from that day on to change my life, regain my health and to live. As time passed and I incorporated healthier living strategies, I felt invigorated, rejuvenated, energized, peaceful and so grateful. I decided to go back to school (for the 3rd time, after nursing and real estate) to study holistic nutrition.

With an open heart and mind, I studied, worked hard and I graduated. Nearing the completion of my course, I committed in my heart a plan to travel to share holistic health and healing. I felt like I had been given "the gift of life" through the knowledge I had gained through my studies. I felt like I was walking around with vials of healing serum and I desperately wanted to share anything and everything I could to help others.

Many years ago, I had a desire to do mission work, but my first priority was my children at home. Not long after graduation, and upon returning home from traveling abroad, I met someone who was interested in going to Haiti to volunteer where members of his church had gone to do mission work. I emailed the foundation directly and received an invitation to apply to participate in an internship.

I also researched other organizations that I felt would be a good fit and where I could make a real difference. I prayed and I sought spiritual counsel from Christian friends and leaders. Soon after, I applied and was accepted to an organization for an internship. I wanted to provide nutrition through education and counsel to orphanages, missionaries, community programs, and to anyone who was eager to learn about sustainable solutions.

In Haiti, I worked in a children's home as an assistant to the special needs students, teaching basics in Creole. I also taught preschoolers and primary students English. I worked filling the gaps in areas where I was needed most.   Together the children and I completed a garden-planting project. With the interest of the Haitian staff and visiting missionaries, I was given the opportunity to do some cooking and food demonstrations. In the clinic, I was able to offer holistic treatments for wound care, treatment of eczema, and taught the importance of removing harmful substances from the body to maintain focus on healing and rebuilding strong immunity. This was primarily shared with the nannies that worked with the children daily. Addressing dietary needs, such as removing dairy from one little girl's daily meal plan relieved her of major breathing difficulty. By making recommendations and demonstrating how to make quick, easy, and healthy alternatives such as coconut or almond milk and frozen banana/mango pops (instead of milk and ice cream) the little girl was recovering from unnecessary congestion.

I studied local trees and herbs and I found research leading me to the most amazing, incredible tree growing in the country.   In English, we know the tree as the "Moringa" or "Drumstick tree". In Haitian culture, the tree is known as "Benzolive" or "D'Olive". The "Moringa" tree possesses the gift of healing from **root to leaf**.

Studies have concluded that the root, the bark, the sap, the gum, the leaves, the pods, the seeds, and the flower ALL have medicinal applications, nutritional applications or both. I was taken aback. I could not fathom that a tree that grew in such abundance was not being harvested and used in daily living.
Eg. Eating the fresh green leaves (gram for gram comparison taken from www.treesforlife.org) was like taking a powerhouse immune vitamin daily containing:

7 times the amount of Vitamin C of an orange
4 times the amount of Vitamin A as carrots
4 times the amount of calcium of milk (cow's)
3 times the amount of potassium of bananas
2 times the amount of protein as yogurt

When the leaves dried, many of the vitamins increased their intensity. Some increased up to 5 times. Moringa had been used in the ancient world records for thousands of years for the following purposes: nutrition, medicine, ointment, insecticide/fungicide, cane juice clarifier, cooking oil, and food.

In traditional medicine, Moringa was used for the following (including but not limited to): anemia, anxiety, asthma, blood impurities, blood pressure, bronchitis, *Cholera, colitis, diabetes, diarrhea, dysentery, headaches, intestinal worms, jaundice, lactation, *Malaria, joint pain, skin impurities, pregnancy, psoriasis, scurvy, semen deficiency, stomach ulcers, tuberculosis, and urinary disorders.

*Can you imagine? In a country where so many people are affected by Cholera and Malaria, the natural antidote, for numerous ailments, is right in their backyard and they don't even know it? Many nights I prayed in tears until I fell asleep.

I was privileged to share this information with universities, trade schools, churches, local communities, orphanages and even in remote neighbourhoods. I hired a translator and driver, we travelled to various schools and homes. I was eager to share this information with anybody that would listen. About 50% of Haitians, that the information was presented to, knew of the Moringa tree; however, only about 25% ever used it in meals. When they used it in cooking, they used the fresh or dried leaves as a "spice" or flavour. Using the leaves, as they did, they ended up cooking the nutrients out of the leaves. 0-1% used the tree medicinally. For me, this became a mission of "the rebirth of this miracle tree", of this healing, medicinal tree, that grew in copiousness throughout the impoverished land.

In a few short months, I was able to present in Creole. I studied daily and practiced with anyone who could tolerate my obliterated version to the language... LOL... I had professors and doctors reaching out to me (via translator and email) about building on some ideas that we had been discussing. Sustainable solutions for Haiti, building production plants to produce oil (coconut, almond, moringa), providing jobs, and ultimately providing health and sustainability to the country.

Through my journey, I came to realize the gift that had been given; a blessing from God in a country that suffered with malnutrition and disease. I travelled through the vast mountains and deep into the valleys of Haiti. I gained insight and perspective on life beyond anything that I could've ever dreamed or imagined. I was taught humility, gratitude and compassion in the midst of devastation.

The first world problems that North Americans face were the furthest things from my mind. To witness 7-8 people living in a shack, with no guaranteed income, little to no food, and yet the children smiled. In North America, as in many parts of the world, we race around doing "stuff," but rarely have we ever had to think about the basic necessities of water, food, and shelter.

Many locals, in the mountains, had to walk close to an hour to bail water, carrying it home on their heads, to provide water for their families. It was not uncommon to see Haitians bathing in the brooks, streams and local waters with animals. I learned to bathe out of a bucket with cold water. You certainly learn to conserve water when you have so little. My priorities for living changed significantly when I experienced no running water, no current (electricity), and minimal resources.

Travelling deep into the valleys brought the term "fear" into a different perspective. We drove on single lane paths (not roads) with deep ditches through the mountains. If you looked to the side, you would see that merely inches or so kept us from plunging down the 1500+meter mountain.

With approximately 500,000 people still living in tents with little to no clean water accessible or available... (accumulative effect of the hurricanes '08 [4] and earthquake '10), disease was and is rampant. Food is scarce and work seemed to be an impossible goal for many. Providing food, water and shelter was their only focus.

In Gressier, I observed and helped treat wounds oozing and filled with maggots. I was astounded that simple wound care is NOT common knowledge. One young boy (12-13 years old) suffered from a minor injury playing soccer. His untreated injury had led him to almost losing his leg, as infection spread through his body. My heart broke.

I asked myself, "HOW could I make a difference?"

I was touched and moved so deeply by the humility, love and hope that was found in so many. This prompted me to remind myself that I set out to share love, hope and nutritional education. Sharing simple techniques for wound care, to harvest locally, to use foods to the maximum potential (to receive the highest nutrition and benefit), and to highlight foods (Moringa) that seemingly had gone unnoted or had been forgotten.

I have a deep sense of appreciation for the Haitian people and their ability to overcome. Faced with such tragedy, the Haitian people have continued to rise up and **with** hope. They taught me to face each day and take hold of each blessing. They reminded me "beauty **can** come from ashes."

I pray for each person that has taken the time to read this, to find an opportunity to give back and IF feasible in the field of missionary work (locally or abroad). If it is something you've ever dreamed of doing, I pray that you would step out in faith and make it come to pass. If by reading this brief story, you feel a desire *"to be the change you want to see in this world,"* I encourage you to make that dream or desire a reality. Step out and be transformed from the inside out. This life-changing experience has given me a profound perspective, an inner peace, greater joy, deeper compassion and **most** importantly an appreciation and *love for life*.

So you may be thinking, "I can't bring people into my house in my position",
"I'm too young" or "too old",
"I don't have a lot of extra money"…
"I just can't afford it",
"I certainly can't go to Haiti"…

So, I ask you, what **CAN** you do?
What **IS** in your ability?

Could you sponsor a child or reputable organization?
Could you write somebody a letter of encouragement?
Could you buy/make someone a tea and chat … listen?

Could you pay for someone's gas/groceries... pay it forward?
Could you donate your clothes to someone or to the local community center/shelter?
Can you bless somebody with your words of love, hope and encourage someone?
Can you offer a hand of help cleaning or moving?

There is NO right or wrong and there is NO judgment.
I simply ask what **CAN** you do?

Many years ago, I was determined to live, now I'm determined to **"LOVE to LIVE"**
because **I can**.

Love others and love yourself.
LOVE TO LIVE because **YOU CAN!**

Take NOT for granted the gifts you've been given.
Bless others and you will truly bless yourself.

"Bondye Beni Ou"... In English... "GOD BLESS YOU."

From my heart to yours,
Rachel Moore

The greatest glory in living lies not in never falling, but in rising every time we fall.
Nelson Mandela

When I was younger, my worth was always determined by what others thought of me, especially boys. Perhaps it was due to my relationship with my own dad. My entire life was spent trying to please others. The biggest mistake one can make is to look outside of themselves for love, acceptance and constant approval. A girl's journey begins with loving herself and accepting her flaws. This builds confidence, which leads to clarity and allows one to see all the possibilities of life. I never truly liked or loved myself and expected my relationships to make me happy. And when my significant other couldn't live up to this ridiculous expectation, I was left disappointed. I wanted to be a journalist or writer, but lacked the confidence to make my dream a reality. It was one person's comment that deterred me from my dream. I remember that day so clearly. I was nine and had a tutor, a woman I admired and was inspired to be like. I thought she cared for me and liked me. However, it became evident that she didn't, for her step-daughter was ever so quick to disclose to me that her step-mom thought I was stupid. I felt unworthy of anything great and this dimmed my light.

As a child growing up I could always sense the slightest human suffering in others. This gift in itself was a curse and a blessing. I was always in favor of the underdog, the unpopular, and the disenfranchised. I believed, even as a child, that if we are here, we must all matter. I remember a girl, in my 5th grade class, who always had a big smile on her face that you would notice from a mile away. Unfortunately, she also wore a wig that you could spot from the same distance, as Michelle had a severe case of alopecia. Every day Michelle's wig would get pulled off exposing her bald head. I remember sitting and observing her response to this demeaning act. She would smile exposing her dimples, and effortlessly place the wig back on her head. I was amazed by her strength, and resilience to keep playing. Watching her being bullied stirred an emotion in me. I vowed to befriend her and help her when the neighborhood kids would bully her. That was me, always trying to rescue everyone from the bullies of the world.

So, at the age of twenty when I found myself pregnant with a beautiful baby boy, I knew I needed to go back to college in the social services field. I needed to help and I needed to do it for my son. I needed to give him a better chance in life. I needed to show him that despite life's obstacles, we need to persevere. I wanted to become an advocate for children with disabilities and mentor adolescents who were afraid to follow their dreams, goals, and aspirations. So, I enrolled in the Child and Youth Worker Program at Centennial College.

After graduating from the Child and Youth Care Worker Program, I was fortunate to get a job working at the York Region District School District. I didn't realize the depth of my calling. Working in education has taught me to be humble and that we all matter, despite the labels given to us or the labels self-imposed. My responsibilities included working with adolescents with learning disabilities and behavioral issues. I walked in the school ready and eager to affect change. I was young, green and naïve to think it would be easy. One of my first challenges was mentoring a student who had anger management issues. I was faced with the opportunity to affect change in this young girl's life and to teach her a new way to cope with her anger.

It was a normal day in any high school. The teacher asked my head strong student to leave the class and my student responded in a reactionary way causing a rift between her and the teacher. The teacher then burst into tears and my student had to report to the Office. I was called in to deflate the situation and get to the root of her anger. I was able to build a rapport with her over time. It was difficult since trust clearly was an issue. There was an English Teacher who I respected and admired, and she noticed early on that this student had made a connection with me. This teacher suggested I work one-on-one with her to complete an English assignment. We would have to meet once a week after school. The first meeting I used humor to lighten the mood, which allowed her to relax and feel safe. In the following weeks, she opened up more disclosing her family dynamics, which allowed us to get to the root of some of the anger. I admired her strength her ability to stand up to anyone. She had a warrior instinct, so I tried to teach her to channel that energy in a more positive way. We continued our meetings every week even though the assignment was complete. After we met, she managed to turn her life around and three years later, graduated with honors, and became a Child and Youth Worker herself. When asked what the pivotal moment for her was, her response was, Ms. Edwards. I felt humbled and elated at the thought that I had mentored a student to strive for more. At the same time, I felt that although I was helping children, there was still that gnawing feeling of disappointment.

This gnawing feeling stayed with me and I wanted to leave education. I felt like we were failing these children. I was mentally exhausted and needed a change. I had students from all different backgrounds with various needs. I noticed early on the correlation between mental health and learning disabilities.

I tapped into some of my learning from my third year placement at Sunnybrook Hospital working in the *Fresh Start Program*. The program was geared towards adolescents with mental health issues who were hospitalized. After being hospitalized and getting diagnosed, they needed a transition period to help them return back to high school (if it was an option). One of the ways to deal with mental health issues, besides the drugs and the therapy sessions, was an hour of exercise. Exercise releases endorphins, which creates a natural high. Remembering this, I decided to open up the weight room at lunch and after school for the kids with learning disabilities to build their confidence and boost their self-esteem. I found it allowed my students to release some of their stress and it created an opportunity for us to talk.

There were two students in particular that benefited from the lunch-time workout. One had a severe learning disability and working out gave her a stronger sense of self, despite her learning issues. This gave her the confidence to advocate for herself and demand she get re-tested. She was able to attend college to become a Personal Support Worker. Another student used the opportunity to make friends and over time improved her self-confidence. Yet, there were still some children who we could not help at that time. To make matters worse, another one of my students had graduated and was later diagnosed with a mental disorder that she could never recover from.

I had seen some success during my career in the education system and some heartache, and I started to question why I chose this path. I enjoyed working with my students, however, I felt discouraged by not giving them the life they truly deserved. I was burned out. I also worried that I was projecting my own fears onto my students -that life could be cruel, that financial stability would always be a concern, and that sadly there would always be barriers and obstacles to overcome. I had no more to give. I felt defeated and ineffective.

"You must be the change you wish to see in the world," said Mahatma Gandhi.

Change is so hard for us. We get comfortable and the thought of moving on scares us. Being comfortable sometimes doesn't allow us to evolve. We become stagnant and even more ineffective. I knew that it was time to leave the community classes and take on a new role.

My new role provided an opportunity to mentor and provide informal counselling to students. I was in charge of monitoring the students through attendance concerns and developing strategies with their guidance counsellors on ways to make them successful. I was also offered the chance to volunteer my time and some of my skills to aid in facilitating a girls group. The group was implemented by Nicole Baxter and Dionne Teape. *S.W.A.G. (Strength within all Girls)* meets every Wednesday, from 3:30pm to 4:30pm. It consists of a small group of girls from grades 9 to 12.

There is a need to have social emotional groups in our schools. The rationale behind SWAG is taken from "the Impact of Enhancing Students' Social and Emotional Learning" (Feb 2011 scholarly article). 40 to 60% of high school students become chronically disengaged from school. 30% engage in high risk behaviors (substance abuse, depression, sex and attempted suicide). A social emotional group will help deal with the rise of the mental health issues which is very prevalent among our young people. It provides a safe environment for girls to share and problem solve in all areas of their lives.

One of SWAG's objectives is to apply the wrap around concept that provides an opportunity for growth, bonding and learning. The wrap around concept was taken from the Native American Community. Through various activities and sharing information on abuse and self-compassion ,the girls are able to learn about strength, resilience and the importance of knowing your worth in order to obtain all your goals. We have held conferences at other schools where other students could attend workshops. Our workshops focus on knowing your self-worth and building confidence. For example, we ran a yoga workshop, abuse workshop, and positive affirmations workshop that emphasized these concepts in a safe and relatable environment. We believe in affirmations and providing the girls the tools to start affirming and believing in themselves. SWAG offers a place of caring and compassion.

Some girls achieve great success through SWAG. One of our girls joined during her tenth year of high school. She, like most of the girls, came with baggage and was acting out. She didn't know her own strength and resilience. This same girl left high school with many scholarships and awards, and a bright future ahead of her. She came back to speak about her experiences and referenced the importance of having a group such as *SWAG*, to help young girls with tumultuous experiences.

Another student who had benefited from our SWAG group was bullied in her early years of high school. She also suffered from depression and low self-esteem. She had very few friends and felt hopeless. She came to SWAG and that day changed her forever. She said, "It was like dropping a heavy anchor that was weighing me down. I felt like there was a break from the stress and hurt."

Since that day we noticed a change in this individual. She started to see that she mattered and the words that hurt her didn't define her. She is in grade 12 and intends to go to university to study law. She is also a mentor to young girls and continues to speak to them about the importance of knowing your worth. SWAG allows every individual to see that there is hope and strength within themselves and that they matter.

I recognize the importance of mentoring and providing an outlet for adolescents to express their feelings in a safe place. In these groups there are opportunities to deal with the many issues facing our young females. Bullying, educational pathways, sex, drugs-you name it, we would discuss it. The reason I felt so passionate about this group was because of my own experience growing up. I was always searching outside of myself for approval and love. Hoping people would approve of my character, my choices. Hoping people would accept and love me, which caused me to doubt myself constantly and dim my light. I did not have a group like SWAG growing up to offer an ear to listen, or tell me that I mattered and that I could do anything. If I just believed in myself, it may sound cliché, but it is so powerful and is needed to foster a strong sense of self. It helps children see their full potential to follow their goals in a cynical, competitive world. We need to give young women the tools they will need when faced with life's adversities.

This new role helped me to evolve and become more effective. Volunteering my time allowed me to stop feeling sorry for myself. The group taught me that I couldn't beat myself up about the issues I had with my own son, and that I did the best I could with the tools I was given. If somehow I displayed strength and resilience for my son, maybe he would be able see his own worth. I looked forward to Wednesdays to gain strength from these young girls. For as much as we teach and mentor them, they offer us the same experience. It was free therapy.

I still struggled with my son who was dealing with his own demons of failure and low self-worth. However, SWAG gave me the push I needed to be strong and to persevere in helping my own son overcome his low self-image. I encouraged him to get up and exercise to help with his own feelings of inadequacy. Every Wednesday after meeting with these dynamic individuals, I felt equipped to share with my son the positive messages I learned. I was able to take steps to help him deal with issues. This allowed me to let go of some of my own feelings of failure and to give myself some compassion as well.

Once you become honest with yourself then clarity comes forth. I was able to get my son the help he needed. I was also given an opportunity to be a part of a conference and discuss the topic that I held dear to my heart. Mental health based on my own journey and what I observed throughout the years working with adolescents. I spoke about how important SWAG was and how rewarding it is to help our young people reach their highest potential.

People believe that to give back you have to be rich and give in terms of monetary funds. However, one of the quotes I hold dear to my heart is from Steve Jobs:
My favorite things in life don't cost money. It's really clear that the most precious resource we all have is time.

Giving others your time is the most precious gift ever. It shows what I believed in even as a small child: that we all matter. To give someone an ear, time and compassion allows them to see that they do matter.

There are days I question why I chose my field and why I volunteer twice a week to mentor girls. The answer comes to me every time I see a young person faced with obstacles in his or her lives that could potentially break him or her into pieces. It amazes me the strength, resilience and determination of these individuals. They taught me to cry, wipe my tears and move on. It didn't matter what hand you're dealt with, what is more important is how you play and keep playing. There were days I remember finding it hard to get out of bed to face my students, feeling inadequate because of my own son's struggles. Students teach me every day that we all matter that it doesn't matter how much money you have or where you live and what you drive. What matters most is time. The time we give to each other, the time to listen, to share, or to mentor is one of the greatest gifts on earth. Charity, mentoring and giving back helps your soul; it allows you to see the abundance you have and to be grateful. Life is full of obstacles and letdowns. This world can be cruel and cynical, however, if we equip our children with a strong sense of self, they will be prepared to fall down and get right back up. Every so often, during our weekly meetings, I would share a poem with them. I wrote it to uplift them, but truly, they uplifted me. I am a better human being because of these dynamic girls and for that I am grateful.

How can words define the soul?
Piercing hearts like darts on a board.
Stupid, dumb, idiot
You are told by ones you love
Who can't refrain their anger, their tongue
How can words define your soul?
Good or bad, they define your worth
Placed on earth it seems this life
Is full of pain and a lot of hurt
how can words define your being?
I say it shouldn't because you're made by god to achieve.
Even if most don't believe that your dreams are for real.

You hold on to what you see when you close your eyes and dream the dream.
Put to action with god's love and compassion
You will see that words are words.
Some may hurt some may heal
But the human spirit is born to achieve.
Beyond, the realms of any imagination.
So say your words to pierce the soul
And think you know a man's true worth.
Who are you to burst the dream in the eyes of the child behind that dream?
Uplift the spirit, hold your tongue
Words can hurt as much as a gun.

CLAIRE KERR-ZLOBIN
NAVIGATING THE VOID THAT LEADS
TO AN AUTHENTIC LIFE

Settled between the Juan de Bolas mountains, overhung by fruit bearing trees, with a river continuously running through, lies the hamlet called, Connors. It was in this naturally beautiful environment where I spent my early years.

My story, like many others, starts out in a similar way. I had a good childhood with parents who loved me, and made many sacrifices in order for our family to lead a better life than they did. I was born in Jamaica and had a wonderful childhood. We were poor, but I didn't know that.

We had everything we needed. When I think about my childhood, I would say I lived in Paradise. We did not have luxuries like electricity or running water, but on the upside I learned other valuable life lessons.

We had a close-knit community. Our parents felt safe with us walking to and from school, even when I was just six, because it was all the kids from our community walking together in the same direction. There were always adults along the way (doing their own thing, but at the same time checking to see if someone was missing from the group). I didn't know it then, but someone always knew where we were, and if we were lagging behind or late. Our parents would always find out what we were up to by the time we got home, even though there were no telephones or email. Our community just worked well that way.

Some of my fondest memories of childhood were our mealtimes. The most vivid memory I have of my early years in Jamaica is when I first saw shrimps being cooked and witnessed the colour change to bright pink. I can still remember the taste, just by thinking of it.

We would tie a string to a can or bottle and leave it in the river water in the evening. By morning, the can would be full of shrimps, and we would run back from the river with our treasure for my mom to fry for lunch. Because we didn't have electricity, I learned how to build a fire and cook meals over it. I like to think of my early years as my own episode of the show, *Survivor*.

As far back as I can remember the years leading up to 2007 went as expected. Whatever plans I carved out for my life was going along as scheduled and I felt in control of my existence, my dreams, and my goals.

When I was 18, I moved from Ottawa to Toronto to start University. That experience was so overwhelming, I ended up not going to university as scheduled. I was torn between a future doing something that made a difference in the world and something that provided financial stability and security. So, I decided to take a few years to figure out what I wanted to do.

I found an amazing job and quickly showed my value. I was promoted to Manager for a Retail Chain where I got to travel across Canada and the USA making $30,000 a year. It was a dream come true at such a young age to have a position such as this. I was really blessed because the owners adopted me into their family and provided me with many life and business lessons that would make it easier for me when I became an entrepreneur.

But, I decided to go back to school for Accounting and Finance. A 4.0 GPA landed me on the President's Honour Roll and I decided I was going to continue in the Finance field because I knew I could make good money. I found a job at the Molson Amphitheatre in the Accounting Department during my final exams, so I was fully employed by the time I had finished my Diploma. I continued studying as I was working towards my designation in Accounting. During this time, I met the man who would become my husband.

Life was good. I was in the middle of planning my wedding to a man I was head over heels in love with. Things were going exactly as planned. But things took a turn for the worst, and my fiancé was diagnosed with a rare and scary pulmonary embolism (blood clot) in his lungs. It still is one of the scariest and most defining nights of my life.

I was woken up in the middle of the night by my fiancé screaming in pain. We thought it was his heart and we called 911. When they came they checked his heart and said he was fine. They thought it was just a panic attack. I insisted that we go to the hospital anyway because my fiancé was not the type to scream from pain, and had never experienced a panic attack before.

Because he thought it was his heart, the same thing happened once we got to the hospital. They checked his heart and said he was fine and it was just a panic attack. The nurses were not taking his pain seriously and even told him to stop screaming because he is disturbing the other patients. Eventually, someone decided to run some tests because the pain was increasing. It seemed like all of a sudden pandemonium broke out, the nurses and doctors were suddenly concerned and then he was rushed off for additional x-rays. The pulmonary embolism was a result of a recent ACL repair surgery.

Up until that night I had no interest in children – I figured I would have children eventually, but being only 25 years old, it had not crossed my mind. The doctor mentioned 7 or 8 times how supremely lucky my fiancé was to have made it to the hospital in time to stop the clot before it reached his brain. I was very worried when they said there were more clots and they'd have to monitor and try to thin his blood before any of the clots go to his brain. They had not yet given him the all clear and it could still turn out to be fatal.

I had a bit of a freak out. I chastised myself for putting my career above anything else.

"Imagine he could have died and I would not have had anything to remember our love, and our chances of having a family would have been over," I thought.

It was an emotional response to a traumatic night. My fiancé was in the hospital for a few weeks and when he got home we decided we would not wait anymore. We would start trying to have a baby. This was huge for us and primarily out of the shock of what was happening. We were still going for daily visits to the hospital, so that he could get blood thinners and other medication. It was still a scary and uncertain time, especially since we were still not sure if he would make it.

In any case, we both thought it would take some time because I was told it would be very difficult for me to conceive. When I was nine, I had accidentally taken *all* of my mother's birth control pills because I thought it was candy and it really messed up my reproductive system. Well, as it turns out I got pregnant on the first try. Unfortunately, I didn't know it at the time.

When I went to the doctor to get the blood test it came back negative, my fiancé and I both had a huge sigh of relief. By this time we had both calmed down a bit, the doctors had given him the all clear and my urgency to start a family diminished as he got better. I wanted to get back to the business of focusing on my career, planning our wedding, and continuing my studies.

But, I was always very tired, falling asleep earlier than usual, and had very low energy during the day. I went to see my doctor and they thought it was the flu – after all I had just had a negative blood test, so pregnancy was ruled out.

In the fall of 2006, I ended up in the hospital with severe pain in my side and the doctors thought it was my appendix. It was during an X-ray that it was discovered that I was 12 weeks pregnant and the pain was from a cyst caused by the pregnancy. Once the initial shock was over, we were overjoyed!

In June of 2007, I gave birth to a perfect, tiny, sweet girl named Katelyn. She changed my life. Katelyn came into the world in a stressful way for me. I had a rare complication, which caused me to be in labour for almost 84 hours. I ended up being in the hospital for over a week.

I was for the first time with a new baby, just released from the hospital and felt utterly alone. I was having scary dreams, which as result of a traumatic birth and would later find out I had a post-traumatic stress disorder. Since I did not know what was happening, I didn't tell anyone because I thought I was going crazy. As a result of all of this, I ended up with severe postpartum anxiety.

Once I got the anxiety under control, I planned to be back at work one day a week when my daughter was 3 months, and back in the office full-time when she was 6 months. I also planned to finish my CGA designation and write my exams.

Yup. That was the type of over-achiever I was, but in all fairness, this served me well in the past, and all my plans always worked out. I had absolutely no idea what having a baby was like, so I was in for a rude awakening.

For the most part, I loved Katelyn from day one – in such a fierce way that I wanted to protect her from everything. Unfortunately, all the stress of the past year, along with the lingering anxiety and stress of the traumatic birth did not bode well for a mom left alone every day. I ended up feeling isolated, sad, lonely and eventually depressed. Yet, at the same time I was wrestling with an old demon of wanting to do something that made the world a better place.

It never occurred to anyone to say to me – *well, you can be a mom and*…it was always, *well, you can be a mom or*…

I had to choose between being a mom and being a professional. It felt to me that our society is not set up to support mothers who want to be a professional and also a full-time parent. I feel that we often have to choose between the two, and I feel that's why mothers today are finding it difficult to adjust to the role of parenting.

I did not have a support network. I did not have the village my mom and other mothers had when they started mothering. While I knew I could be anything that I wanted to be when I grew up, no one told me how to do that while caring for the next generation of decision makers. No one said, you can be anything you want to be when you grow up and this is how to do it while raising your family.

And so began an internal war waged in my head. I felt the struggle pulling back and forth between wanting to be at home with my daughter and pursuing my career. I couldn't imagine leaving my child and being away from her for most of her young life. But at the same time, I wanted to reach for the stars to achieve my career goals. I wanted the world to be better for her, for me, and for all mothers who go through this struggle.

I decided to follow my heart. I would stay at home with my child and try to make a difference in her life and the lives of women with the many roles placed upon us. I wanted to do something to make adjusting to motherhood easier and to support mothers in whatever role they choose on top of being a mom. I wanted to make mothering fun. I wanted the reduce the challenges new parents face after having a family like social isolation and lack of peer support, and lack of a community. I wanted to recreate the village that generations of mothers had before us. I wanted the village, where if you were conflicted, there were other moms around to encourage you, to tell you how they did it, and to say – you CAN be a mom and a professional if you want – or you can be a full-time mom. Whatever you envision for your family, I wanted to help create a system that supported it. So, I created *Life With A Baby*.

Life With A Baby (LWAB) is not just about supporting mothers. It's about reducing isolation for all parents. It's about changing the way we look at the important role of the parent. We provide educational training sessions with professionals who work with parents to help bring the current challenges parents are facing into focus. We have had over 500 professionals from various cities in Canada and the United States participate in our educational training.

We created a charity organization, *Healthy Start, Healthy Future*. We bring awareness to the increase in postpartum depression and share research and knowledge on how this can be prevented as a whole for our society. Through the Life with a Baby program we also provide work from home opportunities for mothers who want to work flexible hours while raising their family. We have 200 moms across Canada and now the United States who have volunteered or worked with LWAB.

We also host support groups and conferences for moms to help them adjust to parenting, like caring for their kids as well as their homes, and reduce the work/life balance guilt they experience.

Once I decided to follow my purpose, my world and the world around me has changed. The 8000+ mothers who have participated in the Life With A Baby program say their lives have changed. They feel supported. They make new friends. They feel like they have a village. I want to continue creating new communities. I want to continue recreating the village of support for mothers and fathers.

We are preventing mothers from becoming isolated. Motherhood is becoming fun and easier. And for the many mothers who may have experienced a Postpartum Mood Disorder or if you are currently experiencing this –know that you are not alone.

For me, I have found my purpose. I am living my dream. I am happy. I am fulfilled. I have found my place and I hope to help other women across the world to do the same.

Often times when I meet people, I tell them about the rapid growth of Life With A Baby and the amazing partners we have. They often say, I make it look easy, but this was one of the hardest things I've ever done. As Samuel Goldwyn said, "The harder I work, the luckier I get."

I think it is important to realize that when we are on the verge of getting what we really want and going after our infinite goals, it *will* be very difficult. It's difficult because there will always be something easier, like getting a job and working for someone else. It will be difficult because of the insane amount of hours and personal time that will be needed to make it successful. It will be difficult because in the beginning we will be putting money into the dream instead of getting any money out of it. It will be difficult and that's good, because if we stick with it, it's because we really want it. And if we really want it, we will not give up.

There are so many things that I could say to other women who want to follow their passion, and their dreams. I'd like to focus on the limitations we often place on ourselves because of our thought patterns. As a visible minority woman, people are always asking if I was discriminated against and if I've experienced a lot of racism. I generally answer in the same way, "No, I cannot say that I noticed any specific negative occurrences."

Although, I generally mention I didn't know I was "black" until I was about 12. Before that, I was always Jamaican or just "me". My family hadn't immigrated to Canada and up until that point, it was never mentioned to me. I was not different, I was not black, I was just, *me*.

I got used to being the only non-Caucasian face at events, clubs, or group meetings. I got used to speaking to groups of people without seeing anyone who looked like me or feeling insecure just because of my skin colour. This came in very handy when I spoke at large events, such as the Health Canada Conference where 98% of the 500 people in attendance were Aboriginal and I was the only Black person in the room. I was fortunate that my early experiences did not limit my thought patterns and my future actions.

So I say to you – please do not let your thoughts limit your ability to be great.

Use my example as proof that when we change out thought patterns, we change our future. If I had believed that the general public did not "like" me because of the colour of my skin, I would have said no to many opportunities. I would not have attended certain events. I would not have approached certain people to speak about funding, sponsorships, or advertising. In fact, I'm quite certain that if I had maintained my limited thinking, I would not have created the Life With A Baby program. I would not be managing an organization of over 200 people and I would not be where I am today.

It is simply amazing the peace and contentment that life can offer when we are living out our life's purpose. I had many internal struggles before I got to where I am today. I struggled when I took two years off from University and decided to work and figure out what I wanted to do. At age 20, I had not yet figured it out.

When I look back I realize that having Katelyn, experiencing the raw emotions, and the fear of what my life would be like if I continued on my current path, that it was exactly what I needed to experience. I was again back to the point of needing to choose between doing something that I felt was important, impactful and life-changing, or choosing financial gain. It was not easy giving up the stability of a regular paying job to branch out on my own. It was a very difficult conversation with my husband, and other family members. I was worried about how little money we would have. But, an amazing thing begins to happen once you start following your heart and life's purpose. The money, and the opportunities, and the security will come.

It is important to live your authentic life. The only way to be content and happy with the success you will achieve is to be your authentic self.

DENISE GARRIDO
AN INDOMITABLE SPIRIT

My parents originate from humble farming backgrounds in Portugal. They immigrated to Canada with hopes of a new life, filled with possibility for them and their young family. I am the eldest of three, first generation Canadian children.

Like most new immigrants, my parents were actively learning English at night school, and obtaining their Canadian citizenships. When I started kindergarten, I was very quiet. Because we spoke Portuguese at home, I did not have any practice speaking English. I could however, understand it perfectly. That was, after all, the language of all my friends in Disney movies. But my inability to speak English made me an easy target at school, and worse, I had no way to verbally stand up for myself.

Cutting comments were made daily, and they never hurt any less. All I could do was pout, whimper, look down, and hope they went away. This continued all through elementary school. I was teased about how I looked, what I wore—essentially anything their young minds could come up with as different, or unappealing, was pointed out. I was afraid of saying anything because if I did, it would bring more attention my way, and that was the last thing I wanted.

In fourth grade, my parents discussed the idea of enrolling my younger brother in Tae Kwon Do classes. It would be an extra-curricular for him to become involved in, as they had us both originally in piano lessons, but he lost interest and dropped out.

I jumped in, exclaiming it would be a great idea for me to join in too! How cool it would be to do those crazy moves—those punches and kicks would make us invincible! My knowledge of martial arts at the time was purely based on action films.

"No Denise, you're already doing piano. Your brother isn't doing any extra-curricular activities right now, so this would be for him. And it's more of a boy thing anyways."

Boy Thing!? Absolutely not! Although I was an introvert outside the home, inside the home I was more of a daredevil. Having a brother only 13 months younger, we were a power duo.

We would plan secret missions throughout the house when Dad was watching TV. Like ninjas, our objective was to go unnoticed. We would sneak up the stairs, crawl across the hallway and into the kitchen, towards the forbidden drawer: the drawer they stashed all the candies and chocolate treats. Reaching that drawer, the "holy grail," was our second objective, and the prize within tasted even better upon accomplishing that mission!

We would have these kinds of adventures often, and because we were sidekicks, there was never a "boy thing" or "girl thing" we would discriminate against. All was equal. We both played with trucks. We both played with dolls. We both did crafts. We both watched Care Bears. So martial arts being a "boy thing" was such a silly statement!

"That's not fair! We both had the opportunity to do piano, and if he dropped out, then that's too bad. But you can't enroll just him in martial arts and not me. It's not fair. I'm older, and I'm a girl. I technically need to know how to defend myself even more than he does."

No retort from either parent. Did I get my message across?

Next thing I remember is pulling into the "do-jang" parking lot. We met this nice lady inside who was working with her husband on renovations to the do-jang and gym. She managed memberships, and her husband was the master instructor. My dad started to inquire about enrolling at their Tae Kwon Do school. Then the magic words, "What would the cost be for two?"

YES!

First day of class, I was extremely nervous. There would be a lot of new kids. Could I blend in enough to not get picked on?

Well, fortunately, we were all wearing "do-boks", the traditional Tae Kwon Do uniforms, so there wouldn't be an opportunity to be teased for my hand-me-down clothes.

And this time, I wasn't going in solo. In school, I was a year ahead of my brother (because I am a year older), so it was just me and the mob that targeted me. I was a one-man army, taking in the insults alone, no one to lean on for comfort or to defend me.

The first day of Tae Kwon Do class, my brother and I blended in quite well. I tried to avoid interaction with other students, in fear they would "discover who I was" and start teasing me. It didn't happen. To my surprise, students were coming up to me, introducing themselves, taking a keen interest in both my brother and I. I still didn't open up too much. It could be a trick. I had built a wall around me.

Class commenced. I experienced the burn of push-ups for the first time. How do people have the strength to actually hold themselves up with their arms? No knees on the floor? A whole 10 push-ups? Then standing arm-out exercises. Stretching your legs so far apart that it felt like they were going to rip right off. This was hurting more than I anticipated. What about the cool acrobatics I saw in the movies? When do we learn that?

We concluded the first class by reciting the "Student Creed" and what "Tae Kwon Do aims to achieve."

To build ourselves, physically and mentally, based on the Tae Kwon Do spirit.

To keep friendship with one another, and to be a strong group.

To never fight to achieve selfish ends.

Tae Kwon Do Aims to Achieve: Modesty, Perseverance, Self-Control, Indomitable Spirit.

At the time, they were big words, and even though Master Delfs explained their definitions to us, it was only in time that their meaning would become clear and alive.

These words would become so ingrained, that they would become my philosophy, an integral part of who I am.

"How was class?" Mom asked.

"It was ok. We did push-ups, a lot of push-ups. And there were students of all ages, adults and kids."

"Did you have fun?" she followed up.

"It was actually pretty good," I replied, realizing that I made it through without being teased.

And so classes continued. And those students, who had introduced themselves to me on my first day, would become my partners in class, and eventually, friends. I finally found a place of acceptance; I belonged.

While learning various techniques, building my strength, improving my flexibility and increasing my endurance, a secret confidence began to grow.

The teasing at school continued, but its impact became less severe, as I would think to myself, "Say and think what you want about me, because you have no idea what kind of secret weapon I have (Tae Kwon Do). I'm a lot stronger then I appear. "

It was during this time that my confidence began to come from within and I began to disconnect more from the need to be accepted by peers at school. I was still quiet, and liked to fly under the radar. And although I still craved friendships at school, my view of life became more long-term.

I knew that I was perceived as someone of equal value in Tae Kwon Do, and this safe place was where a lot of my growth and self-beliefs were developed.

The term "Give Up" was unacceptable in class. Suggesting "giving up" would result in push-ups or "burpies" (jumping jacks with push-ups). If we complained of our arms feeling tired, that meant more push-ups. If something was too hard, it meant extra push-ups and doing it all over again. Giving up was not an option.

There is a little frame in our do-jang that still hangs to this day; and I would read it over and over when standing in line during warm-ups, that says, "Tae Kwon Do is a never ending quest for perfection. An art of developing the mind and body to defeat your constant opponent...yourself."

I truly began to believe that if someone else could reach a physical feat, then I could too. It was just a matter of pushing myself enough to overcome my own mental limitations.

When the time came to fill out my high school course list, towards the end of my final elementary school year, I had the option to select "Academic" (meaning leading to University) or "Applied" (meaning College or Workplace) levels for each class. My parents had often told me that it was important to go to University to have a bright future, as it would allow me to get a good job, which would mean a good life, so I selected "Academic" for all my courses.

One day in class, we all began sharing our course selections for high school--"Academic" or "Applied". When I mentioned I chose all "Academic", a look of disbelief came across many of my peers' faces. One actually spoke out with concern (actually, more to discourage and to put me down), "What are you thinking taking all Academic classes?! I'm not even taking all Academic classes, and I'm smarter. No offense, but if you follow through with that ridiculous idea, you're not even going to make it through high school."

I just listened politely but did not validate her comment with a response. My response was internal, as I thought to myself, "Say what you'd like, and believe what you want to believe, but I know I can do it."

Starting high school was terrifying. This was a bigger pond, older kids, and I heard of bullying horror stories. I didn't want to be one of the victims. I hoped that as long as I kept with my tactic of being quiet, I wouldn't be noticed.

The idea of being quiet slowly began to change as I began to find my place among my peers. That year I began to come out of my shell, little by little.

That was also the year that I began teaching Tae Kwon Do to children, aged 3-7, as my part-time job. I recall the first class; I was standing outside the glass doors of the do-jang, staring in at the room full of little kids running around. Parents sat outside, watching the class. I was terrified. The students were less than half my age, yet I was afraid that they wouldn't accept me as their instructor. I had to change from being the quiet one in the corner, to becoming the focus of an entire class; my heart raced.

Master Delfs met up with me outside the do-jang, introducing me to the structure of the "Kwon Do Kids Class". Fortunately, another red belt student my age would be my partner in instructing most of the classes, so it diffused some of the fear. The first day, I let my partner lead, and did more observing.

To my surprise, the first day wasn't bad at all!

The next class was my turn to be more of the leader, and I tried to go through warm up, and ran through various patterns ("hyung"). I quickly learned that kids have a much shorter attention spans, but for the first couple of weeks, Master Delfs would watch, and provide input on how to run the class more smoothly.

"Sesame Street has been around since 1969, and continues be one of the most popular preschool television programs. What is their formula, that continues to keep children engaged, year after year?" he asked.

I had watched it many times, and I knew I enjoyed watching that show as a child, but I never thought about *why*.

"It's the change of content and scenery every minute or so. It keeps the child's attention locked. The moment their attention begins to wander, the scene has changed to something else. The same goes with teaching Tae Kwon Do (or anything) to children. You need to constantly change what you're doing to keep them focused."

And so I tried it– and presto, it worked like magic! Master Delfs' ongoing advice after each class really honed my abilities as an instructor, and I actually became very good at teaching Tae Kwon Do, especially to children. My confidence grew. The fear I once felt being in front of others began to disintegrate.

In high school, I also began to find my place of comfort and acceptance. By being part of extra-curricular committees, my skills were being used for a greater good. I was learning, I was meeting people, and I felt valued. I found my niche.

I sought out activity after activity to be part of at school. I was kind of addicted! By Grade 12, I was the Yearbook Editor, part of the Drama Club, the Environmental Team, the Ministry Team, did the morning announcements at school, and tutored ninth grade math students, to name a few. If I were in charge of anything, my belief was and is, the final product represents me so it has to be done well.

My lunches were spent in the art room, catching up on work for my visual arts class or in the computer science room, reviewing and editing the yearbook pages for final approval. I'd spent hours after school, finishing projects before heading to teach Tae Kwon Do.

One afternoon at school, a teacher came into one of my classes, promoting the Co-op Program. He spoke of the importance of work placement because "You are all most likely to just be average in work and life, so you may as well get connected with simple job placements now."

His pessimistic assessment of our futures didn't sit well with me. I wanted to be inspired. I wanted to be told that the sky is the limit, and that I can achieve absolutely amazing things if I work for it, not that I'm destined for mediocrity, and to get comfortable with settling.

I was determined to lead by example.

Although I was told that my life was going to be average, my life is far from average. This is because of specific choices. My Tae Kwon Do instructor provided me with an environment of belonging and empowerment, which I strive to provide to my students now.

The choice to be extraordinary was also influenced by my parents, who told me that anything is possible if I work hard enough for it, so don't let anyone else tell me otherwise.

I have been able to do some very exciting things in my life, such as travelling the world and participating in a number of charitable tours.

Some highlights included traveling to beautiful Nicaragua on a medical mission with "Operation Smile." They help children born with cleft lips and palates that without surgery, may not make their 1st birthday.

Other notable charities include "S.O.S. Children's Villages" and "Variety - The Children's Charity" among others. But the most eye-opening experience was with the *Healthy Kids Happy Kids Foundation (HKHK Foundation)*.

I had the privilege, along with 5 other pageant titleholders, to be involved in a two-month tour throughout India with the HKHK Foundation. This experience truly opened my eyes and my heart. We provided food, clothing and medical assistance to children, in some of the poorest slums of India.

HKHK has a vocational college it supports for underprivileged teens and young adults. We were able to visit the students at the college several times. We even assisted with some of their medical camps, in which the students were giving back to their community by providing free medical tests, such as eye exams and basic blood work for those who would never be able to afford it otherwise.

Out of all the students, I really connected with three sisters. One in particular, Fatima, really spoke to me. She was such an intelligent young woman, who was very hard-working, focused, and with so much kindness to give. She was a widow, but unfortunately is not allowed to re-marry according to her religion. A consequence of being a woman without a man, in her culture, is that you become a second-class citizen and rejected from society. She only has herself and her sisters now.

After learning this about her, and discovering what a high achiever she was at the college was very inspiring. Fatima didn't let her circumstances dictate her future, or her potential. By the choices she was making, she put herself in a position to improve the lives of her and her sisters, through education and hard work. The indomitable spirit she showed was something I really resonated with and admired.

We had a final visit at the school, the day before I returned back to Canada. I went throughout the classes saying my goodbyes to all the students. Fatima and her sisters stood in the back, just quiet. They were teary-eyed. I brought my pageant crown with me that day and asked if they would like to try it on and take some pictures– and for a moment to allow them to be the queens that I saw they were.

Fatima, giving me her last hug, quietly told me that she would never forget me. I too would never forget her, her sisters, or the beautiful people I met on the 2-month mission.

It is easy to fall into the belief that I am just one person, what impact can I truly have? That's one thing that the experience in India taught me: the impact of a single person. Sometimes in life, when we feel like no one cares and have lost hope, it is through one person telling us that he or she believes in us that can turn our world around.

One thing that the head of the HKHK Foundation mentioned was that although he appreciates money for his organization, the greatest value comes from people that will give of their time– to give a part of themselves to the people. I began to notice the impact I had every time we would visit certain places. The eyes of the children would light up when their tall, white friend would come back to visit (sometimes with goodies). Just to have a friend who cared, took the time to listen and give affection, really lifted their spirits.

Thinking "I am only one person" implies separation from the whole– from the rest of the world and all its inhabitants. We need to understand that we're connected to everything that's alive. Our actions, even when appearing to be insignificant, strongly impact our global community.

Our intrinsic connection is perhaps where the desire to help others and to give back stems from. For myself, it's whether working in the medical field, training women in health and wellness, or pursuing research, I desire to be a positive contributor to the world.

Everyone possesses the power to make a positive difference. No matter how big or small, the key is taking action and believing in yourself. Sometimes we need a nudge to remind us of our greatness. I enjoy instilling confidence in others, just as my instructor did with me.

If most obstacles are psychological, then there is, essentially, always a way to overcome them. You just have to choose to work harder, be flexible in your approach, and believe you can prevail. And when you do overcome that obstacle, use that energy to encourage and support others facing their own challenges. Show them that they too have a great power within.

Fabiana Bacchini
Changing the world: It starts with me

I remember when I was 8 years old, my mom took off her shoes to give to a homeless woman lying on the sidewalk. She walked home barefoot without saying a word to me. I almost felt embarrassed to walk beside her all the way home, as everybody seemed to be staring at us. As we got home, she told my aunt about it and my aunt said, "You are such a good person. Only you could do such a thing."

Little did I know the impact that gesture would have on my life today.
Giving back was part of us, part of our daily lives. I thought it was not something we only did, but everybody else did too.

I was born and raised in Sao Paulo, Brazil part of the middle class. My father worked really hard to provide for our family. My mom quit her job after I was born because they could not afford daycare. When I was about 4, my parents managed to put me in a private school – this is common in Brazil as the public schools are usually for very low-income families. Needless to say, my parents had to sacrifice a lot to pay for tuition.

I was probably one of the poorest students in the school. The girls on the school bus with me were much older and made fun of where I lived everyday. They threw away my lunch several times. My mom encouraged me to speak up for myself, but I just couldn't do it. Those girls really intimidated me.

In class, on the other hand, I was very sociable. I felt more comfortable around the kids my age. All we wanted to do was play and have fun. No one cared where I lived. Children don't see the differences in other people. There is no such thing as "other" to them. To children, it was only "us."

As we grew older, we developed stronger friendships and had play dates at each other's houses. I got to experience life with more abundance and I began to dream. I started to dream about having a big house, being able to travel abroad like my friends did.

At home, I remember my mom saying, "I wish I could do more. I wish we had more money to buy a little house for a homeless family."

Then, I started to piece things together. What if we had more money so that we could *give* more? I started to dream about becoming successful financially and all the possibilities that would come with it.

I started to understand who my mom was. She wanted the world to be fair.   With her random acts of kindness, she was doing her part. We didn't have the money to donate to charities, so we donated our time and our heart to the people. More than money, our family spread love. We made people feel like people. We listened to their stories. We understood their broken hearts. We actually "saw" them.

Living in a country like Brazil where poverty is so wide spread and in our doorsteps at ALL times, we sort of feel immune to seeing poverty around us. We ignore that the homeless people are actually people with stories, with needs. I realize that the needs are not always a material need. In fact, many people we talked to just wanted to be heard, and just wanted to tell their stories. We were there to listen. We made a human connection in every situation.

My mom's greatest impression on me was during my teen years. My parents' financial situation improved and they bought a cottage. Every Christmas Day, my family gathered together to distribute toys and clothes in a rural area near the cottage. One of my cousins would dress up as Santa (in 32°C weather)! He would ride in a small chariot full of toys, while we were all in cars driving behind it and stopping where we knew there were kids who wouldn't get any gifts.

I absolutely loved doing this. We spent a lot of time preparing for the big day. We decorated Santa's "sleigh." We asked everyone we knew for donations. Our garage filled up fast.

My brother and I got so excited the night before we could hardly sleep. It was the highlight of our holidays. As we drove by the neighborhoods, everyone would come outside to see us. The adults always had a huge smile on their faces and they would greet us as if we were celebrities.

I loved interacting with families we met along the way. Most kids ran after Santa. I could see their eyes shining almost in disbelief that Santa actually existed. In those neighborhoods, Christmas was just another day. I distinctly remember my mother being the happiest in her life during those Christmas days.

I realized that I was just as happy and fulfilled seeing the difference we made in people's lives. They were small acts of kindness, but had such a huge impact.

This was when I started to realize my inner calling or what I believe to be "my purpose." When I was getting ready to go to University, I knew I wanted to do something to change the world I was living in. I didn't find it fair to see so many people with nothing and others, so wealthy. Brazil has both extremes and everything in between when it comes to social classes. I needed to express my indignity in an unfair world and change it.

I became a journalist with the dream of giving the less privileged a voice. I started to work in the newsroom in television while I was still in University. Working as a news producer and a live eye producer, I was even more exposed to the reality of my country. I became more attached to the stories I heard from people, who many were victims of a system that didn't really care about them. Other days I had to interview the law and decision makers, the politicians and people who work in the system. I heard promises made, but those were empty promises that were left on paper, and none of action.

It was frustrating not having control of what news should be aired or how the stories should be told. Even though I loved the adrenaline rush of the newsroom, I started to feel disconnected from my calling. The days I was off, I was more in tune with my heart and I knew I had to do something bold in order to fulfill my purpose of changing the world.

But, I had no idea how I would be able to do something so big.

I had that little voice inside my head asking me all the time, "Who are you to change the world? Only important, rich and influential people can do that."

Sometimes my dream of changing the world seemed overwhelming and unrealistic.

Besides, I had a promising career ahead of me. I could have just settled and took life as it came like everybody else. But I was stubborn and I had to follow my heart hoping I was going to be able to make peace with that voice inside me.

I decided to travel to see the world as it was. My travels ended up being a self-discovery journey. Being alone for the first time in my life gave me time to dig deep inside to discover who I was and question why was I here. I was searching for something, but was not sure exactly for what. I met people from all walks of life, all faith, and dozens of different cultures. I heard hundreds of stories. We shared our beliefs and understandings of the world and of ourselves. I came to realize that no matter where we come from, all we want is to love and be loved. Every woman who crossed my way wanted to contribute to a cause, to her community, and to her loved ones. I discovered that the human essence is the same in all of us. This discovery changed the way I perceived the world. It transformed me into a respectful human being without judgment of other cultures. It also raised my desire to contribute and make a difference in people's lives so we could all live a more fulfilled life. I was still to figure out how.

On one of my trips, I met a man in Israel who shared his love story and how he found his soul mate. Shortly after that, I came across an article about soul mates and I kept it wondering if I would ever find mine to share the journey. A few months later, I met a friend, who I hadn't seen in 3 years, and after spending just a couple of days with him I knew he was my soul mate. We shared the same passion for life, the same desire to contribute, and he complemented me in every way. There was just one problem; he lived in Toronto and I lived in Brazil. However, we did not let distance become an obstacle. And seven years later I moved to Canada to be with him.

We got married. Life was going well. I felt so fortunate to be living in a country where it seemed to be fair and have an equal society. It was not until I started working in Toronto television that I realized that the poverty also exists here. It's not at the same extent as Brazil, but there it is. It's not as visible, but still affects so many people.

Once again, my inner voice started to make even more noise. I had to quit journalism once and for all. But what was I going to do now? I was still unsure.

During the time I was working in television, we covered a lot of fundraising and met incredible people doing events to raise money for their causes. I decided to get involved and help some of these people to fundraise for their organizations and I loved doing it. It was a different way for me to give back. There was a structure, a formal way of asking people to support, and the people involved were truly passionate about the cause. It seemed like a great fit for me and I felt a passion for it. Moreover, I discovered that I was good at asking people to help financially.

Canadian Women's Foundation (CWF) was where I was introduced to many generous women who collectively were changing women's lives right here in Canada.

I was very impressed with a story of a woman I met at my very first event at the CWF. This woman came into a room of 50 women and had the courage to share her story about being a prostitute, who became a devoted mother, and eventually changed her life to become a very successful businesswoman. It all started when she decided to attend one of the programs the CWF sponsors. After that, she was able to turn her life around. It was at the program where she found people who supported and believed in her.

This was my "Ah-ha" moment!

I then realized that changing the world means changing the world around me, causing a compound effect. The CWF was changing the world with one woman at a time. YES! This causes a ripple effect. I felt truly passionate about it and now my dream no longer seemed overwhelming and unrealistic when I saw the changes happening right in front of me.

I knew I had to work alongside women if I wanted to make a difference in the world. I had learned at the CWF that when you improve women's equality, it improves economic and social conditions for everyone.

I was very intrigued by these ideas and I wanted to learn more about them. I found out that women tend to reinvest their income into education and the health care of their families, which improves the overall quality of life for their families, and eventually their communities. When women and girls are educated, they can earn more, but more importantly the gender discrimination declines, their voices are raised in a more informed way, and the poverty cycles can be broken, which benefits all of us.

In life, once you have clear, defined dreams and goals, challenges appear to test how bad you really want it. I decided to embrace the challenge that showed up in front of me when I was 33 years old.

I was faced with a nightmare when the doctor confirmed what my husband and I already suspected: infertility. We tried to get pregnant for one year and after several tests I received this heartbreaking diagnosis. The journey was painful, both physically and emotionally. It's a roller coaster ride with no end in sight. Every month, I took tons of fertility drugs, blood tests, ultrasounds, painful procedures, and at the end of it all, a waiting period for one phone call. Month after month I heard, "It's negative, come back in 5 days."

Some days I felt totally discouraged, but most of the days I kept my faith and the belief that I was going to be a mom. At that time, I also met many women suffering in silence, ashamed and frustrated. It made me think what was really important in life. I surrounded myself with positive people and I started to understand the power of the mind.

After three years, our fertility doctor in Toronto told us that we might not be able to have children of our own. We did not accept his diagnosis and we travelled to Brazil for a second opinion. After one cycle of in vitro fertilization (IVF), I waited for the phone call. Between the blood test and the call was about 6 hours. The longest 6 hours of my life.

The doctor called to say that I was pregnant! I burst into tears. I had to go back for an ultrasound before flying back to Canada. As soon as I walked into the clinic, there were at least 30 couples in the waiting room. I asked what was going on and the receptionist

told me that the doctor does 100 procedures a year for low-income couples that can't afford the treatment. I was blown away.

Again, I witnessed another example of one person making such a great difference in other people's lives. I felt my life's purposes calling me to action, yet again.

My dream of working with women was playing a big part of my life again, especially after seeing so many women suffering and in pain because they could not conceive naturally. I had learned so much from this journey. I learned a lot about me and my belief system. I took several personal development courses. I became highly trained in the power of the mind and its influence on the physical body. I was ready to support a lot of women.

It was at that time *coincidentally* that a friend of mine suggested I take a Neuro-Linguistic Programming (NLP), coaching course. I fell in love with it and I decided to pursue a career as a life coach and work solely with women. My purpose was to help women realize their true potential and fulfill their dreams, so that they could produce a ripple effect in their communities. I loved my new career! I was finally living my life with purpose and this time it was aligned with my career.

I then set bigger goals for myself. I wanted to do more. I envisioned myself having seminars for women to do what I was doing one-on-one, but on a much larger scale. I wanted to empower women and young girls to go for what they really want, to discover their passion, to fulfill their dreams and goals.

Because if I really want to see a big change in the world, I learned that, women and girls would be the best bet. That's my legacy I envision. Knowing that if I impact the life of at least one woman, I will have created a positive change and have made this world a better place for my kids and my community, and then I will feel I have succeeded.

My husband and I always wanted to have 2 kids, and it was time. We decided to have our second child. We completed another cycle of IVF, and I got pregnant again, this time with twins! Surprise!

Just as I was starting to dream even bigger, another challenge was set in front of me. A few weeks later, we found out that one of our twins had a heart condition and wouldn't make it to birth. I put my life on HOLD. We spent 6 weeks in limbo not knowing what was to come. Until I was at 6 months, I delivered the twins at Mount Sinai Hospital in Toronto. Michael was born sleeping and Gabriel rushed to the Neonatal Intensive Care Unit (NICU), which was to be our home for the next 146 days.

When I saw my 2lbs baby for the first time, he was in an incubator with a breathing tube, hooked up in so many different machines, and IVs in his tiny arm. I was so scared. I just wanted to go to sleep and wake up next day thinking that it was just a bad dream. But it wasn't. It was my reality and I had to face it.

I held a positive attitude in the NICU most of the days even though that was the most terrifying journey of my life. I had never experienced life that way, living one hour at a time.

While in the hospital I experienced pain, despair, hopelessness and sadness. Not only mine, but also from so many other families around me.

Seven months after Gabriel was discharged, he could breath on his own and I also was able exhale a sigh of relief and start breathing normally again.

But I also experienced unconditional love, caring, giving and sharing, and I learned to celebrate life's little miracles. That's what kept me going. It made me strong and gave me the powerful feeling that I could really change the world.

My little preemie son taught me the biggest lessons of my life. I learned to live in the *now*, to stay present in the moment by letting go of fear. I learn to appreciate the simplest things in life, to celebrate small achievements. I learned to appreciate what we have and to be grateful for everything that is happening. I understood a concept that I had learned years ago: nothing is good or bad. It is what you make of it.

Often people asked me how could I see any good being in that situation. I must admit at first, it was hard, but I saw good in technology keeping my baby alive. I saw miracles when the doctors gave no hope. I saw the goodness in strangers' hearts devoting their lives to those tiny babies and their desperate parents. I learned the power of gratitude and I felt grateful to be in one of the best hospitals in the world. I felt grateful to have an incredible husband on the journey with me. I felt grateful just to hold my baby when I was once told that it may never happen.

This experience helped me to redefine myself as a woman and a human being. I choose to lead by example because kids do what you do and not necessarily what you say.

I had to follow my dreams so that my kids can follow theirs. I had to fulfill my purpose. I felt strong and determined to make a difference, and to change the world around me.

I made a conscious decision to move forward. What others thought of me no longer played a part in my life. I learned to stay present and live life now. And *now* is the best time to start. We can't wait for something magical to happen so we can start doing things we want to do. We have to create magic in our lives. When I made a decision to take charge, I re-defined my dreams and I re-wrote my personal goals, and slowly one step at a time I started to get back to work. I joined my husband on a part-time business that generates leverage income, so that I could be fully devoted to my purpose.

And the purpose now was very clear: giving back. And everything started to unfold fast.

My husband and I wanted to give back to the hospital that gave us so much. Giving back was part of my upbringing and gives me the immeasurable feeling of gratitude. It came natural for us to do something at Christmas time. I had spent a few years delivering toys to poor neighborhoods in Brazil and my husband, Stelios, donated toys to the Hospital for Sick Children since he was a little boy. However, our reason to give back at Christmas was fortified when Gabriel was admitted in the ICU at the Hospital for Sick Children just days before his very first Christmas.

We felt lonely, but we also felt the love of strangers. On December 23rd, a woman walked into our room and asked me how many children I had. She gave me 2 vouchers, one for each child, to pick up toys at the toy room and a Christmas dinner for two.

I went down to the toy room and I started to cry. The place was filled with all kinds of toys, stuffed animals, books, a wrapping table and coffee for the parents. I could not believe my eyes. The hospital volunteers made sure every kid got a toy, including siblings. The last thing on a parent's mind is to buy Christmas gifts when your child is very sick. As a recipient of the gift, I felt so grateful to know that people cared enough to make others smile and alleviate some of the pain.

On December 25th, we ate our turkey dinner in the hospital lobby silently thinking about how that experience changed us and what we could do for others.

A few months later, Gabriel turned one and we went to Mount Sinai Hospital to say, thanks! We noticed that there was nothing familiar at the NICU we had called *home* for several months. And despite the fact that there are families of all backgrounds and beliefs, supporting families during the Holidays became our choice. We just wanted them to know that someone was thinking of them during a very difficult time in their lives. We wanted to support them as people who had walked in their shoes and who understand what they're going through.

We united forces with my long-term friend Deedee Crosland, who is also a mom of a preemie, and we created, *Great Big Tiny Hearts*.

Our charity is only in its second year running, and the support we have received is so immense that we've extended the project to support low-income NICU families throughout the year with essentials to alleviate some of the financial stress.

I have also been working on a pilot project with the two biggest NICUs in Toronto, and another organization called, "Life with a Baby" to make sure the families feel supported emotionally, and moms and dads have a good start with their pre-term baby at home once discharged.

Bringing the baby home after so many weeks or months at the hospital is a challenge. And many parents, especially moms, feel overwhelmed with the idea of losing the hospital support system. The goal is to bridge the gap, make a smooth transition and support the parents. Our project also works in tandem with preventing postpartum mood disorders and to quickly identify if it's already happening. We are also prepared to provide parents with resources to find treatments.

Everything that has led up to my life now, such as all the courses I took, books I read, and all the people that came into my life were all meant to prepare me to look at my life's challenges straight in the eye and keep pushing forward. Nothing that happens in our life is good or bad; it's how we decide to look at it.

I acknowledge what happened. I acknowledge the pain and the grief. It served as the propellers for me to live my life to its fullest and to go after my dreams.

As soon as I started the charity, I went back to work. Supporting women has been my passion for a very long time and I missed listening to their stories and giving them tools to achieve, overcome and move forward in whatever direction they choose.

In the end, I work on both with the same passion and goal in mind: to provide emotional support so they can feel stronger, inspired, empowered. For me changing the world is one story at a time, one woman at a time. Juggling motherhood (including having a child with special needs), marriage, career, and charity is challenging at times and even overwhelming, but the feeling of living life with purpose is priceless and extremely liberating.

I, like my mom, just want to show the world gratitude and hopefully leave this place a little better than when I arrived.

You are four months old and you are terrified, hungry, thirsty, freezing, and in excruciating pain. You have been starved and standing for the past forty-one hours and have not been allowed any water. This is the first and last time you will ever see the light of day or breathe in fresh air. So many other babies surround you, and you all have the same terrified look in your eyes.

Your life has been hell on earth since the moment you were born - living inside cement walls with no windows, on metal floors surrounded by metal bars, with rows and rows of little ones just like you. You were ripped away from your mom at birth only able to feed from her through metal bars.

Your mother could not nurture you the way she innately wanted. She was never able to snuggle with you or protect you from harm. She could not protect or comfort you when they cut your tail off, cut your front teeth off or cauterized you without painkillers at only seven days of age. She will be raped repeatedly and have her babies stolen from her until she can no longer produce offspring.

You only have another couple of hours of life. You are traveling at a high speed on the highway and today it is minus 31 degrees outside. You have nothing protecting you from the icy cold conditions. Some babies beside you are forced against the freezing cold metal walls and the little body heat they once had is now gone. Their skin freezes to the walls. They will be ripped or cut off the metal, leaving their skin behind.

Once these poor babies arrive at the final stop they will be forced to move off these metal trucks with electric paddles, sending painful electric currents onto their frozen bodies. They will then be forced to wait in line leading to a small chamber that drops into a shaft below ground level. There they will be forced to breathe in CO_2 gas, choking and suffocating them until they breathe their last breath - if they are only so lucky. As the chamber rises back to ground level, these babies will be stabbed in the throat and bleed before being thrown into vats of boiling water to remove the little hairs on their innocent bodies. The sad and horrible fact is that many remain conscious throughout the entire process.

This happens to thousands of pigs every day because people cannot find it in their hearts to give up things like bacon. Every day millions of animals around the world have ALL their basic rights taken away from them. They are abused and murdered by humans because humans enjoy the taste of their flesh.

I was not always a vegetarian/vegan. I was once just as ignorant as are so many people in this cruel world. I don't like to see anyone suffer whether it's a human being or an animal. So if you or I can make choices in life to ease suffering by making the simple choice of not eating the flesh of another living being, why wouldn't you?

I am involved in many different causes and they all are very important to me. It is difficult for me to narrow it down to one core cause, but my work with pigs would definitely be at the top of the list. I love pigs. If you love dogs, then you would definitely be fond of pigs, as they have very similar personalities and are actually smarter than most domesticated dogs. The majority of people are shocked to find out that pigs are very loving, smart, and clean animals. When pigs roll around in the mud, they do so to cool themselves down. It's to protect their sensitive skin from sunburns, as their skin is very similar to that of humans. Unfortunately for pigs, many people care more about the taste of their flesh rather than the pigs' lives.

One day I was talking with a photographer shooting some footage in a cow slaughterhouse. He was traumatized from the experience and told me how the cows cry when they're forced to stand in line to be slaughtered. The floors are covered in blood. These animals know what's happening to their brothers or sisters up ahead. They can hear it. They can see it. They can smell it. He had never experienced something so heart breaking. He never ate beef again. Paul McCartney said it perfectly, "If slaughter houses had glass walls, everyone would be a vegetarian."

I think many people try to convince themselves that farm animals do not have the same basic emotions that we do, or even the same emotions as pet cats and dogs that we love and protect with all our hearts. How did it become acceptable to abuse and murder farm animals? People are outraged when abused dog cases surface. Yet, every day in millions of farms around the world, animals are tortured, abused, and treated with no regard because they are being raised to be eaten, so that makes everything "okay".

I have so many friends that get very upset when they hear about dogs being raised for meat and how horribly they are treated in other parts of the world, when right here in Canada we treat cows, pigs, chickens, turkeys, lambs, goats, turkeys, rabbits, *etc.* the same way. All sentient beings tremble in the face of death. Somehow, we have convinced ourselves that it is acceptable to raise these animals in disgusting and abusive conditions and then murder them, so we can eat their body parts...and to think that we are brainwashed into thinking that this is a healthy lifestyle!

Education is key. I am a firm believer that we are slowly killing our children and ourselves when we choose to continue to eat animal protein. On a karmic and physical level, it really doesn't make any sense. We are consuming the cells of animals that are abused, terrified and sick, many from the moment they are born to the moment they are slaughtered. How can that be good for us?

One of Canada's largest chicken suppliers was in court a few years ago, and I sat in on the trials to learn how these chickens were raised. Maximum profit in minimum time was the take-home message. I was shocked to learn that almost all chickens sold in grocery stores and restaurants in Canada are only six to seven weeks old when slaughtered! They grow a full-size chicken that quickly! Everything is timed, measured, and calculated to the day, so much so that they can never shut down.   Chickens are given the precise amount of food, water, caffeine, anti depressants, and arsenic to grow to a full-size chicken in the shortest time possible. Yes, I did say anti depressants and arsenic...and we wonder why cancer and all other horrible diseases are killing more and more humans every day.

It has been scientifically proven time and time again that many illnesses including colon cancer, cirrhosis of the liver (specifically from processed pork consumption), liver cancer and heart disease are all correlated to eating animal fat and protein. It's not rocket science. We are not carnivores. Do your research and you will learn that those pointed teeth (eye teeth) are definitely not canines; we do not have the enzymes in our saliva, or the intestinal tract to properly digest meat. The multi-billion dollar a year meat industry does not use that information in their marketing ploys.

Eating animal protein is destroying our health and on top of that NO animal wants to give up its life so a human can feast on its lifeless flesh. When you actually stop and really think about it, there is nothing right about eating animals.

I have witnessed this horrible truth with my own eyes, and once you see it, you are never quite the same. Growing up, I was not an animal activist and my passion to help these innocent animals developed later on in life. I saw how animals were used and mistreated in factory farming, as well as in the fashion and entertainment industries. My mission in life is to spread awareness about the unnecessary and horrific animal abuse that happens everyday so that people open their eyes, their minds and their hearts. I want to be a voice for the animals that do not have one. I am working towards one day having a place of peace and love for rescued farm animals as well as having charitable products for sale on my swimwear website that will help both animals and humans around the world.

I decided early on that I wanted to work for myself and be my own boss. I have been fortunate to be able to work as a model, an actor, as well as run a few of my own small businesses. All of these have allowed me to not work in a regular 9-5 job. I am currently working on a line of swimwear that will be launching in 2015, with a part of the proceeds going to different charities and causes that I believe in.

Like I said I was not always involved in activism. In 2007, my website calendar (www. katesteen.com) was produced. It was during the creation and marketing of this calendar that I realized my purpose. I wanted to make a positive difference in this world for animals and decided to use my modeling as a way to spread awareness. I was working on the creative aspect of the calendar, and had some Motley Crue playing in the background. I remembered a really cool picture I had seen of the drummer, Tommy Lee. I did a quick Google search, and came across something totally different....a tattooed, shirtless Tommy Lee in an anti-fur ad for PETA (People for the Ethical Treatment of Animals). The caption read, "Ink not Mink." What an ingenious way to spread awareness. Never being a fan of fur and the repulsive fur industry, I would always try to politely educate people when I would see them wearing fur collars, jackets, boots etc. Usually I'd get a rude remark back. The PETA ads were creative, sexy, and really caught your eye.

That was it! I received permission from PETA and decided to do my own version of the famous, "I'd Rather go Naked than wear fur" poster as a way to promote the launch of my calendar. A portion of the calendar sales were donated to PETA. Little did I know at the time that poster would be the turning point of me wanting to dedicate a large part of my life to helping animals.

At this point, I was still eating meat. I am almost ashamed to say that I think I had a steak dinner the night of the launch of my calendar, but it was then that I really started to think about my choices. What is the difference between wearing fur and going out and eating a steak? Each choice is making animals suffer immensely and both choices are not necessities in my life.

I started to do my own research and decided to make the choice to cut out meat from my diet. I started volunteering my time working with different animal rights causes and organizations such as PETA and IFAW (International Fund for Animal Welfare). The fur industry and the barbaric commercial seal hunt were at the top of my list.

In 2010, I was contacted by a PETA representative who requested that I become more actively involved in demonstrations happening in Toronto. The first one I attended was outside a pig slaughterhouse in downtown Toronto. There, I was introduced to Anita Krajnc - founder of the organization, Toronto Pig Save. During this demo, I was covered head to toe in red paint and put into a human sized "meat tray," cellophane wrapped and labelled as a piece of meat that you would find at a grocery store. It was a very hot day and I remember lying there in the blazing sun, the red paint cracking on my skin, surrounded by so many caring people with signs saying, "Meat is Murder." There was a putrid smell coming from the back of the slaughterhouse that just hung in the air. I could hear pigs screaming and crying in the holding pens inside the slaughterhouse. It's a sound I will never forget.

That demo was put in every paper across Canada and really did make some people stop and think about meat in a different way. I do believe that I have found my "purpose in life" through volunteering to fight for animal rights. I have always been an animal lover, but it was not until later in life that I really thought about what that actually means. It's the reality of facing what is happening to animals throughout the world and right here in our own country.

The type of animal activism I do is not something I get paid for; it is definitely not fun. On the contrary, it is emotionally draining and very depressing. There are no immediate rewards as change often takes a long time. I am verbally attacked by people on a regular basis - ask any vegan or vegetarian and they will all tell you the same thing...it's ridiculous. As soon as people find out you don't eat animals, get ready because you will be "grilled"-strange choice of words there, but it's true.

"Ohhh you're one of those."

"OMG where do you get your protein? Do you take protein pills?"

"Well, your lipstick has whale fat in it."

"Your shoes are made of leather."

"If we didn't eat pigs they would all starve to death because of over population."

"Cows would take over the world."

"These are canines (pointing to their rounded eye teeth). We have to eat meat."

"I once tried going vegetarian and I've never been so sick."

"Evolution."
The absurd list goes on and on but in the end, all I can say is I make my choices for my love of animals. I will never forget an incident where I was out at a bar with some friends and acquaintances. One of the girls showed up wearing a Canada Goose jacket

with the full coyote fur hood, and a pair of rabbit fur moccasins, rabbit fur "pom-poms" and all. We were out for a night of fun and I was not about to say anything even though I wanted to vomit and burst into tears every time I had to look at her outfit. She pulled out her iPhone and started showing pictures of her little dog while going on about what an animal lover she was. Okay, yes, so I said something.

I questioned her love for animals and pointed out she was wearing fur from a wild dog that had been caught in a leg hold trap around her head, feathers ripped out of countless live geese (for down) all over her body, and rabbit fur that had been ripped off of at least 3, maybe 4 fully conscious rabbits on her feet. I told her she might love her dog, but she definitely was not an animal lover. She didn't like what I said to her. She walked away, mumbling something about me trying to save the world.

We have not spoken since and I'm still trying to save the world. It's unfortunate that people don't understand why I care so much. The well-being of animals is extremely important to me. Once you see with your own eyes the cruel reality of what's going on in this world, it would take a very cold hearted person to not do anything about it.

I have changed from a diet consisting of animal protein to a plant-based diet, and I avoid dairy and eggs. I do not wear garments made from any type of animal skin, wool, down, or fur and I use cruelty-free products. No one is perfect, but every compassionate change adds up.

As a young child I didn't make the connection that meat was once a living animal that had to be murdered so that I could eat it. I have one very distinct and horrific memory from my childhood, when I was eight or nine years old. We were going to visit my aunt and uncle who lived in Toronto. We passed the Canada Packers' slaughterhouse to get there. I didn't know what that place was, but I remember the god-awful smell and a horrible feeling when we drove by. It was dark and gloomy and looked old and dirty. Near the top of the building was an opening where there was a metal conveyor belt with a series of hooks attached to it. The belt would come out, loop around and go back inside through another opening.

On that day as we drove by, I saw a cowhide hanging from one of the hooks on the conveyor belt. The skin was dripping with fresh blood and dropped into a metal bin below. I didn't understand it, but I knew it was evil and wrong. I have never forgotten that moment. Today these slaughterhouses are surrounded by high cement walls, and unless you are looking for them you would never know they were even there. One of the pig slaughterhouses in Toronto has a dog park directly across the street. Anyone driving past would never suspect that behind those walls, 7000 pigs lose their lives everyday. The horrific truth is well hidden from the public eye.

Times have changed and with the huge demand for meat every year, animals are raised as quickly and cheaply as possible in conditions that are every animal's worst nightmare. We live in a world where the public never sees the inside of a factory farm, slaughterhouse, or fur farm. What we do see is the end result featuring smiling cartoon pigs on packages of bacon, pictures on milk cartons of open fields where dairy cows are supposed to graze, and ads for fur promoting that fur is green and proud to be Canadian. All are marketing ploys painting a picture of what the consumer wants to see, but is not anything close to the truth.

Most people have pets and love them dearly, and claim to be an animal lover, but does their love for animals go any further than their pet? Do they choose to wear and buy real leather or fur over faux alternatives? Is their pet dog or cat from a pet store that supports puppy or kitten mills? Do they take their kids to the zoo, Marineland, or circuses where animals are forced to live their lives in captivity and "trained" to do unnatural tricks with bull hooks and electric shocks? Many people don't even realize that some of the choices they make everyday are causing so many different animals to suffer greatly. I am involved with so many different organizations and they are all very important to me. I try to spread awareness whenever the opportunity arises. Education is key with the work I do.

With the world running on social media, many of these truths are surfacing, but it is always the choice of the person to choose to educate themselves and make changes, or just click on something else, so they don't have to know. Ignorance is bliss.

I would have to say that Toronto Pig Save is one organization that would be closest to my heart. I have always had a love for pigs from a very young age. It's strange I stopped eating pork around the age of 12. I had done some research on pigs and found out that they are very intelligent and affectionate animals, and had decided that I wanted one as pet. How could you eat an animal that was so similar to a pet dog? The thought actually made me feel sick to my stomach. Interesting how we can convince ourselves that some animals are "pets" and some are "food".

Through the volunteer work I have done with Toronto Pig Save, I have learned so much about factory farming and the lack of laws here in Canada protecting animals raised on factory farms (bless their poor souls). In Canada, pigs are allowed on transport trucks with no food, water, or rest for 36 hours plus a 5 hours starvation period beforehand. That is 41 hours. Think about it. Almost two days. People get so upset when people leave their pets out in the cold in the winter or locked in a car in the summer, but don't bat an eye when they pass a transport truck full of animals on the highway as they race to the closest McDonalds to order a bacon double cheeseburger. It is sickening really.

When volunteering with Toronto Pig Save we often come face to face with pigs on transport trucks stopped at intersections on their way to the slaughterhouse. The abuse and suffering I have witnessed haunts me. One of the things we try to do when these trucks stop is give the pigs pieces of apples, watermelon, water, some kind words of love, and scratch and pet their ears and snouts through the metal openings. Many times the truck drivers will yell, rev the engine and slam on the brakes, which make all the pigs slam into each other and the metal walls of the truck, and could easy snap our wrists.

On one bone-chilling day, it was visible that these pigs had been in transport for hours as they were all foaming at the mouth from dehydration. I quickly started giving water to every pig I could reach. I have never seen animals in such desperate need of water as this day. These pigs were chugging water out of bottles just like a human would. I tried to warm their frozen snouts that were purple from severe frostbite and I told them over and over again that I was so sorry, that I loved them, and I would never stop fighting for them.

I made a video that day with my iPhone and pieced together clips of the horrors we witnessed and captured the heartbreak that myself and other members of Toronto Pig Save experienced. My video went viral and people from all over the world viewed it. People need to know how their food choices can make animals suffer beyond belief. Every piece of meat on a human's plate was once a live being that wanted to live, had feelings, had their own personality, knew what was going on, and did not want to die.

It's from these experiences that I feel I have to do something. I need to spread these stories, as heart breaking as they are, so together we can make a change. My greatest wish is to make this world a better place for all living beings.

Some people hate PETA and think that they exploit men and women, especially when many times they are wearing very little out in public. People have the right to their opinion and when I hear negative comments directed at me or the cause, I try to let them just "float" away. It can be difficult. I don't believe that it's exploitation when you are volunteering your time and energy to bring attention to something that is important for the lives of others. Bottom line is that these demos get attention, attention to topics, and realities that people would rather not know about because the truth is horrific or sad.

Most people would rather continue to live out their lives in an "ignorance is bliss bubble." I have no problem bursting that bubble, even if it means I might feel a little overwhelmed from the attention while standing outside at a busy downtown intersection, for instance, in a lettuce bikini. It's strange that when doing these demos, my passion for helping spread awareness takes over any feeling of shyness, fear, and even extreme cold. I was shy as a kid and still am, but sometimes you just have to have faith and go with your heart.

Modeling and acting was never really a wish or something I dreamed about as a child. I was very shy and a bit of an introvert, so it's a little ironic that I have been quite successful in both industries. Yes, I model swimwear, do film and TV work, and have on more than one occasion, stood outside in next to nothing for PETA. Something happens and it's almost like I "become" another person, especially if it's for something that I truly believe in. I can't really explain it, but I do really enjoy all the different kinds of jobs I have been fortunate enough to land from acting to modeling.

I have been so lucky to have the opportunity to travel all around the world with my work, to many places in Europe and the sunny south. I have worked on some great shows, movies, and filmed many commercials. I really enjoy filming comedy and have so many great memories from filming the second season of "Howie Do It," Howie Mandel's hidden camera show. Some days, I had a lot of lines to remember, which was a little nerve wracking. Although a lot of it was improv, I was still a little nervous before each take, especially because all the attention was on me.

As I said I never dreamed of being a model or actor and am shy, so you're probably wondering how did it end up being such a big part of my life? Well it was a bit of a process. At the age of sixteen, my mom enrolled me in a modelling and a self-improvement course with a big agency in Toronto. She thought that it might help me break out of my shell and be more confident. In this course, you learn about self-confidence and poise, make-up and hair, how to audition for film and commercials, and basic photography skills. My mom put me in the course to try and help me overcome my shyness and awkwardness. I finished the course, and actually really enjoyed every part of it, but especially the acting segment. I remember I had to create a mock Doritos commercial and had a blast doing it.

The time came when I was asked to audition for the agency. I remember I was told to bring a body fitting, short black dress, and heels. The audition consisted of a walk down the runway in front of the owner and booker of the agency, so they could determine if you had a look that they could work with. I remember feeling extremely short on this particular day and a little overweight compared to the other girls there. I was definitely the shortest girl, being a whopping 5'2", while the others girls towered over me. The agents were straight with me - "You're short and you are too curvy, but you have a great face for commercial print. If you could get the hips trimmed down there is potential for work in Japan."

What? I could work in Japan, as a model? I was shocked. Maybe, I'll give this modeling thing a try, it sounded like fun. It was not fun. I didn't even have my first photo shoot before I started going out on auditions. I just had to show up in my little black dress, smile, and have a Polaroid taken. Time after time, I was told that I needed to grow a minimum of five inches, and lose ten pounds, but that it was really too bad because I had a great face.

This started to become extremely frustrating, especially to a 16-year-old. I was just about to call it quits when my booker called and said a job had come up for a "petite" clothing line and that I had exactly the look, height, and measurements they wanted. Well guess what I found out on that audition? A miracle had happened. I had grown 2 inches! I was too tall for the line. That was it! I was done! I hung up my little black dress and went back to my normal life (which at that point was high school and selling shoes at the mall) until another opportunity presented itself.

In my last year of high school I took a co-op placement course. I was thinking about going to university, but was torn between my two major interests - Science and Fashion Arts. I was excited to start the semester off working in a lab at a hospital, but ended up doing filing and data entry all day, which quickly became monotonous.

It was during this time that I started to have back problems resulting in severe back pain. I went through many different tests, X-rays and scans, without any cause being found. I did know that sitting all day long at a desk seemed to be making it worse. My co-op teacher, knowing that I was not happy, had come across a placement in my other field of interest - fashion, at a modeling agency. She figured at the very worst I might be doing some more filing, but I wouldn't be sitting all day. There might be an opportunity to learn about the fashion industry. I had always dreamed of designing clothing, dresses, and had a huge "addiction" to spending my pay cheques on swimwear.

I remember walking into the agency on my very first day. The owner was gorgeous and very friendly. She took one look at me and said, "Look at you! You're beautiful. Have you ever considered modeling?"

I remember thinking I should just turn around and walk out the door. I told her I had given it a try a couple years back, but was not interested. She was persistent. "Have you ever had any modeling pictures taken?" she asked.

I replied, "No, I am too short and too fat."

She kept saying I had a beautiful face, a great commercial look, (heard that one before) and that I should really give it a try. I wouldn't budge, at least not right away. Eventually, I did give in and had my first professional photo shoot, and I had to admit the pictures didn't really look like me, but they did look good! She made me a comp card and started sending it out.

I booked something right away and it was kind of a big deal. It was the cover of a European bridal magazine! Suddenly I was working as a model! I was shocked. I started getting booked for *Today's Bride*, and other popular bridal magazines. I was only 19 and wearing a wedding gown. It is actually a little ridiculous how many wedding gowns I have worn over the years and have never been close to getting married. All those years of modeling wedding dresses was a lesson in itself – wedding dresses are really uncomfortable, hot and heavy. Note to self....get married on a beach in a sundress.

My picture was being sent out for all different kinds of modeling jobs for make up, catalogues, and print ads. I booked a national campaign for Bonne Belle cosmetics (I literally didn't need to buy make-up for the next 20 years!) The day it actually dawned on me that I kind of "made it" was when I opened up a *Vogue* magazine, no I was not the editorial model (let's stay realistic), but guess whose smiling face was in between the editorial features that month? Me, in an ad for a tooth whitening product!

I started to get booked for swimwear and lingerie catalogues on a regular basis, the curves were finally starting to work for me! Things were going great. Making the switch from working in the lab to the modeling agency really was a huge step towards where I am today. Not only did I make it as a model, but I learned a lot about how the business worked. As well, I was trained to teach the modeling and self-improvement courses that I had been enrolled in only years before. I was now teaching classes on make-up and hair, runway, modeling, TV auditioning and self-confidence. It was during this time that I was sent out on my first TV commercial audition and I landed it - a national 3-4-1 Pizza commercial. At the time I was non-union, so I got paid very little and it played for years, all day, all night. Every time I turned on the TV, there I was selling pizza.

Constant auditioning for different parts really helped me overcome some of my shyness and I learned to deal with so many personality types. I was booking commercials and small bits in TV shows, and my career (one where I never thought I would be a few years earlier) was really starting to take off. (Even though by "model standards" I was too short and too curvy.) I feel as though my earlier unpleasant experience in the industry almost prepared me for my future career as it really taught me the business is very harsh and to not let it affect you and your self esteem.

You have to have a very thick skin in the entertainment industry and what you see in fashion magazines and on TV is not reality. That perfection does not exist. We are all beautiful and talented in our own ways.   As I continue with different businesses and goals throughout my life, I will also continue to work in modeling and TV....at the end of the day playing a different character for a commercial or a TV show or being made to look a certain way for a photograph, (even if it's only for a day) is actually a lot of fun!

I've had some very meaningful jobs throughout my career.   I landed a job that lasted for over seven years when I was hired as "Barbie" for Mattel Canada. You're probably wondering what does working as "Barbie" entail? It meant that Mattel would create an exact replica of the dress of the most popular or newest doll at the time to fit me. I would wear the dress at special children's events and sign autographs and postcards. Working with Mattel I was honoured to be able to work with different charities and visit various children's hospitals. One of my first experiences working with a charity was with the Children's Wish Foundation.

When working with the Children's Wish Foundation, a day that will always remain in my heart was one spent with a little girl who had lupus. This little girl was dying and her wish was to spend the day with Barbie. I was asked to spend the day with her at a Toys R Us store where we would have lunch together and she would go on a Barbie shopping spree. The day was so much fun, but there were times when I would look at this little girl and have to fight back the tears. Her time on this planet was limited and she was so thrilled to be spending the day with Barbie and picking out toys. We spent the entire day together and she was ecstatic!

It was a very eye opening experience to see how such a simple act of kindness brought such joy to this little girl. I walked away from that day realizing that we take many things in life for granted, especially our health. That day really taught me that every day we are given is a gift and we should not let the little things in life that don't matter get to us. In the grand scheme of things, it's those precious moments that mean so much.

That same year, I was asked by Mattel if I would like to visit some children during Christmas at the hospital for Sick Children in Toronto. This day only reinforced what I learned from that little girl suffering from lupus. That day I really learned to be grateful. Your whole life can change in the blink of an eye as it did for one of the little girls I visited with that day. This one particular girl burned a hole in my heart. As I did the tours of different floors in the hospital, a nurse would go in first and ask the parents and the child if they would like a visit from Barbie. I would talk to them, sign pictures, and give out colouring sheets and stickers. As you know if you are a child at Sick Kids Hospital you are more than likely dealing with something that most children, thank goodness, never have to even think about.

This one special girl was about seven years old. She had been in a serious accident and had both her legs amputated above the knee. She struggled as she used a device that hung above her bed to pull her little body up into a seated position, not wanting any help, and with the biggest smile across her face, she shouted, "Barbie!!!!!"

I am actually tearing up writing about this.

She was so excited to meet me. This girl's life had changed so severely and would never be the same. She had just lost both her legs, yet, she was so happy for the visit and the colouring sheets and stickers.

I changed that day. Something that was so simple for me to do, brought so much happiness to a little girl, if only for a few moments. It's moments like this in life where you realize that you can make a difference in the lives of others....in the lives of people, and in the lives of animals by the choices that you make. Most of us have absolutely nothing to complain about and we take so many things for granted. It really drives me nuts when people complain about meaningless problems and are in bad moods over nothing important. It shouldn't take something bad to happen for people to realize how blessed we truly are and how simple acts of kindness towards others can make a difference in their lives.

After a few years at my first agency, as hard as it was, it became time to cut strings and move to a larger downtown agency. That's when my career really started to take off. I was doing a ton of print work, landing commercial after commercial, even some small movie roles, and making a ton of money. I had an audition for an upcoming swimsuit issue that was for a Toronto newspaper and that's when my life really took another turn. It was there I met an incredibly talented photographer, Silvia Pecota. I also met absolutely the best make-up and hair artist in the industry, Gig Szabo, whom I consider family. I booked the swimsuit editorial, shot locally in Elora gorge, which is a gorgeous area here in Ontario.

The pictures turned out amazing and it was after that that I began to travel to many beautiful and exotic locations, modeling swimwear, and doing shoots all over the world with Silvia and Gig. We were a great team and worked on many unforgettable projects together. The most memorable and closest to my heart is a postcard of me wrapped in the Canadian flag, which we dedicated to the Canadian military when the troops first went over to Afghanistan.

I have been very fortunate to continue to work in this tough industry. I have shot over forty national commercials, everything from Nissan to Casino Rama, Canadian Tire to Sears, Miller Lite to Advil, and everything in between! I have had the opportunity to meet and work alongside many interesting individuals and celebrities. I have worked alongside Pamela Anderson, Russell Peters, John Levitz, Matthew Perry, Susan Sommers, Ivana Trump, and Gene Simmons, to name a few. I've even had dinner with Mick Jagger! The industry in Toronto is highly competitive, but I have been fortunate to have had numerous small roles in film and TV, with my all-time-favourite being a regular cast member on "Howie Do It".

I am very fortunate that I have been able to live a lifestyle that I want, never having the stress of a 9-5 job. I have always chosen the entrepreneur road instead - working 80 hours a week, so as not to have to work 40 for someone else! I have devoted much of my spare time to helping animals and trying to spread awareness. I also try to use my modeling and business adventures in ways that promote causes I believe in.

There are some situations where I can only do what I can do. When I go into a grocery store, do I want to save all the lobsters I see waiting for their horrific death in the tanks? Yes, of course I do. Do I have to leave the store without them? Unfortunately yes. Do I have to wipe back tears and walk away after every pig transport trucks turns into the slaughterhouse? Yes, I do. What I can do is spread awareness in other ways, to get people to think about and hopefully make changes in their lifestyle.

I am definitely not saying that the things I do are easy because that would be the furthest thing from the truth. There are many nights when I can't sleep because of the horrors I have witnessed. When I go outside and it is cold, I don't think about how cold I am. I instantly think about how cold the pigs and other animals in transport on the highway must be, and in the summer how much they are suffering from the heat and lack of water. It may not be easy, but I do have purpose in my life and I believe that a lot of people are missing that.

I have always wanted my own business and started up a cosmetic line a few years back. I was personally making some of the products such as lip balms, and bath balms, and privately labelled a whole line of cosmetics. The line was called, *Kiss Me Kate Cosmetics*. It was definitely a learning experience, and even though I loved it, I had to put it on the back burner as it was becoming too expensive to produce the packaging in Canada. I am hoping to re-launch the line in the future and, of course, it will be cruelty-free and vegan.

I am a firm believer in always having a few businesses on the go. I am an independent consultant for Arbonne, a botanically based cosmetic, supplement, and skincare line. I also have my own vegan and organic spray tanning business called, *Tikki and Bombshell Spray Tanning*. One of my lifelong dreams is finally materializing and I couldn't be more excited....I am launching my own line of swimwear!! Yes - MORE bikinis!!! The line is being manufactured in Canada and a portion of all proceeds will be donated to different charities involving human, animal, and environmental causes. The line is called, *Hot Mess Swimwear*, and the website will be up soon! You can find the link on my website at www.katesteen.com. I am really excited as to what the future holds. With my swimwear line I really want to promote a message and focus on cleaning up the oceans and keeping marine life in the ocean where it belongs, never in captivity.

It's so interesting when you look back on your life and you see how all the pieces fit together to bring you to where you are today. I mentioned earlier how I stopped eating pork at a young age because of my love for pigs, but it was during the launch of my calendar that I decided to cut meat completely out of my diet. I remember the moment I made up my mind. I was out on a date! It was during dinner and we were discussing my calendar launch party. I was telling him about the anti fur postcard and the promotions for the event. I was very happy with how everything was going and felt good about the anti fur message I was spreading, but had these underlying feelings of guilt with other areas of my life - my diet. I was telling people not to wear fur, but then I was going out and ordering a steak for dinner - where was the logic? He looked at me and said, "Kate, why don't you just stop eating meat?"

That was it! Nothing more, nothing less. I turned a new page in my life. I started with beef. I cut that out. A few months later, I cut out chicken. About three years later, I cut out fish. I went vegan about three years after that. At that point I was doing it for the animals, however, I did not know that it was the most beneficial choice I could have made as I had underlying health issues that did not surface for a while.

It's odd that as a society we are so easily brainwashed. I certainly was. During my early twenties, I fell for the whole high protein low/no carb diet. Sure, you lose weight quickly, but eat another carb again and you will blow up to five times the size you were originally. Stick to that high animal protein diet, no carbs diet, and you will lose some weight, but you will pay for it in other ways. I did.

My doctor couldn't understand why my iron levels were so low. Yes, I did say low - I was eating large amounts of meat and was borderline anemic! I had to go on iron supplements, which did nasty things to my stomach. My results also showed that my liver wasn't functioning properly. My doctor asked if I had a drinking problem!? No, I didn't. My cholesterol levels were also high for someone my age. As far as my doctor and I knew, I was eating a healthy diet.

I couldn't sleep and was literally going on fifteen years without a decent night's sleep, so I was given a pill for that. I had severe anxiety...I was given a pill for that. Bouts of depression...I was given a pill for that. Neither my doctor nor I realized that my diet was the underlying problem.

I started to notice significant changes in my health after I cut out meat. My anxiety was starting to lessen. I was also able to do more cardio at the gym. Within the first year of cutting out meat and not taking any iron supplements, my doctor did some blood-work fearing the worst. (She thought I was crazy for cutting out meat). My doctor was floored with the results because I was no longer anemic, my cholesterol was normal, my liver levels were normal and my blood work was perfect. I noticed even more significant changes when I cut out dairy.

I could sleep well for the first time in years, my skin cleared up, and I felt better than I ever had in my life. I walked around feeling so content; I had what I can only describe as "inner peace". My connection with animals was always there, but something strange happens when you go vegan. I think animals can sense it. It's something that you have to experience for yourself. It is beautiful.

People start to notice differences about you too. Different people constantly told me that I had a "glow" about me, a comment I never got when I was eating animals.

About a year and a half ago, I started having some problems with my eyes. I woke up one morning and couldn't look at any source of light. I called my friend who rushed me to a walk-in clinic with a towel wrapped around my head to block out all sunlight. Had I somehow turned into a vampire overnight? All kidding aside, I came down with Iritis, which is inflammation of your iris. The doctor told me that it's not something you catch, it's one of those fluky things that usually goes away and you never know why it happened. Mine wouldn't go away, and I had it in both eyes, which I later found out was very unusual.

I was put on prednisone for two months and gained fifteen pounds. I was sent to one of the best eye specialists in the city and he was the one that finally put all the pieces together. When nothing changed after a couple of weeks of treatment, he asked me a strange question coming from an eye doctor, "Have you ever had any back problems?" He tested me for some scary stuff including lupus, autoimmune disease, and an array of genetic disorders. And sure enough I was positive for one of them.

This particular condition attacks your spine, including your neck, your joints, and your eyes. It causes severe inflammation, which is never a good thing. All those years of misdiagnoses from doctors and specialists, and an eye doctor figures it out! During the countless tests, MRIs, and x-rays (I wouldn't be shocked if one day I glow when the lights go out).

Treatment for this disorder is with drugs that are outrageously expensive and I am not a huge fan of pharmaceuticals, especially if there are possible natural remedies. I was shocked that one of the first things people asked me when learning of my condition was, "Did you get that because you are vegan?"

I guess some people are more brainwashed than others. Turns out that a vegan diet is absolutely the best possible diet for this condition and it was almost like my body was telling me to go vegan years before. This is a genetic disorder that I was born with. It was not caused by eating too many vegetables LOL.

I took matters into my own hands and started doing my own research into natural remedies found in food. Some simple changes I made were adding things like turmeric (one nature's best anti-inflammatory remedies) to my diet as well as avoiding nightshade vegetables whenever possible, and eating less gluten and wheat. I was already way ahead of the game by not eating dairy or animal protein, both of which cause inflammation and acidity in your body, which is NEVER something you want. Cancer for instance is only found in people who are acidic. (Look up alkaline foods for more information.)

Going vegetarian and then vegan was the best decision I ever made. Once you do the research and look into what meat and dairy actually does to your body, you will be shocked! We are taught from a very young age that we need meat and dairy to be healthy, yet, these are the very foods that are killing us, contributing to heart disease, cancer, and so many other illnesses. It's unfortunate that many people often realize after they have been diagnosed with life threatening illnesses, that many times their diet is the cause or a contributing factor to them being unwell.

The very fact that 75-90% of humans are lactose intolerant is not rocket science. Cows' milk is for baby calves, not for humans. All mammals produce milk for their young while pregnant. (Cows are the same - they do not "magically" produce milk; they are continually raped on dairy farms to always be pregnant and produce milk).

We live in a world where the majority of people only think about themselves. So many people are living in a bubble, where the highlight of their day is how many "likes" they get on their latest Instagram "selfie". I have to be honest when I say that I am happy I grew up when I did, before all this social media garbage. The massive social pressure on the younger generation these days is at an all time high. With Facebook, Twitter, Instagram and all the other social media platforms, it can be very overwhelming.

These platforms can be used to your advantage if you are promoting a business or staying in touch with friends that live far away, but don't let these platforms be the "centre" of your universe. They really waste so much of people's time and there is always going to be another picture or another "big" story. Be different and use these things to promote positivity and good in this world.

I have a Facebook account where I promote mainly animal rights, and share some personal info with my friends. I have two separate Instagram accounts, one for my modeling and swimwear business, and one for animal rights, and I combine both on my website. Technology is not going anywhere so just make sure that you use it in a positive way that will benefit your life.

Never think that you are only one person and cannot make a difference. I receive letters and emails almost daily from people thanking me for opening their eyes on different issues, thanking me for promoting a plant-based diet, and for the health benefits that they have experienced as a result. Often I have no idea that these individuals were even following me on social media or they had listened to what I was saying at a demo or an event. I have seen and witnessed how people who you think will never change, do change, and sometimes it's all about just being informed. There was a time, many years ago when you could catch me saying, "Why would anyone ever be a vegan? That's just crazy."

Not so true now. Being vegan is one of the smartest and best choices you can make for yourself and the creatures of this planet.

There is a severe imbalance in this world. Most people will refer to themselves as an animal lover, yet will go home and make dinner using various body parts from an array of dead animals. These animals on factory farms are severely abused and tortured. If people witnessed what happens to these animals, I know their eating habits would change.

We need to start educating children at a young age to live with compassion for other life. If people want to teach their children about animals, take them to an animal sanctuary, not a zoo. There is NOTHING natural about zoos or marine parks, where many of these animals have been caught from the wild and forced into captivity. One of the saddest images I have ever seen was a picture of a polar bear captive in a zoo, looking so depressed and bored sitting on a cement floor, staring at a painting on the wall of snow and ice. Zoo and marine parks are not natural, and therefore, the animals are not acting naturally. These animals are stressed and depressed.

We should not be teaching our children that it is proper to take animals away from their families and natural habitat to be thrown into a cage or a tank, all for human "entertainment." We should not be teaching our children that dolphins and elephants do tricks for fun. They have been tortured for hours with bull hooks and shock therapy. When they can't take the torture and pain anymore, they submit and perform.

I have so much love and respect for people who are out there trying to make a difference in this world, and for the celebrities who use their star power and personal funds to help animals in need. Bob Barker is definitely at the top of my list. I will be forever grateful to him for getting the elephants, Toka, Thika and Iringa out of the Toronto Zoo and into the beautiful PAWS (Performing Animals Welfare Society) sanctuary in California. He does so much to spread awareness, and to make a difference.

My dream is to one day have my very own animal sanctuary. I want to rescue animals that have been raised on factory farms. Animals lucky enough to be rescued from factory farms will have life-long scars of abuse and trauma. Pigs will be missing their tails as they have them cut off on day seven of their lives, as well as having their teeth clipped, and testicles ripped off if they are male. Baby female chicks on factory farms have their beaks snipped, and the males will be thrown into grinders just moments after birth (as they have no profit). Cows have their horns burned off. All procedures are performed without anesthetic, freezing, or painkillers. Cows on dairy farms are continually raped and have their babies taken from them moments after birth. A mother cow will cry for her baby for days. Once she can no longer become pregnant and produce milk, she is slaughtered for low-grade hamburger meat. The majority of animals that humans eat are only babies. Life for all these animals is hell from the second they are born to the moment they are slaughtered.

Globally animals need help. Bears are suffering and slowly dying on bear bile farms in Asia, sharks are being finned and left to drown in our oceans, fur bearing animals are being anally and/or vaginally electrocuted on fur farms. The shelters in your own city are full of animals that need to be loved and adopted. All zoos should be eliminated. Chlorinated prisons like Marineland, Seaworld, and Ripley's Aquarium are completely unnecessary. The marine life that live in captivity were once wild and free in our oceans before being captured and thrown into tiny tanks full of unnatural chemicals and artificial light in order to entertain humans for an afternoon. All these places need to be exposed and shut down.

Every choice we make matters. We are all connected: humans, animals, and the earth.

Why do I choose to spend my time fighting for causes I believe in? Once your eyes are opened, your heart soon follows and the choice is obvious. My hope is to make a difference in this world - to help humans and the environment, but my greatest wish would be to stop the unnecessary suffering of animals and give them lives full of love, respect, and peace.

As Mahatma Gandhi said, "Be the change you wish to see in this world."

LEIGH NATURKACH
HOW FEMINISM CHANGED MY LIFE

Sometimes it feels like the more I learn the less I know. However, there are two things I *think* I am certain of.

- I talk a lot. Like, a lot. It's been said by some of my nearest and dearest that I came out of the womb mid-sentence.
- I am a feminist. And I love bulldogs. Okay, that's three things, and dogs aren't relevant here, but they're pretty awesome, right?

The first two, I couldn't change if I tried. It's these things that have helped me to explore who I am, pursue my passions, give back to the community, and be part of a global movement.

I don't remember the moment I became a feminist, it's been within me for as long as I can remember. Feminism fits me, like a favourite pair of shoes (heels, running shoes, slippers, whatever). That doesn't mean it's comfortable. Feminism is a constant challenge to my thoughts, relationships, values, actions, and backbone. Calling out a sexist comment at a dinner party with friends doesn't exactly earn me any points. Feminism is difficult, heartbreaking and enraging, but also inspiring and soul-fulfilling work that anyone can be part of, with the added benefit of making the world a more inclusive and equitable place for all genders.

There are many different perceptions of feminism and feminists. It is not any *one* thing embodied by any *one* person. People have a hard time understanding a living, breathing, multi-faceted thing. Society likes baselines, figureheads, and easy judgments.

There are outdated stereotypes and always common, but false generalizations including that feminists hate men, aren't funny, anti-family, and/or reject femininity. Some women who identify as radical feminists might declare they hate men. I don't believe hatred or prejudice is ever okay. Some women aren't funny. (Some men aren't funny either.)

Other feminists are hilarious. Some feminists are married to men, have children, or wear lipstick. Others don't. Feminists are all living a thousand different kinds of lives. The point is it is their choice to do so and THAT is feminism.

Roxane Gay, author of *Bad Feminist*, said in an interview with *Time* magazine, "I think one of the most important things we can do as feminists is acknowledge that even though we have womanhood in common we have to start to think about the ways in which we're different, how those differences affect us and what kinds of needs we have based on our differences."

So what is central to being a feminist to me? Feminist writer Chimamanda Ngozi Adichie says it best, "The person who believes in the social, political, and economic equality of the sexes."

Feminism is a movement that includes people of all ages, cultures, and areas of society such as academia, politics, pop culture, mainstream and social media, sex, work, law, sports, business, literature, childcare, medicine, science, fashion, social services, and more. Feminism today exists in role models such as Shadi Sadr, Julie Lalonde, Aung San Suu Kyi, Laverne Cox, and Hillary Clinton, to name a few.

It exists in large organizations like Planned Parenthood, or global movements like contributors to Twitter #activism, like what we saw in Ferguson and the New Brunswick fight for reproductive choice and access. It exists in small gestures like making sure someone is okay after experiencing sexual harassment on the street. For me, it's a part of everything I do. To not practice it would be like trying to unsee a colour that I love.

I am not an expert on feminism, race or gender. The closest thing I'm an expert in is probably 5-pin bowling and eating peanut butter on crackers, while standing in my kitchen at 2am. However, the point is we don't have to be experts in order to care about something or to critique it. I have learned so much, from my own experiences as a woman, from the women in my life, from books, novels, documentaries, articles, other activists within the feminist and anti-oppression movements, and on social media. I have listened, educated myself, and learned. Remember when I said I talk a lot? One of the best things I have ever learned to do is shut my trap (sooo hard!). We must use our voices, but also actively listen to the experiences of others to help amplify theirs.

The good feminism I see is intersectional, personal, evolving, questioning of itself and the world, and addresses larger issues in society that are difficult to take on. I want to say it's positive or optimistic, but I don't think that's always true. While feminism envisions a better world, which is positive and optimistic, and carries empowering messaging, the work of feminism addresses hard realities about our societies and our roles within it. We disagree with each other. And yes, sometimes we are angry. Table flipping angry. This makes many people uncomfortable. However, some realities of the world are outrageous and deserve our outrage. Change is not easy.

Some people say to me, "We don't need feminism, I just want human rights."

So, I respond by saying that the only way we will make true progress is if we as a society, as individuals, identify when, where, and who has less human rights, talk about *why* that is, and do something about it.

Because, when we talk about the when, where, who has less and why, inevitably we are talking about identifiers such as gender, culture, sexual orientation, race, ability, age, class and more. As one of my favourite feminists, Rosemary Brown, the first black woman in Canadian history to be a member of a Canadian parliamentary body, once said, "Until all of us have made it, none of us have made it."

As a person who is white, able-bodied, heterosexual, middle class, I do not face the same barriers and challenges as people who are not these things. I live with privilege even though I live in a male-privileged society. Though people of all backgrounds can be prejudiced, for many of us to acknowledge how we benefit from privilege is uncomfortable. It forces us to consider how as individuals and collectively as a culture we might have or do harm others, intentionally or unintentionally. It forces us to take a good, honest look at the systems we have inherited and are upheld that disproportionately affect certain groups as well as address our own prejudices and actions, and what we need to do change them.

I moved into a career in social justice work because I not only wanted to explore this on a personal level, I wanted to learn how to create change on community and systemic levels.

One of my biggest challenges in social justice work is that I am an incredibly emotional person. How many times can one person cry during the movie *Up*, I ask you? Crying attempting to eat popcorn is pretty pathetic! While it's important to remain empathetic and passionate about what you do, it's also important to think critically. This is one of my biggest battles. This means looking at facts, seeing new and different viewpoints, asking questions, admitting if and when you're wrong, but also standing your ground when you're right, and not letting emotions become centered because it distracts from the issue at hand. I try to ensure (with varying degrees of success I might add!) I don't get lazy, or carried away by my feelings or group-think.

While emotion can work against you, it was emotion and raw passion that drove me into social justice to begin with. It's a balancing act.

I grew up in a small town called Fort Frances in northern Ontario, the kind where everyone knows each other's business, fishing tournaments are the social events of the year, and there isn't a bookstore (which horrifies me now, come to think of it). I was surrounded by a community of family, friends and neighbours. I was, and am, truly lucky because this is a huge, helpful foundation to build from that many of us take for granted.

I developed passions for many things, including social justice, but I had very limited ideas of how it worked. I thought you either had to be a Prime Minister or work for the Peace Corp. I wasn't exposed to a lot of activism, and philanthropy wasn't a word I knew. I didn't have anyone in my life who I strongly identified as feminist, though I had many strong women around me.

When I was in middle school, I got my hands on a copy of *Ms. Magazine*, learned about its co-founder a famous feminist author, journalist, and activist, named Gloria Steinem. My feminist seed was planted. It took me years to realize Gloria was mainstream feminism's most recognizable face likely because she was white, heterosexual and gorgeous in addition to all of her qualities, for a movement that was built on the hard work and leadership of huge networks of women from a variety of identities, races, and cultures who all worked in their own ways to improve the lives of women, their families and communities. Her contributions are incredibly important, but I recognize now that no movement exists without the individuals within it, and examples of leadership can be found in the people who are not seen, heard, or recognized by the mainstream.

One of the best lessons I remember every day is from one of the greatest leaders I have ever had the chance to work with – former CEO of the Canadian Women's Foundation, Beverley Wybrow. She simply taught me that kindness can change everything. While Bev had changed the lives of tens of thousands of women and girls, if not more, she also took care of those around her, by simply sharing a seat at a lunch table.

Growing up in Fort Frances, there were two elements that really only informed my thinking later on. In my extended family, there were situations of domestic violence. This is still hard for me to reconcile. I always wonder what I would have done about it if I'd been an adult while all of that was going on. Would I? Could I?

It's hard to think about.

Also, my hometown was mostly white people, with a large Indigenous population who lived in town or on the reservation just outside. Racism was and is a reality, and though I had friends and Indigenous members of my family, I didn't understand the colonialist history, challenges, discrimination, and trauma that the First Nations community had faced and continue to face.

I always believed in hard work, messages like "Girls can do anything!" and that we can create our own opportunities. While some elements of this are true, not everyone starts off on equal footing because of systemic inequality or family situations they have no control over. When I was younger, I was full of confidence and self-importance, which blinded me to the fact that other people didn't have those things. It's only in the last few years that I'm realizing how much my experience growing up shaped my perceptions and prejudices back then. A young Indigenous woman who lived in my town and I have reconnected on social media after many years, and we have talked about how growing up there shaped our experiences, and how we are grateful for how much we are aware of now. What drives my work today is realizing how much I have to learn, and unlearn. The biggest personal challenge I had was when I moved to a middle school. Here I encountered the "mean girls". These mean girls were a part of my larger group of friends. It was a few girls in this group who fundamentally affected my self-confidence. I remember they would take turns picking on another member of the group. It became kind of a sick game where we just tried to do anything we could not to be the one who was on the outs, made fun of, or gossiped about. It got to a point where I woke up every day, dreading, positively dreading what might happen that day in school. I can still feel the weight of that dread all of these years later in the pit of my stomach.

One day I remember clearly sitting in a music class, and two of my "friends" sat beside me, talking about me negatively, and putting their backs toward me. I felt like everyone was staring, and I felt so alone. I had no idea what I had done. It was several instances like this that changed how I felt about myself, conducted myself, and instilled a paralyzing fear of saying or doing the wrong thing, or acting the wrong way.

I remember thinking it was so weird, sad, and awful that this was how female friendships could be. I had other friends who had their turn being on the outs, and other friends who never made me feel that way. It was a confusing and painful time. Because it was a small, isolated town, there wasn't a lot of room for not caring what other people thought, or privacy. That's not too different than growing up in a big city, but with limited exposure to any cultural or social diversity, it often felt like a fishbowl with no way out.

While it may not be a big deal compared to what so many go through, it left a scar. I've learned that experiences are valid, and while it's important to keep them in perspective, it's important to recognize the impact they can have. My experience introduced almost paralyzing self-doubt into my life for the first time.

In some ways I'm grateful for it – it's made me more empathetic to others who have or currently experience the same kind of thing. Toxic relationships can be a lot like bullying.

After a few years of this drama, I realized that these bad relationships weren't an inevitability. We would all be going to high school where that kind of garbage wouldn't fly. It took confronting one of these "friends" one day in the hallway about something she had wrongly said about me to realize I could stand up for myself. I was terrified. Admitting that now feels so silly, but it was. It was the first time I saw fear and powerlessness in *her* eyes, and I realized things started to change. I can still remember how freeing that was. The daily dread started to go away.

Years later, after high school ended, I wanted to have a completely different experience from where I grew up. I was torn between going to university for something to do with social justice or pursuing a broadcast career. I got into the country's best broadcasting program, Radio and Television Arts at Ryerson University, and my decision was made.

After graduation, I got an internship in TV, which turned into my first full-time job. I stayed in the industry seven years, from production to programming, to marketing. I met creative and hilarious people, and it fulfilled my love of documentaries and storytelling. I soon realized though, that compared to many in my field, I didn't carry the same passion for that work, the same technical know-how. There were some values that didn't fit with me – the media and entertainment industry can be very sexist and shallow. Values conflict is often inevitable at one point or another in any industry. But, I listened to the fact that I had a lot of questions about what and how I was contributing to the world, so I also explored volunteering. I was still curious about a career in social justice.

Volunteering allowed me to explore a number of causes and roles, and meet people in the sector who would help shape my experience and my opinions. At one point I volunteered for Youth Assisting Youth, being a big sister type to a young girl. I loved working with her, but I found myself increasing interested in her single mother's story, her life and what it was like for her to raise two kids on her own. I realized then that women's advocacy was where I really wanted to focus my efforts after all. I had known this all along.

I continued to volunteer for different things, including women's shelters and service organizations. Then one day early on in my career in TV, my boss gave me tickets to a fundraising breakfast by the Canadian Women's Foundation.

I went. I was hooked.

Everything they spoke about –building resilience in girls, ending violence against women and girls, helping women to move out of poverty, creating better communities and connectedness, all of it deeply resonated with me. It was like hearing a different language that I somehow already knew. This was the feminism I wanted to participate in.

I reached out to someone at the Foundation to inquire about how I could get involved. Soon I was volunteering and helping coordinate a young women's group. This group involved young women early in their careers learning and talking about the importance of supporting other women and girls in Canada. They also wanted to continue the work of the incredible women who'd come before us, who worked so hard to provide us with the freedoms, possibilities and choices we have today. I wrote a few pieces for their newsletter, and spoke at events. I learned what philanthropy was, and that we can use it to invest in those who need to get on equal footing to then pursue their goals.

I began doing information and job interviews with people in the charity sector. I wanted to get more awareness about what roles might be a good fit for me, find out if I did need to go back to school, and get a feel for what my value would be if I were to make the career move. I had numerous meetings and interviews, and was even offered a few jobs. During this time, I received a Citizenship Award for volunteerism from the company I was working for, which came with a $5,000 reward. I chose to give it to the Canadian Women's Foundation. I gave my own money too, in much smaller amounts. I learned that no matter how big or small the gift, philanthropy is a powerful tool. It does not take the place of justice, which is something I am constantly learning and questioning.

Not long after, out of the blue, someone at the Canadian Women's Foundation called me about a new position they were hiring for. I practically jumped out of my desk and ran down the hall outside to take the call, like a new contestant on the *Price is Right*, arms flailing and me shrieking. As she told me about it, I already knew I would take it. There are times when decisions are like a hard multiple choice test, and other times when it's an arrow of big flashing blinking green lights pointing toward an open doorway.

I took the job managing a $6.25 million fundraising campaign to help women living in low-income situations become financially independent and build better lives for themselves, their families, and community.

It was my dream. I loved it so much, the work and the people, I considered it my home and many of us who have come through its doors are still very close. Those four years were a whirlwind tour of the charitable and social justice world, traveling the country, working with amazing donors, companies, volunteers, event people, and most importantly, the organizations and women themselves who benefitted from the funding. I thought I had to leave my skillsets from TV behind, but I realized so many of my skills were useful here too, while building new ones. The day we announced we reached our goal of $6.25 million, on International Women's Day, was one of the best and most rewarding days of my life. Again, of course, I cried. Probably for two days.

Soon after I had finished that campaign, I was interested in applying for another job in the Foundation on the program side. The role managed work focused on preventing violence against women and girls. I applied. I was rejected. I didn't have all of the skillsets that were required. I made peace with that. Rejection has come to be a friend instead of a fear. It makes you more willing to try new things.

As luck would have it, the person who got the job turned it down. The job was mine. Over the time I did that job, I learned more about feminist and anti-oppression work being done across the country and around the world, I realized I again needed to get out of my comfort zone from within the organization. So much of what I had learned was from the lens of the Foundation. While this was wonderful, I knew didn't have the experience I felt was necessary to do the work with that critical lens I talked about earlier. I needed to expand my horizons, get experience, question what I was part of, challenge my thinking, and learn about the work from different perspectives and communities.

It's like travel. It's one thing to see the pyramids of Egypt in a picture. It's another to stand looking at them in person, and feeling the sand blowing on your skin, the sun beaming down on your head, and smelling the Pizza Hut breadsticks in the air (true, weird story).

So I resigned from the Foundation. It was a difficult decision, but it was the right one. Challenging yourself to find out who you are and what you believe in without the titles, affiliations, comfort, and supports is an amazing and important growth experience to have. That said, I was in a position to resign after I found a new job to support myself and pay my bills. Sure, people can change the world and go on epic personal journeys, but they also have to eat.

Now, as I write this piece, I am working as a fundraiser for a community-based AIDS service organization that incorporates feminist values. Even in this short journey, my thinking has changed. My values haven't, but my understanding of the non-profit sector, activism, anti-oppression work, and people who are facing multiple barriers has deepened and broadened. It's been a huge learning curve, and one that will continue to curve. To help supplement my learning, I am also going back to school, to the same university I went to 17 years ago, only this time for a completely different program rooted in Community Development. For me, it's important to get academic, theoretical, historical context, as much as it is to get front-line, practical, professional, and personal experience. Not everyone feels this way, but I've realized it's important to me.

There are many moments where doing social justice work has been rewarding for me. As I get older, the benefits become more rewarding when it's not about personal recognition. Being part of the feminist movement that has made so much change for societies around the world is pretty incredible. My thinking has changed. Titles are no longer important to me. Hey, I'm not a selfless person. I am usually always first in line when people are doling out pieces of birthday cake when it's not even my birthday. But I've realized that there are truly brave, gifted and strategic leaders, speakers, activists out there who should be acknowledged, visible, and lead this work. Some of the bravest acts tend to be unacknowledged.

I heard a story from a woman I'd gotten to know through my feminist work. Years before we'd met, Jinger was in a really rough spot. She'd had a string of bad luck, one thing after another that ultimately resulted in her becoming isolated from her family and friends, homeless, and battling depression. At one point she was living in a shelter. The shelter was for abused women, and one of the only ones available. She was at risk of being put out on the street to be replaced by a resident who had experienced domestic violence. She became even more withdrawn and fearful about what the days ahead would bring.

One day a woman came into the TV room at the shelter and said to Jinger, "I see you haven't eaten."

Jinger thought this woman was angry with her, perhaps for "taking a spot" of a woman who'd been abused, or was assuming that Jinger was stealing food from the kitchen. She left the TV room and immediately went to her bedroom down the hall and closed the door. A few minutes later, she heard a knock. It was the other resident. The woman, who was at the shelter because she was a victim of domestic violence, held out a $20 bill and a can of soup. She said to Jinger, "Here. Take it. This is half of what I have."

It was with this gesture that Jinger decided she would one day pay forward that $20. She did. She went on to become successful in business after finding her way, and she volunteered, donated, and extended kindness to so many others. This is one of many stories of courage, leadership, kindness, and giving back I've heard over the years that tells me that all acts of giving back are important, and some of the biggest go unnoticed.

It's rewarding when someone, a friend, or an acquaintance contacts me privately after a talk or shares something that I post on social media about issues like violence against women, reproductive rights, sexism or other feminist priorities. This means someone has gained knowledge about the issue, realizes they or someone they love are not alone, that there is help for themselves or a loved one, or just recognizes that this work is important. Helping individuals and witnessing change on an individual level is as incredible as a global movement, because it's all part of the same picture.

From where I started, I've redefined what success means for me. Success is continuing to explore new things (like writing!). Education doesn't just come from academic institutions. Education comes from people and activists in your community, family, mentors, friends, travel, books, personal stories, and so much more. Social media has been a huge influence for me because it has connected me with incredible people, it questions mainstream media and the larger systems we are a part of, and you have to use critical thinking constantly to decipher the messages, perspectives, and conversations. It elevates voices who we otherwise would never have access. I'm also a connector by nature, and have huge capacity for conversation and engagment, which is an important part of social media and the learning you get from it.

Another marker of success for me is still giving back, with my talent, time, resources, and using my voice to speak out. I'm still putting a damper on dinner parties wherever I go. I recognize that although I work hard, I would not be where I am without the advantages that I have been given, and without the efforts, work, and courage of the people who have come before me to make the path easier to travel. I feel it's my responsibility to continue that legacy for women around me and women who will come after me. We each can contribute positively to this world, it matters to ourselves and it will matter to someone else.

We can never be certain of what path to take or what will happen, but if you stay true to who you are, and contribute to that notion, that is the best kind of success. Of that I am certain.

KRISTINA EVANOV
BEAUTY FOR ASHES

I often wish I could go back and tell my 15-year-old self what I now know about self-image, self-worth, and love. I wish I had someone who spoke the words of truth that could have prevented me from much pain and suffering. Yet, I can't go back. I can only go forward and tell others the lessons I learned through my experience. I hope to be a voice of truth, to speak to other girls, and young women to tell the truth that I now know. This truth has brought so much joy and peace into my life since those days of strife. Over these next few pages I'd like to share the journey that led me there. I am so thankful to be able to stand on the other side of that valley, able to tell happy news, a hopeful story, and some words of wisdom learned in the battle for self-worth.... for it could have gone another, darker way.

Hungry to be Beautiful

I was 6 years old when I first felt "fat". Fat, a word that no 6 year old should ever even have to think about, but many do. I was 7 years old when I first put myself on a diet. Diet, another word no child or adolescent who is still growing and developing should have to worry about, but still many do. I was 14 years old by the time these feelings turned into the full-blown eating disorder of anorexia. I was 18 years old when I finally stopped the vicious cycle of starving myself for long periods of time. I was 23 when I finally felt beautiful and the mindset of the eating disorder had been broken. It was a long and a cruel journey, one I would like to prevent any other young girl from experiencing.

But somehow within this journey, God was merciful and I learned of truth, love and kindness. I developed compassion and wisdom. The things we suffer through in life can make us bitter, or they can be a refining process. It can transform us into pure gold, full of more strength and grace than ever. I want to encourage you that you don't need a perfect start to have an incredible destiny. There is a God-given strength, hope and resiliency inside of you to overcome whatever challenge you may have.

It was the beginning of high school when my life really started to crumble. It started with my own self-image. I saw myself through a distorted lens, through a lie that I believed. I believed the lie that I was not beautiful enough to be accepted, to be liked, or to be loved. Not only did I believe this lie... I lived for it, worshipped it, entertained it constantly, and let it control me. In feeling unworthy of life... I pushed life away. Feeling unpretty, I pushed the beauty of life away. I turned my eyes away from all things good, nourishing, healthy and healing. I was hungry, desperate to push food away, desperate to see myself the way I wanted to, as "beautiful enough."

Throughout this year my exercise became excessive, I counted calories relentlessly, and I would weigh myself obsessively several times a day. It was as if I was looking on the scale to see how much I was valued or how much I had fallen short. It was a terribly cruel test to put myself through. The thing about an eating disorder is no matter how much weight I lost and what size I was, I could never measure up. Because the problem wasn't really with my body, the problem was with my mind, how I saw myself and the fact that the thoughts about my body were not of love, but of hatred. I would be so hungry I would cry myself to sleep, and still not eat. Learning to love my body was a process of many years ahead of me.

By the end of 9th grade, I was a sick and broken girl. I had lost 40 pounds, as well as my hormones, some of my hair, my ability to laugh and most devastatingly, my self-worth. I had given myself completely to this lie and its demands. My body was starting to warn me that the consequences could be deadly.

I went away to summer camp, and something unusually miraculous happened. One day I looked in the mirror and I finally saw reality. I had seen myself as "fat" for so long that even when my body was wasting away, I still saw that same image of a girl who was unlovely and fat. Yet as I said, one day, I looked into the mirror and I finally saw... reality. I saw a lovely girl who looked skinny and sick, with bones protruded, frailty within my frame and insecurity within my eyes.

I would say it was by the grace of God that my eyes were opened and I could finally see for the first time what I'd been doing to myself, and the effects it was having upon me. I lay in bed at camp and that night for the first time in a long time, I started praying. I prayed for forgiveness for the abuse I had inflicted on my own body. I prayed for healing for the damage I had cause to my health. It was at this dark time in my life, I knew I needed light. I wanted light. I returned to church and into a relationship with God that would be the source of so much healing and freedom.

Choosing Life

It was a gift of Grace that after all I had put my body through, I began eating normally again and enjoying life. Unfortunately, the struggle was not over at that point. For such struggles come from a deeper place of wounding inside us, and there is no quick fix. My high school years were tumultuous indeed, and I went through several bouts of starving myself, even ending up in the hospital. But the story didn't end there.

I remember some of the people who judged me. I could tell they thought my life would be stuck there; my issues too great, my struggle too big. But beyond those years, there was beautiful life to be lived. My mother would always say to me, "Why are you doing this to yourself? God wants to give you a full and abundant life."

It took me hearing those words so many times, until I finally believed them for myself, until I finally received them as my own. The following quote became one of my life-verses. They're words that rescued my soul. The words we believe can be poison or can be healing. The moment I decided to believe these words, is the moment I decided to truly live.

"I came that you may have and enjoy your life and have it in abundance. To the full, till it overflows. " (John 10:10) ~ Jesus

The Power of a Choice

When I was 18 years old I made the decision to never starve myself again. I am so honoured to say that throughout the past 12 years I have remained healthy and committed to that choice. In essence, I made the decision to receive life. By receiving food, I received life again. Sometimes, when we deny ourselves of food, we start denying ourselves of life in other ways too. We deny ourselves of hope, of enjoyment, of health. But when we open ourselves up to life and all its blessings, we are honouring life, we are honouring ourselves, and we are honouring the One who gives life. I have experienced that beautiful things flow from that place.   This choice cleared the way for something beautiful.

I could put my identity in something so much greater than a number on a scale or the size of my physical being. I could put my identity into my heart and my spirit, into the authenticity of who I was. I let go of the superficiality of those high school years, which I let control me. I began to live real life, with real friends, and a realistic view of myself. I have lived out so many dreams because of this choice.

Learning to Love

Although many of you reading this may have never suffered with a full-blown eating disorder, I would say that the false beliefs, self-hatred, and self-loathing that triggered my experience with anorexia are all too common for young women in our society. Self-hatred is the root of so many destructive choices in our culture. Learning to love yourself truly, may be a life-long journey, but it's worth taking.

Even long after I had stopped starving myself, the mindset of the eating disorder stuck, and it would take many years to deprogram and reprogram my brain. It was habitual in my mind and emotions to feel fat, to feel ugly, to feel guilty when eating, to look in the mirror and be unhappy with what I saw, and to reject myself.

Feeling truly pretty, beautiful or attractive is not something I enjoyed in life until after I was 23 years old. To be honest, I think these feelings also kept me from dating or being open to a man liking me for a long while. I kept myself from men's acceptance because deep down I didn't feel I was worthy of it. I felt my physical being was unattractive, so I didn't let anyone get close to me. I needed that time on my own to find my own love for myself first.

Steps to Freedom

There were many steps I took to break free.

1) I stopped weighing myself. Being defined by a number was too harsh of a definition for me, so for over 3 years I never stepped on a scale. It was so liberating for my mind, and I felt better over time.

2) I stopped saying negative things about myself and my body. I felt challenged to not verbally criticize myself anymore. "Fat" became a forbidden word in my language. A famous proverb says, *"Life and death are in the power of the tongue."*

Words have power and the more negatively I spoke about myself and my life, the more I gave that negativity power. As girls and women we should lift each other up , not tear each other down.

3) I chose to listen to the voice of my Creator, instead of the chatter in the media, the magazines, or even the critical words of people in my life. I knew my Creator saw with truthful eyes. I knew he saw me as His masterpiece. These words became my own. I celebrated them like winning first prize.

"You made all the delicate inner parts of my body, and knit me together in my mother's womb. Thank you for making me so wonderfully complex. Your workmanship is wonderful, – and. how. well. I. know. it." Psalm 139

I chose to listen to what Love thought of me. And I dismissed the chatter and the voices that would hold me to an unrealistic and superficial standard. I rejected the messages that taught me to reject myself. I accepted this message of acceptance that made me feel at peace with myself.

4) I redefined the way I saw food. Eating is a vital part of life and to reject the enjoyment of it is bad for the body and the soul. Instead of seeing food as something that may make me fat or make me skinny, I saw food as life, as nourishment, as enjoyment. When

this happened, I actually ate much healthier. I also enjoyed food more fully for the first time ever.

5) I redefined the way I saw exercise. Exercise used to be self-punishment for me. I exercised in an effort to change myself into a certain image. So instead, I started doing things I liked, with the motivation of enjoying my body and appreciating my Creator. I spent a summer, biking, swimming and dancing. It brought me a sense of vitality and joy, so I continued to exercise.

6) I found when giving to others, it took the focus off of my appearance. I felt joy in giving selflessly, and my sense of self-focus and self-hatred diminished.

After all these choices, I was so free, emotionally. I was soaring with a sense of joy. My body was reaping the rewards. I was healthier and in better shape than I'd been in a long time. We can pursue a healthy body from the inside out. Our bodies are created in order to be nourished, to move, to do beautiful and wonderful things. We don't need to treat it harshly or deprive it. It works best when we love and care for it, when we give it what it needs.

I learned I can love my body through healthy food, through not overloading it with junk food, and through exercise that brings me a feeling of vibrancy and life. Every good choice I make sends a positive message to myself and my body....

"I am worth it.'"

"My health is important."

"I love my body."

This mindset has made all the difference for my health.

Loved Back to Life

Throughout this whole journey, I attended University for Sociology and Religious Studies. These years were a learning platform academically, as well as for life. I acquired life lessons that made me the person I am today. I learned the most important thing in life is... Love. The Love of God changed my life forever.

At this time, I realized that growing up without a father in my home left a void of rejection and abandonment within me. I felt unloved. I tried to fix this and earn the love I felt was missing through striving and starvation. But nothing, I did outwardly could correct this void. Nothing, but receiving the love of God. In those years, I experienced the love of my Heavenly Father in a very real way. He filled my void and healed the wound within me. I learned that I was a beloved daughter of God. A piece of writing that I read over and over again was, "The Father's Love Letter." You can find it online at www.fathersloveletter.com.

I always say, "God loved me back to life."

After I experienced that, I started to want to love others back to life. I became sure of God's unconditional love and mercy towards me. And this changed my life forever.

Words from My Heart to Yours

You may wonder what all these personal struggles have to do with "Making It." I have learned that true life and success flows from the inside out. What you believe about yourself may be one the most powerful things in your life, leading to blessing or to pain. It is the undercurrents of who you believe you are and what you believe you are worth that makes the greatest impact on your ability to succeed as a complete person. I once heard the story you tell yourself about yourself in the middle of the night, when no one else is there, is what determines your life. **So girls, tell yourself good things, true things, lovely things about yourself. Because you truly are lovely.**

Perhaps it's time also for you to stop listening to the chatter... to put the magazine down, turn off the television, to walk away from cruel people... and to stop looking for your worth, for it is already inside you. You are filled with true worth, and this is something that can never be taken from you. No matter what this world or this life puts you through, and no matter what you think of yourself, you are so highly valuable, greater than pearls or diamonds. Your worth is highly set, non-negotiable, and undoubtedly always present within you. May you fight to believe this until you know. I mean truly **know** it.

The Beauty of Giving

One of the lessons I learned through very trying times was great preparation. There is a quote by recording artist Kirk Franklin that has always resonated with me. "The pain was preparation for my destiny."
If you have been through anything challenging, you have an edge of wisdom and strength that can empower you to accomplish greatness in your life. I developed compassion through my experience. I knew this love and compassion was within me for a reason, a purpose greater than my own life.

One of the purposes was in Uganda, and the children I would work with there. My journey towards Uganda was most profound. I prayed about the possibility of volunteering in Africa. From that prayer forward, literally ever step brought me closer. Everything lined up; the finances, the opportunity, the support, the courage, the faith, the peace. I stepped into the greatest adventure of my life so far with the greatest sense of peace. I was in the right place, in the centre of my destiny, and I knew it.

Uganda was my home for seven months. The people were my people, my family, my friends. The babies I cared for became like my own. I worked in a home with over 70 little ones who had been orphaned or abandoned. Every day I was like a mother; holding, loving, feeding, comforting, and singing to the most beautiful treasures on earth. These treasures that had literally been tossed out, thrown out, and were unwanted. These treasures were hidden in the darkness of poverty, abandonment and pain. Yet to God, these are royal ones.

It became my pure joy and honour to find them, to love them, and show them affection. They are precious, worthy of love, chosen, honoured, adored, glorious, children of God.

Everything in my heart resonates with the knowledge of the love that these little ones so deserved. Everything within me wanted them to feel, know, and experience their preciousness.

They were worth me leaving my comfortable Canadian life for. They were worth getting completely heartbroken. They were worth being sick for months after returning to Canada. Love is always worth it; when it's pure, and when it's authentic. I experienced the blessing of giving love to another who couldn't repay me. Jesus said, "It is more blessed to give than to receive." (Acts 20:35)

These words became colourful, vibrant and alive for me in this experience. The most fulfilling and rewarding time of my entire life were the months when I let go of all my petty, self-focused worries, and I spent my life loving others.

The beauty of giving is something the beauty magazines will never tell us. Advertising never tells us how rewarding it is to **take off** the make-up, to **remove** the jewellery, to dress **simply** and to care for others with **love**. This is the beauty of living against the grain of culture. This is real life... to love another. My favourite quote from the musical *Les Miserables* is, "To love another is to see the face of God."

And I tell you, I've never seen the face of God like I did in Uganda, in the faces of those beautiful little ones.

If we live our lives for the promotion and exultation of our own self image and reputation, at the end of the day, we will have a shallow and empty list of accomplishments. But if we live our lives beyond ourselves and reach out to make an impact, our accomplishments will be those of genuine contribution and peace.

And please know that you don't have to go to Africa to give that kind of love. I love everything that Mother Teresa ever said. But one of my favourites is, "You don't need to do great things. Just do small things with great love."

You can make a difference by loving the person sitting next to you, your neighbour, or the person in your class. I have always believed that one of the most important things in life is how you treat the person next to you. Whether you live in the luxury of Beverly Hills or the simplicity of a Ugandan village. How you treat the person sitting next to you is one lasting effect you will make upon this earth.

If we all did that, life on planet earth as we know it would change. We never know the poverty of loneliness of the rich and glamorous person beside us. And we never know the wealth of wisdom and character within the person sitting next to us in the poorest slums.

Never assume and never judge by the appearance of others, whether beautiful or ragged; whether brilliant or worn. To everything there is a story behind the surface and layers beyond the superficial. In our day and age, we are trained to focus so devotedly on the outward appearance of a person, that we rob ourselves of knowing the richness within a person. Let's see and accept people, the way we wish to be seen and accepted. Let's treat others the way we would love to be treated.

Beautiful Lives Beyond Vision

As girls and women, we are bearers of beauty to this world. This is a wonderful thing. Beauty gives refreshment, life and joy. Imagine if this world was only functional. Yet, it's not just functional, it's also beautiful. The beauty of nature and humanity refreshes our souls and gives us peace. The desire to feel beautiful is natural.

But striving after society's definition of beauty will leave you depleted and heartbroken. You don't have to buy your beauty or achieve it, because you were born with it. My hopes in writing this is that you would be able to know, feel and accept your innate beauty. You are meant to enjoy things like make-up, fashion and hair styling. You are meant to possess them, they are not meant to possess you. You can own your own sense of beauty, so don't let the drive for beauty own and control you. You are already a beauty.

We often try so hard to validate ourselves with external things. We look to the opinions of others, the opinions of guys, the number of likes we get on Facebook, and our external accomplishments. Those things are not bad in and of themselves, and should be enjoyed. Yet, when we look to them to feed our souls, they will always leave us empty and craving more. We need to find that validation from within.

I personally find that in my relationship with God, for His love is a constant source of identity and approval. But I also tell myself: I am loved, I am worthwhile, I am beautiful, I am powerful, I am significant, and my purpose on earth is real and is great. I decide this for myself. No one else can do that for me. Not a guy, not a friend, not an accomplishment, and not a position in life. In the same way, you need to decide this for yourself about yourself. When you know the truth about yourself and when no one can take that away from you, there is great freedom.

Eleanor Roosevelt said, "No one can make you feel inferior without your consent." So, do not give anyone consent. Your ideas and thoughts are unique and worthwhile. Your dreams are important and valid. Your words are powerful and impactful. No one else has the gifts, abilities and calling that you have. You are a unique design and no one else can fill your place on this earth.

You're like a vibrant colour on a blank canvas. The canvas of the universe would not be the same or as beautiful without you. So don't give up, hold on, love yourself and let light and love in. You do have a purpose on this earth. I encourage you today to see yourself with new, kinder eyes.

India Arie is a great singer, known for motivating girls and women. She sings, "Are you a popper or a superstar? So you act, so you feel, so you are."

So see yourself as a superstar. You are a princess. And by that I mean, you were born to be honoured, to be royal, to make an impact, to be a leader (whether it's of a family or of a nation). You were born with significance and great capabilities. So give yourself the permission to feel like a princess, like a superstar, like who you truly are.

Life These Days....

These days, life is much sweeter. There is a beautiful quote in Isaiah that says we will receive beauty, instead of the former ashes of our life, and great joy, instead of sadness. It says we will rejoice and sing praise instead of living in the former despair. This has been true for my life. Everything indeed turned around with a blessing instead of a disgrace. The places of sadness have become places of joy. I am so thankful for this wonderful promise and that it became my own.

To grant those who mourn.
To give them a beautiful headdress instead of ashes.
The oil of gladness instead of mourning.
The garment of praise, instead of a faint spirit. Isaiah 61: 3

I am happy. I almost never have a day where I feel ashamed of my body or appearance anymore. I can truly say I feel beautiful from the inside out, most of the time. This is a true transformation from the days when a constant sense of shame haunted my thoughts. There is always a vulnerability to feel that way. But in general, I am a free woman, eons away from the bondage of my past. I've moved miles and miles on from that place of restricted insecurity into the open fields of freedom. We are meant to be free.

Those heavy and burdensome worries and expectations that the world puts on us were never meant for us to carry. That is why they feel so unnatural, so painful and why they stunt our growth into a happy and healthy person. We can be so free from all of that if we choose. If we choose to stop believing the lies about our identity, and start believing that we are free.

Freedom is yours and it is mine. I pray that as women, we can enjoy the freedom of feeling beautiful without the addition or subtraction of anything from our lives and beings. May you feel beautiful to simply be exactly who you are. When you are just sitting there, just being you, you are perfectly complete. May this sense of quiet beauty settle in your bones, calm your heart, and put a gentle smile on your face. You are worth it.

Worth It

Upon coming home from Africa, I went through a time where I learned to give to myself and love myself again. I started to realize that for my whole life this sense of unworthiness had lingered upon my soul. It had caused me to hold myself back in many ways. I started letting go of that negative sense, and instead opened up to the goodness life had been offering me over and over again. Previously, I had stubbornly decided I wasn't worthy of these lovely offerings. I had denied myself of food, dating, enjoyment in life, opportunities, and even of friendships because a root feeling of unworthiness.

Feeling unworthy is a prison we can keep ourselves in. We look out on all these beautiful aspects of life we wish to enjoy, but we doubt ourselves and keep ourselves from them in the prison made in our mind. Yet, we are the ones holding the key, and the way out is simply to have a little faith in ourselves. May we dare to believe that *maybe* we are good enough, talented enough, strong enough, and brave enough to go for it. And let's see where that new and adventurous thought pattern may lead us. When that *maybe* becomes a *yes, we are*, we can really start living.

I once thought others were holding me back, but I started to realize that I was the one holding myself back. As my mindset started to change, many good and wonderful things began to happen. My self-doubt diminished and my self-love increased; I became bolder and more confident to go for my dreams. I began to be open to the idea of actually being a successful woman. The walls caused by fear and a belief of unworthiness crumbled to the ground. Behind them abundant life sprouted up, and I was filled with a new sense of hope and adventure towards this life. Finally, I felt worth it. It's moved me so far forward and I've never gone back.

I started using some of my gifts that lay as dormant dreams within me for a while, such as singing, song-writing, photography, dancing and acting. I've explored the arts and creativity in many ways, it's been so fulfilling. Although, it's not quite as drastic as moving to Africa, these things have still been adventures to me. Anytime we try something new, go somewhere new (even in our own city), or meet someone new; it can be a great adventure. That is what I live for and how I most love to experience life.

I also recently started my own radio show with a focus on inspiration and faith. It was something I never thought I would do, but opportunities can arise when you least expect them. If they aren't happening yet, keep going and keep growing; they will happen.

Hidden Treasures

There is so much within you that you have not discovered yet like your dreams, gifts and abilities. The world and life is yours to behold. Don't fret if you haven't discovered all that you want to do yet. I encourage you to do the things that make you happy. Do things that make you come alive.

"Don't ask what the world needs, ask what makes you come alive. Then go and do it. Because what the world needs is people who have come alive."
Howard Thurman

The beauty inside you is endless and it will take an entire lifetime to discover it all. I encourage you to plunge into places undiscovered, even the places in your own heart. There's a lovely song by Yael Naim called *Far Far*.

Some of the lyrics include:

Why do you stay outside? There's a beautiful mess inside. Take a deep breath and dive. There's a beautiful mess inside.

You may feel like a mess, we all do some days. But you are a beautiful mess. In the words of Leonard Cohen,"There is a crack in everything. That's how the light gets in."

So don't be afraid of the cracks or the mess or the beauty or the light within. We are all a complex mix of all these things. The journey to accepting yourself in all these ways will make you grow into the beautiful queen that you are. You are a light, meant to shine in this world.

Nelson Mandela said these words in one of his famous speeches, written by Marianne Williamson.

Our deepest fear is not that we are inadequate.
Our deepest fear is that we are powerful beyond measure.
It is our light not our darkness that most frightens us.
We ask ourselves, who am I to be brilliant, gorgeous,
talented and fabulous?
Actually, who are you not to be?
You are a child of God.
Your playing small does not serve the world.
There's nothing enlightened about shrinking so that other
people won't feel insecure around you.
We were born to make manifest the glory of
God that is within us.
It's not just in some of us; it's in everyone.
And as we let our own light shine,
we unconsciously give other people
permission to do the same.
As we are liberated from our own fear,
Our presence automatically liberates others.

So that is my story of "Making It in High Heels." Notice it says "Making it," not "Made it." I don't consider that I've reached it, or arrived, I'm still just on the brink. All of us are on a journey of making it. Sometimes we're in the comfort of running shoes upon familiar streets, or the freedom of flip-flops in sunny places. Sometimes on painful stony paths with bare feet or in the glamour of high heels on busy city streets.

We are all on a journey somewhere and it's not always easy or glamorous. If we can walk in love, that is the most important thing. It's ok if we take a different path from others, make our own path, or take a bit longer to get to our destination. We are heading somewhere brilliant. The exciting part is.... the best is yet to come. :)

Megan Shaw
Mind over Matter: #MINDOVERALZ

It's our fourth year and you would think the novelty would have worn off, but tickets for Memory Ball 2015 are almost sold out, and I am glued to my registration tool, constantly hitting refresh. It's been less than one month since tickets went on sale and still two months from the event, and tickets are... almost.... yes! They're sold out!

In 30 days, we have sold 400 tickets, and the requests on Facebook for people who didn't get them in time are already being posted. It's surreal that we've come so far so quickly, and we've learned some important lessons along the way.

While in university, a few friends and I had the idea of planning a fundraiser. We weren't sure where, when, or even what charity would benefit, but we knew giving back was important to us and something we really wanted to do. We all spent time volunteering for different causes in our communities and we loved planning parties and nights-out. So what better way to mix these two interests, we thought, than planning a night out for charity? With busy schedules, different school locations, and limited resources, however, it remained just an idea for a number of years.

After graduation we all moved to Toronto to start our careers and not long after, the desire to plan a fundraiser resurfaced. This time we had a cause; unfortunately, we had all been personally impacted by Alzheimer's disease. Watching loved ones lose their memories, their independence, and themselves, motivated us to spread awareness and raise money for this devastating illness.

We did some research and soon realized that Alzheimer's disease was much more prevalent than we originally thought. We learned that every four seconds, someone around the globe is diagnosed with Alzheimer's and yet, there is no viable treatment and no cure. We also found that there are approximately 50,000 people under the age of 50 living in Canada with Alzheimer's and other forms of dementia; a staggering statistic, since it's usually a disease associated with aging. The more research we did, the more confident we were that this was our cause, and soon Memory Ball was born.

Before we got too far in the planning process, we decided to set up a meeting with the Alzheimer Society of Toronto, our beneficiary. We met to discuss our skeleton of a plan – we were going to host a couple hundred young professionals for a night out in Toronto, raising money, but also really focusing on awareness. We wanted to explain why Alzheimer's was an important cause to support, and we wanted to share the statistics we learned during our research. It was important to us that our guests knew why we were hosting this event and that is wasn't just another night out in a fancy dress.

The Society was excited and supportive, but also realistic. They told us that both fundraising and awareness are very important, and while it would be great if we raised money on top of spreading awareness, they wanted us to make sure we didn't end up losing our own money by hosting the event. Their advice to us was to focus on breaking even in year one, then to expand from there.

This surprised us. It was the first time we considered that we might lose money. In all of our discussions, there had never been a question in our minds that we would at least raise *something*. We had talked about how much we wanted to raise, but hadn't really discussed the apparently very real possibility that we wouldn't have any proceeds to donate at all. What if we booked a venue and no one came? What if people came, but didn't have a good time? What if people came and had a great time, but we didn't offset our costs and in turn didn't raise anything?

We discussed all of these concerns and had a very real conversation about the "what ifs." We wanted to do everything possible to ensure that the event was a success and that we could donate money even in our first year. It wasn't an easy discussion because when you're really excited about a new idea, it can sometimes be difficult to take a step back and consider the potential faults and risks in your plan. Yet, it's so important! It can truly be the difference between success and failure.

I really feel like that conversation set us on the right path for our first event. By considering the worst-case scenario (no one comes), we set more realistic expectations for ourselves and for the event. We still wanted to present the Society with a donation, but we became more reasonable when discussing how much. We also took a look at our plans for the event, and our proposed budget, and tried to scale it back a little to make sure we were being responsible.

Even though we were trying to be more realistic and conservative with our planning, we all still hoped and believed that we were going to raise some money. If ever someone doubted that our event would be successful, we didn't let it bother us. We believed in ourselves and the event, which was so important, especially in our first year.

To be successful we needed to not only convince people to buy tickets, but also convince individuals and corporations to support us financially without any proven track record of success. We spent a lot of time pitching our event to anyone who would listen, and at times it became discouraging when people would say no. But because we believed so strongly in the cause and our event, we were able to attract a number of sponsors in our first year, each one adding more and more to our credibility as a Toronto event.

Filling the venue was also a difficult task. Our group of friends were eager to buy tickets and were happy to invite a few friends each, but we were hoping to sell close to 300 tickets and our friends only made up a handful of that. We faced a similar issue with ticket sales as we did with sponsorship – we had no track record, so people were hesitant to spend money on a brand new event. Why would they spend $100 on a ticket to something they knew very little about? We were telling them it was going to be great, but why should they believe us?

We knew if we got them to buy a ticket, they would have a great time and become part of our attendee-base for years to come. It was all about making those initial sales. Luckily, as more and more sponsors came forward, our credibility slowly increased and through some of those partnerships, we were able to add more value for our attendees - like giving out late night burritos! Slowly ticket sales picked up and we started to see people on our attendee list that we didn't even know! It was working!

In spite of everything we were doing right, we had only sold about 200 tickets a week before the event. We were getting anxious because it wasn't close to the 300 we had hoped for and our fundraising goals seemed to be slipping out of reach. Don't get me wrong, 200 was great and we were thrilled that 200 people believed enough in us to buy tickets, but we had so strongly believed that we would be able to sell 300 tickets, it was still a little disappointing. A few tickets were still selling, but not very quickly, so we reluctantly gave the venue our final guest count of 225.

BUT THEN, 24 hours before the event, it was like everyone suddenly woke up and ticket sales skyrocketed! We sold 100 tickets in less than a day and ended up selling out on the morning of Memory Ball 2012.

I remember sitting at home watching tickets sales flood in, being so conflicted. On one hand I didn't want to turn anyone away, it was a dream having so many people attend! But on the other hand, our venue and catering were only set for 225 people and I didn't want the event quality compromised for the attendees who had supported us from the beginning. As a group, we hadn't expected this sort of sales rush, so we didn't have a concrete number to "sell out" at, which made it even more difficult. Eventually, we capped sales and announced for the first time that Memory Ball was officially sold-out!

That year the event was a huge success and everyone had a great time. More importantly, we were able to raise $25,000 for the Alzheimer Society of Toronto – way above anything we had ever expected!

We have since expanded our team, increased our event capacity, and hosted two more Memory Balls, raising a total of $120,000 to date. We have an extensive list of sponsors and people are now approaching us wanting to get involved! Each year, we have sold-out our event faster and faster. This year, we sold out in just under one month.

Along the way, we have learned some very valuable lessons that have ultimately lead to our success.

I think one of the most important things we have done from the very beginning has been believing in ourselves and our event. Throughout the process we did come across some critics and sceptics, urging us to consider the worst-case scenario. This is a great practice for risk management and I think it ultimately lead to our success in that first year, but it's also so important to believe that you can achieve whatever goal you set out for yourself. Whether it's planning an event for a few hundred people, trying out for a team, or applying to your dream job, attitude counts for so much! If you don't believe that you can do it, why would someone else think that you can? On the other hand, if you believe you will succeed, you are more likely to take chances that can lead to even greater success. This is exactly what happened when we moved to a larger venue space and opened up tickets to 400 people. We were nervous, but still managed to sell out a week before our event and raised even more money for the Society.

I also learned there is really no harm in asking for what you want! When we started Memory Ball, we weren't sure where to look for sponsorship. We approached family and friends and asked them to reach out to their connections, but it was only getting us so far. We were relying on sponsorship and donations for most of what we were donating back to the Society, so it was crucial we look outside our immediate networks. We started cold calling and stopping into local businesses asking for monetary or product donations, and we were so impressed with the results! People were happy to help, often giving us whatever they could. Some people had personal connections to the cause and wanted to help as much as possible, while some people just had extra inventory that they were happy to give to a good cause. Whatever it was, we were very glad we had asked, and I was really impressed with how generous people were to perfect strangers. It may feel uncomfortable at times, but there is no harm in asking for what you want. Oftentimes people are happy to help, they just need you to tell them what you're looking for!

A challenge I faced in our first year was recognizing our limit and cutting off ticket sales. It's easy in the moment to get carried away and excited and take-on too much, or not want to say no. I could have left ticket sales open a little longer and maybe we would have made a little more for the Society, but it would have negatively impacted the experience of all of the guests who attended. Being confident enough to say no when you need to is so important. You can't take on everything, and if you try to, other elements end up suffering. For us, quality is more important that quantity so we would rather turn people away than compromise the attendee experience.

Lastly, it is so important to HAVE FUN! As a group we all love what we do, and believe strongly in the cause that we support, but we also have a really great time planning and attending Memory Ball each year! Because we enjoy the process, we end up spending more time and effort on the event than we would if it was something we *had* to do. We also do fun things throughout the year to refocus and reenergize whenever we feel like we need a bit of encouragement. Whatever you're doing, make sure it's something you enjoy; whether it's a team, a project, or a job, the more fun you are having the more motivated and successful you will be.

Meghan Sherwin
Creating Safer Streets for Our Children

Four years ago, pregnant and hopeful, my husband and I moved to a small, community-centric neighbourhood, just north of the city. We believed it was safer to raise a family in a tight-knit community rather than in the heart of downtown. We spoke to our realtor and gave clear direction that "location" was more important than the "house" itself. When houses came on the market, I'd spend time just standing on the curb watching the street, the people who walked by, and the cars driving past. I'd imagine my children wandering out of the house and I'd judge the home and community against how safe I felt it was for that child. Was it okay to have a swing in the front yard? Could they ride their bike down the sidewalk? Could they pass each other a football on the front lawn?

After eight months of house hunting, while I'll admit not our perfect house, we knew it was the perfect neighbourhood, and we felt lucky to move in. After unpacking our home, with a one-month old in our arms, we sat on the porch and watched the community wander by and we knew we were home. There were families walking their dogs, kids riding bikes, and even a house down the road had a tree swing in the front yard. It felt wonderful.

But the honeymoon didn't last long in our new neighborhood. After about a month we realized that traffic was a big concern on our street. What didn't seem too bad when we were looking at the home on weekends, turned into a traffic nightmare during the work week. We had delivery trucks and commuters using our streets as a through-fare. We were 10 minutes north of the city, and people were driving through our community to get to work downtown. While we had originally believed that being so close to downtown was ideal, we now saw that our neighbourhood was seen as a barrier for commuters coming from the suburbs into the downtown core.

As new parents, we were protective and we became increasingly concerned about the road traffic and how safe our streets were for the kids. We watched trucks zoom by day after day, month after month. We tried parking on the street to slow cars down, we tried driving slower through our neighbourhood to remind drivers of the speed limit, but we felt nothing was making a real difference. So we started reaching out through email and phone calls to our elected officials, our city councillor and the police. At first asking questions about what the plan for traffic was in our neighbourhood, and when we got no response or just standard answers, we escalated to asking for these councillors to support initiatives that specifically improved road safety. Unfortunately our requests for help went unheeded and we felt abandoned by our community leaders. We sent email after email, asking for a traffic study. We asked the police to monitor the 4-way stops and watch as cars rolled through the intersection. But no leaders did anything substantive.

We were friends with our neighbours, and as we stood on our front porches after cutting the lawn or raking leaves, we always started our conversation with the traffic, and the cars and trucks that drove by. And what we realised was that we were all sending emails, and asking for help and none of us were happy with the results. We all felt ignored. And what was worse, we knew in our hearts it was a dangerous situation for our children. It would only take one rolling stop on a four-way intersection or a car driving around a corner at high speeds, and a child crossing the road to break our world. We were kindly asking for help and filing police traffic reports, but it wasn't making a difference.

What more could we do? While frustrated and concerned, we had followed due process. We had complained and asked for help. Even though no one was listening, we were asking people to do their jobs. While our neighbours lived on the street longer than us, and they may have championed longer, our personal complaining lasted four years. Every now and then I'd get upset at a particularly fast driver and send another email or make another phone call, but nothing changed. Not one visible difference (to our street) was made in four years – while I was upset and frustrated, I did nothing else.

That is, until this past July. I was at work and got a phone call from a friend in the community. A child had been killed. Walking home from the park at the end of our street, a child had been hit by a car. That's as much as we knew. We tried to connect with all of our friends. What was the age of the child? What was the sex of the child? Whose world just changed forever? I knew it wasn't one of my children because they weren't in the neighbourhood that day. But it could have been my friend's or neighbour's child.

Out of some instinct to be home and with my children, I grabbed my things from work and I drove home. I prayed it was a mistake and the child was okay. I've heard so many stories of children surviving incredible accidents. I repeated over and over to myself that it was going to be okay. I spoke to my friends and we counted all of our children one by one. We all picked our children up from day camps and play dates, we all immediately went into a protective mode and corralled our children.

On a summer day, with an ambulance at the end our street, and our kids wondering why we were all crying and holding them, we found out the harsh truth. Our worst fear had come true. A young girl was struck by a car commuting through our neighborhood. A car making a right hand turn on a red light killed a little girl who needed to cross a single street to get home from day camp.

My husband and I didn't know the young girl or her family. But it didn't matter. The fact was that she was killed. My husband and I were devastated because it should not have happened. We were devastated because we knew our streets weren't safe and we didn't stop it.

Later that same day, six neighbors stood on the sidewalk in front of our home and we started talking about how we had complained to everyone and anyone. We talked about the unanswered emails and how, while we hoped no one would be hurt due to the traffic, we had always known it was dangerous for all of our children. But we had offset our blame and our own failings at not finding a solution because we had asked for help. Was it our fault or theirs? Who was accountable? We blamed inaction on our own failings to find a solution. We grieved for the family's loss and looked at one another as the night grew darker. We couldn't leave each other. The kids hung on our legs and asked for dinner and we all stood there just trying to keep the day from ending. We didn't want to be alone with our thoughts. We wanted to share our grief to make it less painful. We finally left the street that night, but we agreed to connect the next day. So we all went to sleep that night and I can't speak for others, but I hugged my children tightly. And as they fell asleep, I promised them I'd do more.

Within the next 24 hours, everyone we had asked for help over the past four years (including the police and our elected officials) were interviewed by the media. No one took responsibility or talked about how it could and should have been prevented. They said it was a tragedy (and they were right). But we were outraged that they weren't acknowledging their own failings to keep our community safe. Emotions ran high and we decided, as a group that enough was enough. If they wouldn't take responsibility, we would. We decided that we would act and make a difference. We were tired of just complaining and asking for help. We looked at one another and asked what could we do? What single step could we take to make a difference?

We brainstormed different ideas and we decided that there were two big hurdles or issues. The first being a collective voice, everyone was asking for the same thing, but at different times with different messages – we need to connect our messages. And second, we needed to empower individuals – we felt like we had no way to help or act, no way to make change. We felt our society was built around people doing their own jobs and we could ask them to do something we wanted, but they weren't held accountable to those requests. We felt as a group that we would make a difference from the ground up, a grassroots initiative. With no help from the police or elected officials, the six of us decided to rely only on ourselves to make positive change with a collective voice.

Within 24 hours, we had a clear plan and within 14 days we had implemented it. We designed signage that asked drivers to slow down for the safety of our kids. It was a simple message, delivered in a creative way to drive an emotional connection, and could be implemented easily. We then spoke to local printers and businesses for funding and support. We called our friends, and friends of friends and asked humbly for favours. And we were shocked when everyone we asked, said yes. Yes, to wanting a sign, yes to a small donation – everyone wanted to do something.

So we printed as many signs as we could and gave them out freely to our neighbors. And we started hearing from strangers that they also wanted a sign. We were humbled by the community engagement. So we kept printing signs with donations from community businesses and started giving them to everyone who asked.

Within 8 weeks, the campaign had gone viral, the media picked up the story, people started paying for the signs and we were on top news channels on a daily basis. Why did it connect with people and the media? Why did we suddenly get noticed? It was because our community was asking for the same thing, at the same time. It was because we had a consistent message. We had a large collective of individuals participating, and it was easy to see the traction of the campaign. Finally, our councillors and local police were being asked by the media to be accountable, take responsibility, and to make positive changes for the community. All eyes were on our community leaders – with a collective, visible voice, and the media watching what would they do. How would they act?

Within 10 weeks, we had new by-laws in place, minor traffic improvements completed and increased police presence. All small changes, but every step makes a difference. Every instance made our community feel like someone was finally listening to us. All we had to do was work together towards a single message. We started succeeding in creating change where four years of complaining had not.

I think it was because of the simplicity of the message, the ease in which to participate, and our design that inspired communities across the country and globe, to pick up and take notice. We have been asked to mentor and help communities around the world create their own road safety initiatives and create change in their own neighborhoods. We have recently won a national award for our community initiative, and by all intents and purposes, as of right now, with multiple individuals bringing our campaign to their communities, we see the initiative as a success. We are thrilled to be able to help and inspire others to join together as a single voice. While absolutely nothing brings back that little girl, if we can prevent one more senseless death – then we have succeeded.

The story doesn't end here. While there is still work to do in our own community to make the streets even safer, we have as group of neighbors realized something very special. That empowering others, through a shared vision, simply and with humbled grace – can truly create change in the community. I've learned that we must all take it upon ourselves to make a difference. But you don't have to do it alone, nor should you. If we can join efforts with other like-minded individuals, and then empower others to help deliver change, you are more than a single voice – you become a tidal wave that can't be stopped and *must* be listened to, because you are moving forward and gaining traction and support. It's an incredible experience; I wish everyone could be a part of something so wonderful and positive. So dig deep, find that kernel of truth in you for what you believe and find others with that same kernel. Decide to step up and do something. It always starts small, that's the point, but it can grow into something impactful, fulfilling and life changing.

And you'll have to keep digging deep. As a mom of two young children with a full-time job, it is hard to keep going. It's far easier to make an excuse and after the kids have gone to bed, curl up on the couch and relax. And while I admit I do that some nights, most nights I'm answering questions or resolving issues with the campaign. But that night in July, I promised my children I'd do a better job of keeping them safe and I wouldn't lean back anymore. I do what I can to create a safer world for them. So that's my drive, my children. And every day and every night, when it would be far easier to put the responsibility on others, I do what I can to create a positive change. And surprisingly enough, it's created this sense of pride that allows me to stand taller and keep going.

Melanie McGregor
Every Experience is a New Opportunity

This is my life story; an account of the trials and tribulations of starting a business from scratch and my life lessons that have shaped me into who I am today.

I would not say I'm the best performer, the most graceful, beautiful or flexible, but performing is my passion. Performing, to me is an escape from everyday living. Growing up I was very shy and timid, yet my inhibitions were lifted when I was in front of a large audience. Performing sets me apart, and allowed me to play a character outside of my everyday life, which I then learned to use in my everyday life performing in the roles of a dancer, model, sister, business owner, daughter and friend.

At first, I thought I was going to be a writer or a journalist. Growing up I found the only way I could express myself was through writing. My parents knew I was really upset when they got a letter from me expressing my feelings. I had journals amongst journals, yet dance was another form of non-verbal communication I learned to use as a way to relieve myself from the stress of everyday life. At a very young age I was introduced to theatre, which I fell in love with. Every Christmas my family goes to Toronto to watch a live theatre production, such as *Mama Mia!* or *Cats*. We've seen it all! The performers have always mesmerized me and it was instrumental in shaping my future.

Every year when we were getting ready to go to our annual theatre show, I would raid by piggy bank and pack my purse with as many coins as possible to give to the homeless. I enjoyed giving all my coins to the homeless in hopes of making their day better. I always had the urge to give back and my parents cultivated this quality by giving me the freedom to do what I believed to be right. They didn't stop me when I'd approach a homeless man to give him the coins I had in my purse. They believed it was important to nurture this type of kindness because they knew it would help me to develop into a good-natured adult. That giving quality in me grew as I did. When I was asked to write my story for the purpose of giving charity back to youths, it just clicked because this is exactly what my business and life-mission stand for.

It all started at the early age of three, my mother put me in dance lessons. I grew up taking recreational lessons in every dance style I could immerse myself in: tap, jazz, ballet, hip-hop, acrobatics, modern and lyrical! This gave me the confidence to produce my own plays and perform for them at family gatherings. I have always enjoyed entertaining people and seeing smiles on my family's faces, knowing that it was me who made them feel this way.

It wasn't until I entered high school that I was asked to join the competitive dance team at my studio. Words can hardly describe how ecstatic I was. However, my mother had concerns about my grades slipping in school. I was determined to make this dream a reality. I had to learn to fit into a team of girls who had performed together competitively since the age of 5, were very close friends, and were much more skilled. Yet, I wasn't going to let it daunt me or hold me back! I already had my height of 5'10" working against me. I was taller and older than most of the other girls on my team. I had to overcome these challenges and, I refused to give up! These challenges only made me want to work harder and become stronger. I knew I could not let my team down.

I remember my mother bargaining with me and saying, "You can only dance once all your homework is done." They knew school wasn't my strong suit. They cleverly engaged my need to thrive in school by providing the consequence of taking away dance should I fail. This plan was a big success! By dedicating myself to dance, my grades actually went up. My parent's plan worked perfectly because I knew I had to effectively finish my homework before I could jump into what I really wanted to do. I went from almost failing grades 9 and 10 to a straight-A honor student in grades 11 and 12 with multiple university scholarships across Canada. On top of it all, I was working part-time at a retail-clothing store and had a normal social life. I learned by keeping busy, I was able to prioritize my tasks and manage my schedule more efficiently. Having my focus on what I love only made me more successful in the other areas of my life.

Growing up, I spent summers with my mother, also an entrepreneur, who managed two childcare centres in a low-income area. My mother wanted me to spend time at her work with less fortunate individuals to realize and appreciate everything I have. It really helped me learn the value of giving back my time as the children were always very excited to see me when I came in. One of the staff members suggested that I teach the children to dance and play sports, such as basketball and volleyball. That's when it all began. What a great idea!

I quickly began to create programs to teach the children dances they would find enjoyable for both boys and girls, such as hip hop. The children really enjoyed it, and once again I felt the enthusiasm of helping the children, while learning new skills in teaching and performance. I learned a classroom of students from all diverse cultures could come together in unison and work as a team through dance. It allowed more opportunity and motivation to practice my dancing while bestowing my knowledge on the community and education curriculum. I continued doing this every summer while at school and found myself falling more and more in love with dance and sharing this passion with others.

At the age of sixteen, I decided to register this idea into a business called *Get Low Dance Co.* The goal behind my new company was to spread awareness of fitness, exercise and culture through dance and share it with other communities and educational facilities. Having the opportunity to provide children a place where they could share a common interest with other kids was really important to me.

I found the shyest of children would be able to express themselves through dance and actively involving themselves with the other children. There was one little boy who was autistic, but through dance he developed the self-confidence to actively take part in my dance program just like the other children. He thrived with the others and all the children were now team members working together.

At the end of the summer, we put on a dance recital for the parents who were amazed at their child's creativity. It brought joy to both children and their parents. This was my reward and, to me, made all my hard work worthwhile.

My mother's daycare became a place where children could be physically active through dance and a place for them to express themselves. I saw how critical it was for low-income families to have access to these kinds of services. It allowed me to discover my passion and love for performing, dance, fitness and built self confidence, responsibly, team work and leadership skills at a young age. I truly believed I could share my knowledge and experience with these children. There was a lot I had to offer. Not only did I believe this, but also it was verified by my success. At the age of 17, I went from two locations to seven. This was right about the time when "So You Think You Can Dance" and other talent reality shows became popular and dance became a craze!

While at high school, I was known as the "super tall girl in class". I was very self-conscious about this and I just wanted to look like all the other girls. My height was my physical challenge. For example, when it came to playing piggy backs with friends, I would be so embarrassed of being too heavy for someone to lift me up. So, I would always make sure I was the one carrying the other friend. I never wore heels during my first two years of high school and would either crouch or lean to one side to try and look shorter. A few of my friends, however, were always telling me that I should try modeling.

It took a couple months to overcome my hesitation and doubt, but I eventually decided to do a little research on what it took to become an actress and model. At the time I had more of an interest in acting, as my favorite class was dramatic arts. I was very intrigued by the possibilities. I always love to have my hands dabbling in different avenues. I never wanted to turn down an experience and miss a potential opportunity. I grew up always ready to take a risk, although I am a deep thinker, I will try anything once, work hard at it and hope for the best. I believe if you don't take risks and try new things you will never know your full potential. Although the modeling industry was a very intimidating world I had already promised myself I would do my best.

My mother was always a protective parent. For good and bad, I loved and loathed that about her. She would demand doing her own research on the acting and modeling idea and would of course have the final say. Luckily, she read good things about an acting and modeling school and agency. This was one of my happiest days of my life when we went to go for an interview. I originally went to the agency looking for acting classes because I always wanted to be like Julia Roberts. At the meeting, the agents were impressed with my height and walk, and arranged an audition as a model.

My first audition! I was so nervous! I had to walk the runway, (which I had never done before), state my name and agent, and take photos. I went in and got the job! Words couldn't express how amazing I felt.

However, this was a whole new skillset for me and I hadn't received any formal training. It made sense at the time that I should take advantage of what the modeling school had to offer. I signed up for a few modeling and acting courses as hastily as possible.

Within no time at all, the modeling life pitted me against another glass ceiling. Being a dancer and having muscles in my legs actually hindered me as a model because for fashion and runway they want you very slender with little muscle. I had a curvy figure. This is why I always felt I wasn't model material. Nonetheless, I planned on giving it an honest attempt. From that point on I switched from flats to high heels –in the modeling world, at 5'10" was a normal height and with a 5 inch heel I was now over 6'4"!

I had finally found a place where my height was actually a good thing! Modeling reaffirmed my confidence and boosted my self-esteem. In the modeling industry you come across a lot of rejection–causing some people to fall apart. But I didn't let adversity bring me down and convince me that I couldn't succeed. Rather I would pick myself back up, rally my wits, and try again. The modeling lifestyle continued to help shape me into a stronger woman. Especially since you could audition every day of the week and maybe lucky enough to obtain a job here and there. You could be rejected 90 out of 100 times as it is a very competitive industry. At 17 years old I was going to auditions by myself, which were always downtown. This taught me how to be responsible. I had to drive thirty plus minutes to an audition, ensure I was on time, prepare full hair, make up, and discuss attire and sometimes a script.

There would be hundreds of girls who all looked exactly like me to audition for the exact same role. Only one can make it. The one that makes it is the one that fits closest to the idea in the producer's head. When I first started, I would hope for days to get that special call back from my audition. Yet, if you didn't get the job, you never hear a word, any feedback, and no way of knowing how to better yourself for your next audition. I used to take this rejection personally, but it's all the luck of the draw. Knowing this made me tolerate rejection a lot easier.

I came to the realization that the modeling world is hard and brutal. I was told several times to "tone up and lose weight," although I was at normal weight for my height. The stress was very difficult to handle and the industry has the power to break and tear you down. At times it makes you feel almost miserable and beyond regret, until the special day when your struggles and hard work are finally rewarded. Lessons like these: never giving up and never losing focus, really helped to build character. A character that I used to forge myself into the person I am today.

My Girl Guide lessons kicked in, "always be prepared" when I saw others chewed out for not bringing enough wardrobe attire to sets or because they had changed their look without notification. I never wanted to feel that embarrassment, so I would always ensure to bring everything with me.

The struggles and rejection I faced in modeling were lessons that I could reflect on as I continued to build my business. I harness it in my mind and use it to empower myself during life's hardest moments. Plus, it didn't hurt having the wisdom of my greatest teacher: my Nana. Her fine words still resonate with me to this day, "Whatever happens, happens for a reason."

Even though I had my struggles, that's not to say good things didn't happen too! By staying positive and gaining strength over my experience in the modeling industry over the years, I landed two major commercials, MTV and TK Maxx, along with other major fashion shows, such as MAC Fashion Cares, Toronto Fashion Week, and more. Although, I did not become an international model super star, I did get a taste of the lifestyle. When you are in the game, it is never what it's all hyped up to be. Yet, it was still a world I understood and wanted to be a part of. The lessons I truly took away from this experience were those of fortitude and responsibility. Hard earned wisdom that continues to help me in life to this very day.

As I continued to improve myself both physically and mentally, I had a rare opportunity come my way. Most of the modeling and performances I had done up to this point were local. However, I was invited by my agency to a modeling convention in New York City. I pleaded with my mother to let me go! After much deliberation, she finally agreed – predicated on the stipulation of her coming along with me. My self-confidence may have been better since I started, but I still questioned if I really had what it takes. I wondered, *do I really stand a chance at modeling in New York City?* I didn't have the standard "model body", I could have been on a stricter diet, and I could have been training harder, but I did the best I could. At only 17, I was recognized by three different New York modeling agencies that offered to have me work full-time for a well-known fashion magazine. But, this was the moment my luck finally ran out. My mom's patience and understanding had reached its limit and she did not want to me to move to New York City. It seemed negotiations were terminated and there would be no compromise this time around. She wanted me to finish high school and university first before anything. I had a hard time focusing on school at this time and certainly did not have an appetite for university. Modeling and entertaining were my focus! My parents pulled rank and demanded, "Get a degree first, then you can do whatever you want after."

I had finally realized that I had to continue my education and I graduated with a BA in Arts, a minor in Dramatic Arts and a Post Degree diploma in Advertising Media Management and Marketing. Yet, I never lost my passion for the performance arts. My university offered extracurricular activities, in which I joined the University Dance Team. There, I was able to test my ability in diverse dance styles I had never tried before, such as Irish and Highland dancing. I also volunteered for every fashion and arts event. In addition, I found promotional modeling companies to work with on evenings and weekends where I was able to meet and connect with people who had a passion for entertainment and arts. Of course, never forgetting my dance company, Get Low Dance Co., which I worked during every summer break. The most beneficial part of university was the relationships I built and the network of great people I connected with.

When I completed my education, I was well rounded, which ultimately served as a distraction from my focus: entertainment. With a marketing degree from University, my parents really pushed me towards the idea of getting into a stable job. I convinced myself that my parents knew best and I should take their advice.

I applied for a full-time position to work in a large Marketing Corporation. It was a milestone in my life. I was feeling more and more like an adult. I worked there for just under a year managing a team of brand ambassadors across Ontario. I loved the youthful atmosphere of the office I was in. I felt a part of a team I could grow with. Also I was working at special events with multiple brands so there was always something new and exciting to learn. I learned the ropes of working for a corporation; which ultimately had expanded my business knowledge and continued to teach me valuable lessons in management (as I was still continuing to run Get Low Dance Co., on the side as a part-time business). I was the only coordinator for my region and I had to ensure all my events were covered from the hiring of staff, training, set up, scheduling, equipment distribution then providing closing reports of results from events. It was very demanding and stressful at times. Yet, I extrapolated the wisdom from working in this corporation and applied it to my own business. I now had real life experience of how a large corporation was run professionally. I paid a great deal of attention to how it handles employees, infrastructure, clientele, and team management. I gained great business knowledge and experiences that I would not have been able to gain if I went directly into running my business full-time directly from school.

All of these lessons were tested when I was let go from my job. It was devastating.

A physic reader once told me, "Bumps in the road come when you fall off your track to your destiny."

Even though I thought this was where my career should be –it's not what I truly wanted to be doing. Of course it isn't easy saying goodbye to notions of a new career. But, my entrepreneurial family always told me, *"Working for someone else...you can only go so far."*

I wanted to set my own hours and do what I love to do. When you work for yourself, the opportunities are endless! Plus all your failures and successes are yours to own alone. Whether it flops or thrives, it's all on your own shoulders. Some people may find this frightening, but not me! My best friend always told me she had no idea how I do what I do and that she would live in anxiety if she had my life. The flame in my mind had been rekindled with the loss of my marketing position, and I was ready to push my company and modeling career to new frontiers.

With more free time on my hands now, I took Get Low Dance Company to the next level. With the new knowledge of how to handle employees, I was ready to recruit a few of my own! It was such an exciting moment for my business and me. Up until now I had been running the whole business solo. Taking on new dancers would really open new portals and opportunities for my company to new heights. Luck seemed to finally be back on my side as I met four incredible dancers during my first round of hiring. With my new dance instructors, Get Low Dance Co. was ready to teach summer programs full-time. Plus with a little extra push from my marketing skills, I really got the ball rolling; so much that I was beginning to consider more than just a summer program. My company now had the potential to run year round and take on more challenging clients and venues. With the advent of new dance instructors, Get Low Dance Co. was becoming more self-sufficient. It was reaching further into numerous communities and attracting a wealth of diverse children from low-income regions. Yet, even with the growing popularity of my business, I still did not want to put all of my eggs all in one basket. As I've demonstrated already, I like keeping myself busy. Even if it means I end up taking on too much at a time; I'd rather be too busy than not busy enough! That's why I started modeling for jobs promoting various products, supported research projects, paid photo-shoots, and more. Daily I would be on the Internet bringing awareness of myself, my business and reaching out to partners in the industry. I found by continuing to work with other companies I was able to learn from them and apply my skills and knowledge gained toward my own company.

Going back into the industry as a freelancer model can be very risky, as you will get a lot of people who want to take advantage of you and exploit you. You never know someone's intentions, another lesson I had to internalize. Going out there on your own can expose you to unexpected and dangerous situations, so it became crucial for me to be smart about my choices. Occasionally I would run into unprofessional clients who would try to convince me to do exotic work for extra money. When out of work, it may seem very tempting, but I steered clear from anything that didn't feel right, as I knew it could hinder my career in the future.

After awhile, I was not achieving what I hoped to on my own in the modeling world, so I went back to look for a new agency to represent me. I was 22 years old, and quickly was rejected by well-known agencies such as Ford and Next and Elite, for being too old, curvy and not meeting their standards, but I did not give up there. After several rejections from top agents, I found my current agency, who accepted my curvy girl, next-door-neighbour look. But I still wanted to push for a new horizon. I wanted to challenge myself into a different world of modeling: pageantry. So I entered my first pageant, Miss Canada Tourism 2011. I thought, "Why not give this a try and see what happens!"

After preparing for several months and working very hard, to my surprise, I won my first competition, and once again new doors were opening for me. I was asked to participate in charity events such as Camp Jamoke, Carivaughan, Canada day Parade, Special Olympics Toronto, Light of Night Marathon, and many more.

It was an amazing experience to take part in a cause, and to learn about the many other organizations that give back to the community. Learning how they spread the word of their cause and seeing how many lives they touch by their fundraisers. My experience with other organizations brought me back to see exactly why I started Get Low Dance Co. To give back to the children and bring the passion of dance into lives to those who may not be able to afford the costly studio prices. While volunteering at these events, I worked with children, adults and families with disabilities and illnesses that changed their lives, but were still living life to their fullest. Watching them enjoy themselves at these events, learning about their successes and having them tell me how thankful they are to have me there, made it a true honour to meet them. These moments will always stay dear to my heart.

My pageant director, Karen, always told me, "Though you may not think volunteering at these events are beneficial, you never know what opportunities will come your way. Plus you never know what kind of people you will meet."

That has always stuck with me, and really taught me to appreciate the small things in life. From winning this title, it led me to an opportunity to travel to Thailand to represent Canada in "Miss Tourism World Pageant" where I met 60 wonderful girls from around the world who I still stay connected with. My crowning moment was winning Best National Costume. I was then asked to represent Canada in Ecuador the following year in the "Miss United Continents Pageant" followed by "Miss Tourism International 2014" in Shenzhen, China. Though, internationally, I was not the overall winner, I was able to network with fifty plus countries each trip, gain new experiences, obtain a complimentary trip to foreign countries (I would of never have had the opportunity to do otherwise), and challenge myself to new heights and learn new cultures. One opportunity after another! Which constantly reinforced the lessons I had learned over the years: when one barrier comes up and you think you are about to fail, another barrier falls and provides the opportunity to succeed. You just have to keep positive and your mind open so as not to miss the chance.

At this point in my life, I felt I could only make success in one field at a time. When I put my energy into the business, it hit new heights. When I was given the freedom to pursue modeling full time, I did very well for myself. Yet it seemed I could only cause one facet of my life to thrive at a time. Despite Get Low Dance Co. becoming more self-sufficient, it reached a threshold. My dance instructors were doing their jobs adequately, but without a true leader at the helm, an idea can only go so far on its own merit. Because I tried to let the business run itself, I began falling away from dance. It wasn't something I ever wanted to fall away from! Especially since it helped change my life. I had to make the honest choice of which career I wanted to pursue. And once I made that choice, I would devote myself 110%, no regrets, and no looking back. My final choice fell to dance. Yet I was aware of the threshold my company faced, and to continue forward I needed a little extra help. I simply couldn't do it alone. I needed at least one other person who had effective knowledge on how to run a business.

It wasn't too long before I came across a company looking for dancer performers. This is when I met with the owner (another entrepreneur, and soon to be my future partner). She was so positive and powerful in all of her thoughts; I thought she was the one who could make my business and myself grow. She was intrigued by my business. In fact, she was so intrigued that the possibilities of combining our companies quickly became a serious consideration. Our verbal partnership blossomed within a very short time and I had at last found a reliable source to count on, so I thought. She brought a lot of knowledge and resources to the table, but so did I. Rather than butting heads, we synergized our talents and used them to build a powerful company. I quickly took the role of executive director of her company and on the Board of Directors of a Not For Profit company in which we created together. I was able to thrive on my passion full-time as an entrepreneur and performer, yet I had set Get Low Dance Company aside.

I thought I finally was on track with my dream –which soon became a reality. Yet, this was too good to be true. After two years of successfully working hand in hand with my new partner, I began to believe we had a life long partnership, and she reassured me every step of the way. At that time we never ran into any conflict and both handled our departments. After another year went by our responsibilities became uneven and I was handling all of the business to the point that she would be unreachable, while she moved towards a different career direction. In good faith, I believed we were on the same page, yet I quickly began to feel taken advantage of and abused. My entire life was dedicated to the good of her company and I had forgotten all about Get Low Dance Co. When feelings were laid out on the table, I was laid off of her company, any talks of partnership was dismissed and many investments I personally put into her company would never be seen again.

I quickly learned, when it comes to business, you must be extremely careful with who you put your trust in. It is important to put yourself first before others, ensure proper contracts are set in place and to triple check your Ts are crossed and your Is are dotted. A very hard and costly lesson I had to learn and in the future I will be more careful in my business dealings.

This was a huge turning point in my life; I did not know how I was going to be able to get out of such a tragedy. For several weeks I pitied myself. How could I be so stupid to not see this coming? I grew up being very business savvy since a young age, yet I did not realize how vulnerable I made myself to the point I was manipulated and taken advantage of. I had no ambition or drive, as I was back to where I started 4 years ago. Then a childcare centre contacted me, as they had heard about my dance programs for educational facilities and asked me to create a program for their children. This was my door opening to continue to push forward. I brought the focus back onto my true dreams.

I am now fully committed to Get Low Dance Company providing diverse dance programs to low-income regions and bringing dance and fitness into the school boards and childcare centres to reach out to large groups of children. I have also become an ambassador of Operation Smile to spread awareness of their cause through dance. Get Low Dance Co. organizes dance-a-thons across the city to raise awareness and funds. I had auditioned and successfully become a delegate for Miss Universe Canada 2015. Through all of these organizations, I will be able to spread my passion to give back to our younger generation through the arts. I have realized by putting all my eggs in one basket, I was living life for someone else, not me. By spreading my love and passion out through multiple avenues, though it is not for everyone, I am able to live my life to its fullest. Every success story has its trials and tribulations, believe me I had plenty in mine. Yet at the end of the day, I'm very proud of where I am. I truly believe that everyone has a destiny. Yet at a young age, you don't know what you want, and therefore you want to do it all. I for instance have been told in the past that I do "way too much". However that's just because I can't stand the idea of missing an opportunity! I was a "yes" person, and luckily I was granted the ability to dabble in many different fields at a young age.

This allowed me to remove restrictions and experience everything I desired to try. Though you may not think of it at the time, each experience builds you to be a strong individual, especially through the hard times. You need these experiences to really appreciate what you have. You need to take those chances and be willing to accept failure. For without them you will never know how successful you really could be. Even though doubt and fear tried to restrain me, I just simply never gave up. I always wanted to do more, and I took pride in everything I did. Hard work, passion, conviction, determination, and resilience are the weapons of my personality. I use these tools every day to wage war against laziness and apathy. And I truly believe if I can inspire myself, others may find strength in my story too.

As I've mentioned before, helping people and changing their lives are some of the most rewarding experiences I've ever known. It's the foundation of my life-mission and my company alike. I hope to some day reach the hearts and lives of others worldwide. With my business having a stance that seeks to help people through dance, physical fitness, and healthy living, I know that even greater things await for me over the next horizon. And it's my sincere promise that I won't quit, I won't stop striving, and I won't back down from reaching above and beyond the next step in this amazing journey.

SHAUNESSY SINNETT

My dream was always to dance on stage in front of thousands of people. I loved the idea of performing: the allure of the lights, costumes, music, and applause from an approving audience. Even as a young child, I would dance around the house, and ask my parents, "Is my skirt twirling?"

I knew I wanted to be on stage, but the path to get there involved a strange, enlightening and arduous journey.

I was born and raised in Goderich, a small town in rural Ontario. Here, as limited as the opportunities were, my supportive parents were sure to expose my sister and I to the arts. As children, we studied dance, drama, and music. We didn't study in world-class conservatories, we studied in the basement of the Legion, or in the public school gymnasium; wherever the lessons were available.

My first gymnastics class was at age three, and ballet at age four. I fell in love with performing at one of my first ballet recitals. I had a solo in the show, and I will never forget waiting anxiously backstage.

When I stepped on stage, my heart fluttered, and I felt buoyant. There was something unearthly about being in front of that audience; I felt hundreds of eyes focused on me, but I saw only the glare of bright lights from above me. I felt as though I was watching myself in my little tutu and tiara, pirouetting under spotlights. I was in love with every second I spent on that stage.

I continued training in ballet, and when I turned seven, my sister and I enrolled in Irish dance lessons. We quickly became interested in the world beyond recreational dance. We competed locally, and after a few years, we drove 1.5 hours from Goderich to London, Ontario for more advanced lessons.

Balancing an active school life, Irish dance lessons, ballet, and our new endeavours of competitive jazz, hip hop, and acro-gymnastics was never easy. We'd finish school at 3:15pm, quickly attempt a bit of the day's homework, then load ourselves, and a lunch bag into the car. Mom would drive us to dance and our routine continued for nearly six years.

My competitive dance career began to flourish in 2007. I joined the Corrigan School of Irish Dance, and Nora, my new teacher, was very inspiring. She was a former *Riverdance* principal dancer, and she had a great understanding of how the competitive Irish Dance World worked. She was willing to dedicate the time needed to help me succeed. I was sixteen at the time, and I didn't believe that receiving a medal at the Canadian Championships was even possible. Nora made things sound so simple. She would say, "You can do anything you want if you work hard to achieve your goals, and believe in yourself," and "You're just as good as anybody out there, if not better."

Before this, I believed there was something special about the girls who achieved medals. I believed it wasn't for *regular* people like me. The truth is, everyone out there is *regular*. The medals are for the girls who work incredibly hard, and dream big.

Together, Nora and I worked on new dances for local competitions, and she helped me set goals for myself for the Canadian Championships. I'd dance several hours a week in class, and then practice independently each day, too. Over the next two years, I attended the annual Canadian Championships, where I placed 15th, then 10th.

In my third year, I waited anxiously as an announcer called the top six dancers by number. I was number 114, and was called into the top 6 places. I knew, then, that if my number was not called next, I would have achieved my goal of placing in the top 5.

"In sixth place," he started, "is competitor number 113."

I smiled and gave a sigh of relief as the audience clapped for the top five. He called the next two places, and I was still left standing.

I knew I was in the top three.

I remember my body going a bit numb, and my heart was racing. I hoped he wouldn't call my number until announcing first place.

"In third place: competitor 114, Shaunessy Sinnett from the Corrigan School of Irish Dance."

I was disappointed for a split second; I thought I miraculously won the entire competition! As I walked up to collect my trophy and sash, I realized what I had accomplished, and I was grinning wide. I proudly stepped to the third place spot on the podium.

I'll never forget that moment. I was walking up the same podium that I had once believed was an exclusive podium for a special type of dancer. Now, *I* was that special kind of dancer. I was the one who works hard for what she wants, the one who relentlessly pursues perfection, and the one who doesn't give up on a goal or a dream.

It was only through Nora's encouragement and coaching, my family's support, and hundreds of hours of hard work that I was able to achieve my goal of ranking among the top 5. At eighteen years old, I had learned a lot about how to win and lose, and most importantly, how to persevere.

After the Canadian Championships, I competed in Glasgow in 2010, and received a medal at the World Championships of Irish Dance. With this accomplishment, I felt that I was closer than ever to beginning a professional Irish dance career. Now I was faced with a serious quandary. While I was passionate about my dance and my artistic activities, I never allowed them to interfere with my academic studies. I graduated second in my class in 2010. Although I was performing well academically, I gave my future much consideration, and I chose the road less traveled.

I deferred my acceptance at the University of Western Ontario and pursued a career in dance. Originally, I thought my only option would be to join the *Riverdance* tour for a few years before retiring and focusing on my University studies. But spaces in *Riverdance* were extremely limited, and even after flying myself to Dublin for the audition, I wasn't guaranteed a spot in the show right away. I emailed what felt like hundreds of other dance shows. I only got a few replies, but that's all I needed.

I was flying myself around the world on a bi-weekly basis to audition for shows. When I wasn't auditioning, I was working long hours at home to pay off the expense of the flights. I was in England and Ireland on four separate trips over three months. I was always anxious, nervous, and full of self-doubt at auditions. It never gets easier. You're always vulnerable. You give everything you have, and then a panel of stern-looking strangers judge you.

Finally, I was placed on a tour in Dubai. This was my first taste of a dance tour, and I loved performing in the evening, sightseeing during the day, and meeting people from different backgrounds. I enjoyed the experience so much that I knew it wouldn't be my last tour!

Next, was a three-month tour of Canada and the USA. During our first week of rehearsals, things went smoothly. We practiced during the days, ate meals together in our temporary home in the evenings, and even managed a few evenings out to hockey games. Two weeks later, though, our situation worsened.

The evening of our first preview show, we were backstage when a few police officers showed up at the venue looking for the person in charge. After speaking to the police, Brian, our choreographer and dance captain, told us in his thick Northern Irish Accent, "There's been a fire at the house. There's $50,000 worth of damage. All I know is that we can't get in until tomorrow."

A bit of panic struck the room. No one knew the extent of the damage, if any of our belongings were safe, whether the whole house was still standing, or whether it was burnt to the ground. We had no other information. It was only ten minutes until the show started, and, well, you know what they say, "The show must go on."

So the band entered, the curtains rose, the show started, and we danced as if nothing had happened.

It wasn't until the next day that we were allowed back into the house to collect whatever belongings we had left. Luckily, my room was quite a distance from the fire, and despite everything being covered in ash and soot from the smoke, I still had most of my belongings. Two days, and about 21 loads of laundry later, we left on a flaming start to the tour.

Things only went downhill from there.

On our first weekend, we traveled 14 hours overnight on a refurbished school bus with a broken heater in -15°C temperature from Ontario to Connecticut. Subsequently, some of the cast fell ill with colds and flus. After performing on the east coast, the bus broke down in Fredericton, New Brunswick on our way back to Ontario. We were delayed almost 10 hours.

The next week, the company manager told us that would have to accept a pay cut for the tour to continue, and that the catering provided for the performers would no longer be an option. Halfheartedly, we accepted the pay cut, and continued to Michigan for the next part of the tour. Because of work permit issues, some of the European performers we not allowed into the USA. The rest of us pressed on, and did a few shows trying to cover for empty spaces in choreography, as well as a shortage of instruments in the band.

Our bus broke down week after week, in Illinois, Wisconsin, Minnesota, until our final destination: Sherwood Park. We never made it. About 60km outside of Edmonton - you guessed it - the bus broke down. That was the end.

Our manager told us there was no money left in the budget to fix the bus again. So the next day, we were all put on flights back home, and with that, the tour finished as abruptly as it had started.

You'd call me crazy for not giving up on professional Irish dance after that experience. There were days when I wanted to give up entirely. But, there was some part of me that wanted to continue, and strive for something better. I knew I could succeed in a show as famous as *Riverdance*, and that thought was enough to help me endure any challenge that would come.

My next tour was in Germany, England, Scotland, and Ireland. It was a fantastic opportunity to see Europe. That's what I have to remind myself because I worked for over 2 months and I didn't get a single paycheck. No one did. The company went bankrupt, and we were left to purchase our own flights home.

I don't know if I believe in destiny, but something was at work in the late summer of 2010. I was flying to Dublin for a rehearsal. I started to chat with the woman beside me, Jamie, and I learned that she was heading to Ireland too. I told her that I was traveling for a professional Irish dance show rehearsal, and I talked a bit about my previous auditions. I remember her staying quite silent, and smiling at me, until I asked why she was traveling. Jamie smiled again.

"I work as a producer at PBS, and I'm traveling to Ireland because I'm producing an Irish music and dance show for the network. I know they just hired a new dancer, but I think you'd be a good fit for the show."

I couldn't believe it. My eyes were wide, and I think my jaw dropped in disbelief. What were the chances that I'd be sitting next to her? Or even the chances that we'd speak about our careers? She showed me some clips of the show that had been filmed for PBS. It was called *Celtic Crossroads*. It was brilliant. It was a smart mix of traditional Irish music and dance fused with bluegrass, gypsy, classical, and jazz sounds. I loved the idea of the show!

Jamie gave me her business card, and I gave her my name, phone number, and email address on the back of a duty-free receipt. (I was just starting out, after all, and I didn't have a business card!) She told me she would get in contact with the director of the show, and send along my details.

Sure enough, the director contacted me. It wasn't until the very end of the European tour in 2011 (the one I unintentionally did for free) that he sent me a formal offer and contract for a position in the show for Spring 2012. It was the best contract I had ever signed.

I joined *Celtic Crossroads* as the youngest cast member in February. With a small, but fantastic group of dancers, and six outrageously talented musicians, I performed in nearly 40 states in the USA within three months. I was part of the show's PBS Television Special, and Universal Music's release of *Celtic Crossroads*. I couldn't have asked for a better experience. The people were great. The management was great. And they brought me back for two subsequent tours in 2012 and Spring 2013.

By this time, I had almost forgotten about *Riverdance*. It was still a dream of mine, but I was so busy with *Celtic Crossroads*. I figured *Riverdance* was winding down and didn't have much work for me.

In March 2013, Charlene, another female dancer in *Celtic Crossroads*, showed me a video advertisement for *Riverdance*'s new show, *Heartbeat of Home.* It was a fusion of Latin dance, flamenco, afro-Cuban, and Irish dance. It was *Riverdance* for a new generation. The video was calling for online dance auditions to be submitted. I watched it a few times. I researched the show on their website. I was waiting backstage during the intermission of a *Celtic Crossroads* show when I said to Charlene, "This is what I'm going to do next. I'm going to be in *Riverdance*'s new show."

Over the next week, I spent time choreographing for an online audition video. The videos were to be submitted and then voted on by the public. The 10 dancers with the most votes on their video submission would be invited to audition in Dublin. Charlene helped me film my audition video, and I submitted it on the second day the voting began.

The good people of Goderich campaigned for me. They shared the voting link on Facebook and Twitter, the town newspaper wrote a story about the competition, and I even went on the local radio station to talk about *Heartbeat of Home*. After a few tense weeks, I ended up second place in the voting competition. I was on my way to audition in Dublin!

We did a whole morning of press interviews, photos, filming, and then finished off the weekend in the studio learning choreography and performing our prepared dances.

Two weeks went by, and on a Friday evening, I returned from dinner to find a missed call on my phone. The same happened on Sunday. I suspected these were the audition results, as it was just over two weeks since I'd left Dublin. The next day, I was on my way to work, and my phone rang. It was the assistant director of *Heartbeat of Home*.

"You're a hard person to get a hold of," he said.

My heart skipped a beat as he began to talk about the auditions. "We want to thank you for taking the time to submit a video, and for auditioning in Dublin. It was very difficult for the creative team to cast the show. I'm sure you understand."

Every word he said was drowned out by the sound of my own heart beating. I knew that this news could mean eight months work with my dream company or missing out on the opportunity entirely. I was so anxious.

"At this time, we are in a position to offer you a full contract with *Heartbeat of Home*."

I said nothing. For almost a minute, I was entirely speechless. All I could come up with was, "Are you joking?"

"No, I'm not joking. We're offering you the contract," he said.

I was ecstatic! I was so proud to begin the journey as an inaugural cast member of *Heartbeat of Home* performing in its world premiere in Dublin, and touring Beijing, Shanghai, Toronto, Chicago, Detroit, and Boston over the year. The show is more fast-paced, dynamic, and multicultural compared to *Riverdance*, but I still had my heart set on being part of the original Irish dance show.

Only a couple of months after touring with *Heartbeat of Home*, I received an important e-mail. I had waited for that e-mail for three years. I had visualized for so long what it would be like to read it, and there it was in my inbox on a lazy Tuesday morning. It was an offer to tour with *Riverdance*! My dream job!

I danced my first week of *Riverdance* shows in Dublin. The rehearsal process was physically and mentally exhausting. We had just four days to learn the whole show before performing live, so we rehearsed full-time during the day, and practiced again at night. It was grueling, overwhelming, and exciting all at once.

While performing with *Riverdance*, I felt the same spark I had felt during my first ballet solo 13 years prior. There was a likeness in my nervousness, and in my sheer delight. Since that day, I have enjoyed touring the world with *Riverdance*, and the young, innocent, and impressionable Shaunessy that once dreamed of being on stage has been beaming from the inside, out.

Somehow, I'm a bit more proud of being in *Riverdance* now because it took me three years, and several trips around the world to get here. Sure, I would have loved the opportunity to join straight after my audition. But it would have been too easy. I had to endure long hours of rehearsals, sore legs, blisters, bruises, exhaustion, mistreatment, dishonesty, and pay cuts. But that's what makes me proud. I overcame these obstacles and I have such an appreciation for my experiences in dance because they've taught me important lessons about independence, discipline, trust and perspective. I've learned so much on my journey to becoming a *Riverdance* cast member, and I've grown as a dancer, a performer and as a person along the way. My story is certainly one about perseverance, and one of my greatest ambitions is to have the opportunity to share the lessons I've learned with young dancers.

I spend a lot of my time in between tours tutoring and teaching young performers. I began in the studio assisting my Irish dance teacher, but now I teach workshops in other styles of dance too. I love choreographing for children. It's a challenge to incorporate basic dance techniques with the music the students enjoy, all while promoting elements of fun, creativity and fitness. Teaching dance can be chaotic; it's as high energy as a Phys-Ed class, combined with loud music and leotards. But it is so rewarding to see students progress.

I'm always proud when my workshop students ask to show their parents a new gymnastics trick they've perfected, or when they practice and perform their choreography with classmates outside of lessons. It feels very natural that I share bits of my dance experience with a younger generation of dancers. You never know where the next Fred Astaire or Ginger Rodgers could come from! I hope one day to be able to offer more workshops in my hometown, and give the young dancers of Goderich the opportunities I never had as a child.

I've volunteered in local elementary schools teaching dance workshops as part of the Physical Education curriculum. It's gratifying to reach out to students who wouldn't normally have the opportunity to take dance lessons. This is important to me because everyone can do it! Dance, integrally, isn't about cheesy performances, costumes, lights, or makeup. Dance is a reflection of life. It's moving art, and it's a way to speak without words.

I hope I can inspire a few young people by sharing my experiences. Whatever your goals, dreams, and ambitions, it's important to realize that you can find ways to achieve them. Go after what you want, even if it seems improbable or impossible. Shooting for the moon sounds cliché, but I'm proof that if you do, you might land among the stars.

Special thanks to Mom and Dad: I owe all of my success to my parents who gave up dozens of Florida holidays for weekends at competitions, expensive dance classes, and time spent driving nine hours a week to and from lessons. I owe you a vacation. (And now you have that promise in writing.)

Natasha Hope Morano
Vice President, Economic Club of Canada,
Founder, Gadfly Academy
The Girl who didn't wear High Heels

Hope. What does it mean? Well for my parents it meant, **h**old **o**n, **p**ain **e**nds, and have faith.

I am the only survivor among four pregnancies and I appreciate the gift of life. My parents honoured me with the name Hope, which I try to live up to. I am their "miracle child."

I knew from an early age that I was a little different from my peers. I would always try to look at the glass as half full as opposed to half empty and dwell on the positive. I have difficulty separating myself from wearing the pain of others and taking on their burdens. I am an empath and truly appreciate learning about people and the stories that reveal who they are.

I was born on October 3rd, 1985. My parents still reminisce about the drive home from Toronto General Hospital. Majestic coloured trees lined the roads home, as my parents carefully navigated through traffic with their precious baby girl. I grew up with Barbies, horses, and spent as much time outside as possible. My grandfather played a large role in my upbringing. He was a modern day philosopher. He taught me the importance of critical thinking, which has become one of my most treasured attributes.

My teenage years were filled with horses, and long hours at the stable. My best friend and I would spend any spare moments at the barn, while a lot of my peers would be at malls and movie theatres. Upon horseback, everything else in the world would fade; and I would get lost in the beauty of the moment. It was a spiritual connection.

My mom quit her career in social work to give me her full attention. She imparted her wisdom and equipped me with the skills for life. She is my mentor, best friend, and guardian angel. She taught me to live everyday like it's my last, take nothing for granted, and treat pauper or prince with the same respect.

My dad is my warrior, my buddy, and mentor. He looked death in the eye and defeated it. Throughout his illness, I had to hope- live it, breathe it and believe it.

Watching my father suffer in a hospital bed for over a month through hospital neglect, helped shape me into who I am today. You may ask, who am I? Yesteryear, I was an eternal optimist always trying to find the positive in people, making them comfortable and avoiding conflict. I would often sacrifice my own needs and wouldn't stand up for myself, as it was peace at all costs. I am a changed person today.

After the episode with my father, I was catapulted into action. I learned how to constructively apply empathy by becoming an advocate for what is morally and ethically expected in health care and society at large. Morality dictates my behaviour and it is this inner fortitude, which has and continues to stand me in good stead.

The first twenty-three years of my life was wholesome and positive. I was fortunate enough to be spared from the dark side of humanity as I was never actually bullied or victimized. And by today's standards, this is rare. I moved out for university when I was 17 and never returned. I completed an undergraduate degree in Political Science, English, and Philosophy with my end goal to become a teacher.

I then went on to complete a Masters in Political Science. I assisted teaching a first year political science course as part of my Master's Degree and learned first-hand that youth lack the basic skills needed for the workforce. This subconsciously was the beginning of what would be called the Gadfly Academy. The ingredients for what is to be my greatest achievement began to sift about in my head.

Now bear in mind, in my earlier years, I was always a very shy, timid girl. In high school, undergrad and grad school I would sink down in my chair in fear that I'd be asked a question. I cannot begin to tell you the anxiety I felt just thinking about having to speak in public and being the centre of attention.

I had a serious lack of confidence. I have been 5'12" (I don't say 6 feet) since the age of 14. I was always taller than teachers, boys, and well, pretty much the entire population. Prom shopping was a nightmare. While my friends bought stilettos; I bought flip-flops to wear under my dress, so no one would know my actual height.

I was always the first to be noticed and could never quite blend in. I never told my family just how uncomfortable I was. I just tried to suck it up and no one truly knew the awkwardness I faced. Whenever out in public, whether it was a mall or movie theatre, I was highly conscientious- I stood out like a sore thumb. It was only upon my horse's back where, I was truly comfortable in my own skin, as no one knew how tall I really was.

Intellectually, I grew into my own skin during my final semester of my graduate studies. I became more confident. My intellectual capabilities and potential were actualized. Defending particular hypotheses regarding an international relations paradigm equipped me with a new external confidence, which later morphed into a full "all encompassing confidence."

Once I finished grad school, I ventured out to into the real world and hoped I would find something that nurtured all of my interests and talents. I was into research, political affairs and teaching. Who actually finds the perfect first job right out of school? Well I did. I began an internship at Queens Park, as I wanted to gather practical political experience. The days were long, and the trips tedious on buses and trains to Toronto.

However, it eventually paid off, as I found myself in the right place, at the right time and met a contact who told me about The Economic Club of Canada. I was captivated by this company and had to learn more. Through this contact, he set up a meeting for me with the President and CEO of the ECC. Days later, I met with him and spent an afternoon discussing political affairs. Before I knew it, I was hired as Director of Research and Innovation at the ECC.

Life was perfect; I was working in Toronto and contributing to something that I believed in. The ethos of the ECC is to provide a platform for the most prominent and influential world leaders to break news, and in turn spark discussions with Canada's business community regarding important public policy issues. With the fragmented and biased news aggregators in Canada, the ECC's business model struck a chord- I had to be part of this! Sign me up!!!

Only one month into my gig, my world crashed down, and I almost lost my father. For one torturous month he was in the hospital, in and out of isolation, and the Intensive Care Unit. I cannot begin to express the emotional rollercoaster my mom and I went on. An accident took him in the hospital, neglect kept him in, and it ultimately caused him the battle for his life.

Experiencing the underbelly of the health care system, lack of critical thinking and compassion caused more ingredients to come off the shelf and mix into my master recipe– Gadfly Academy.

My dad had to be transferred to another hospital because of the lack of resources available. The juxtaposition of the two hospitals was polar opposites. The rural hospital in Richmond Hill was completely inept, the teaching hospital in Toronto, was so advanced they saved my dad. How is it possible that one's geographical location dictates the quality of health care one receives? This is a sad reality.

My dad slowly began to recover and a sense of normalcy returned. Lady Luck was on my side, as within a few short months of working at the Economic Club, I was named Executive Director. My political science background and research skills contributed to my promotion. I was noticing my prompt ability to critically analyze the news and then secure the big influences of these stories to speak at our podium. It wasn't an easy journey, proving myself at work, while being preoccupied with my dad's health- a fine juggling act.

I always try to keep a composed exterior although inside, I am a mess trying to calm the internal storm. My grandfather taught me this; have faith in yourself, you can do it! Stiff upper lip, chin up, and all that jazz. Well I guess it worked, I was able to establish myself at work and pour my energy into educating my audiences regarding the most important issues of the day.

Through my role at the Economic Club, I was able to raise awareness and expose the lack of quality health care. It became my therapy, my mission, in coping with what had happened to my dad. I organized a panel with Canada's most prominent health experts discussing the state of Canada's health care system. Within a few months, at the age of 26, I was handpicked to open the first satellite office for the ECC and move to our nation's capital, Ottawa.

I knew only one person there. I left a boyfriend, my family, and entire network behind. I knew it was the right decision and I haven't looked back since. I have been in Ottawa for three years to date. That move was the beginning of me growing my confidence and becoming the businesswoman I am today.

I expanded the Club's reputation and started hosting the who's who of the country. I couldn't be the timid girl scared to speak. I had to eat my fear of public speaking and emanate confidence. The first year of this transition, I will admit was filled with a lot of nail biting and sleepless nights... I couldn't believe the responsibility and carte blanche I was given. Prior to every event, I had to instill an inner confidence by embodying the same mantra I employed during my equestrian days. Do not be a wimp, be strong and do not let the judge, (and in this case, the audience), know your fear. Own it and rock it- this is your life and you are solely in charge.

I still remember my first event, the room was packed, national media everywhere, spotlights a glare. I stepped onto the stage, speaking notes in hand, trying to still the trembling hand holding my remarks. I remember thinking, do people see my sweating brow, shaking limbs, and is my heart pound as visible as it feels? My first words out of my mouth, "Good afternoon ladies and gentlemen," – I remember the big gulp I took after these few words, the lump in my throat was so large, I thought I was going to be sick... The inner voice said, "Natasha get it together, no one knows this is your first time speaking to a large audience, pretend you have been doing this for years."

This worked, as the three pages of notes, turned into two, and then one, and then one word was left to utter. I had developed my own rhythm and was actually beginning to enjoy it.

I cannot begin to tell you the sense of pride and accomplishment I had that evening, as I collected my thoughts and watched the coverage on the evening news. With the passage of time and the frequency of events came a confidence, which ultimately led to that inner voice taking a hiatus. I don't need her anymore. She is now obsolete. Practice does reduce anxiety. However, to say practice makes perfect is a stretch. It doesn't. None of us are perfect, although some of us perhaps strive too hard to be so. The little mistakes we make along the way add to our patina and character. Gradually, that pretence of confidence has been replaced by true outer confidence.

Now, I no longer have to pretend. It's engrained into my entire ethos. I get a thrill every time I take the podium and have morphed into a confident self-assured woman, who stands tall! I have finally embraced my height. This confidence led me to become the Vice President of the ECC at the age of 27. Taking on this responsibility was exhilarating. I was the master of my own destiny.

Gaining the knowledge, accolades, and respect in Ottawa elevated me and I began to examine the serious deficiencies in the world. Inequality amongst youth became a primary focus. I researched different programs available to assist underprivileged children, especially in known lower socio-economic areas in Ontario. I discovered there were less "free" resources available than I thought.

There had to be something I could do.

It hit me like a tsunami. I remembered the book, *Born to Rise* by Dr. Kenny. They say don't judge a book by its cover. I did. The cover displayed was a middle aged blonde woman surrounded by African American children. I instantly was intrigued. It was about a woman's struggle to obtain a Charter School in New York. She opened Harlem Village Academies, schools designed to help underprivileged youth receive a quality education and revolutionize public education. I instantly went into research mode and learned that Ontario does not have a Charter policy in place.

Well, when I truly believe in something, I don't back down. I stand by it entirely. When my head and my heart work in tandem, I am a force to be reckoned with.

I met up with Dr. Kenny in New York City. I felt the passion and love radiate off the walls of *Harlem Village Academies.* It brought tears to my eyes to see the affect of this fairy godmother's genuine desire to help youth in need. She is heroic. After meeting her and learning more about the state of public education in NYC, I saw many parallels in Ontario and wanted to replicate her model north of the border.

The problem in Ontario is that the educational system's big players seem to be opposed to some of the options parents and teachers want. Teachers, parents and children have limited options to pursue fair education. Monopolies that govern Ontario Education are inefficient, lethargic and unresponsive.

There are remarkable success stories of charter schools in Alberta, Florida and New York. The quality of education in these respective locations has risen exponentially. It's time to look at schools as market driven business institutions, where innovation and entrepreneurship are rewarded. When competition is introduced, it stimulates services from surrounding areas, and the threat of parents withdrawing their children becomes a reality.

Teachers benefit from the ability to choose schools. There is a correlation between the degree of choice for teachers, parents and students and how well students perform academically. So why not let teachers have that choice if it can benefit our children?

I needed to learn everything I could about charters in Canada, so I flew to Alberta and met with some of the founders of education reform. I also met with as many education advocates as I could in Ontario. I was a sponge, absorbing every last bit of information I could. I knew I was on the brink of something big.

In partnership with the Society for Quality Education and the Economic Club of Canada, we hosted Jeb Bush, the 43rd Governor of Florida, who is an education reform expert. The educational reforms he implemented in Florida (including choice) was the central theme of his address. This was the message for Ontario's business community. National and International media were present. And, we certainly achieved our goal - get this on Ontarians' radar.

Given the inability to obtain a charter, in the province of Ontario, like in the state of Florida, what could I do to provide underprivileged youth free education and promote choice?

A charity based institution. Yes! That's it!

A charity based independent school funded by Corporate Canada. I knew the partners and members of the ECC, who had already been privy to the Jeb Bush speech, would be interested in this initiative and would want to support me. I am fortunate enough to have a boss who is not only fully supportive and on board with this, but who is also helping me make this dream a reality- thank you RT! Hosting education reform experts and holding roundtables regarding the topic of school choice through the ECC has been a tremendous help in gaining the respect and legitimacy of this project to future partners who will fund my school.

What would I name it? Where would it be? How would I manage this on top of a full time job that is certainly anything but a nine to five?

Well ladies, let me tell you, where there is a will, there is a way. The internal passion and drive give you the extra motivation and energy to make it happen. Balancing this side project and running the ECC in Ottawa is difficult at times, but somehow I manage to figure it out. The time restraints I faced during grad school certainly taught me the importance of time management and I squeeze every second I can into doing something productive. Sometimes sleep is secondary and you just nap when you can. I learned flights are great for writing, you are uninterrupted by emails, texts, calls- the outside world so to speak. I use my time traveling to and fro to collect my thoughts, and put pen to paper.

After meeting with alternative education and private school experts, I discovered I knew nothing at all. I needed to go back to school. I decided to complete the Private School Principles Courses at York University. I completed this in the span of a year, and had to travel back to Toronto to take the courses. Thankfully, they were offered Friday through Sunday, so I didn't miss too much work. I was the only individual coming from a non-educational background, so times, I did feel like a fish out of water. However, the support I received was invaluable, and I am still in touch with some of my peers.

Part of the program was preparing a final project, whether it is a new policy for an existing school, or succession plan. I was the only one preparing a business plan for a school from scratch. I named the school, The Gadfly Academy, after my favourite philosopher, Socrates.

The Gadfly Academy will be a charity-based institution giving hope to children who are not privy to "quality" education. Children enrolled at this school will have exhibited potential that was not maximized under the public system. There is no simple "one size fits all" approach to education at the Academy. The Gadfly Academy is centred upon the goal of ensuring students feel that they can make a difference in their own lives and in the lives of others. I want my students to feel trusted, respected and empowered. They will develop life skills for the future and will be engaged in both social networks as well as real-life experiences. My students will walk through the doors of Gadfly Academy infused with positive energy that will support them at school and at home.

Gifted teachers will be selected based on their ability to grasp the importance of critical thinking as well as their creativity, community involvement, and over-arching knowledge of world issues. GFA teachers need to genuinely believe in changing the discourse of education. There will be no hierarchical structure; students and teachers will work together to create a culture and atmosphere of mutual respect and shared responsibility.

I chose an area my mom used to frequent when in social work- Jane and Finch in Toronto, Ontario. Schools in this corridor of Toronto face many challenges. I hope my Academy serves as the stimuli to raise quality education for all housed within. Quality of education is often dependent upon income. Those in the confines of low- income housing, such as Jane and Finch, need mentors, role-models, and an education system that can nurture their natural talents, push them to the best they can be, and eradicate mediocrity.

The number of children falling through the cracks in the Jane and Finch area is disconcerting. We need to address and resolve a multitude of issues, while realizing education is the ultimate tool for success.

If Gadfly Academy creates competition in this area it will ultimately result in challenging the public education system's current restraints. If my school can ignite hope within even one child, take him off the street, give him an opportunity to be the best he can be, then I have lived up to my name, hope, in all its entirety.

As I write this chapter, I am still in the process of officially opening the doors of Gadfly. I am sure there will be many more challenges in front of me, but I am ready for them. I know this is what I was called to do. I know I am fulfilling my God-given talents. Each Gadfly that comes through my doors of GFA will be given hope.

My advice to young women is to always listen to your gut and know that everyone can make a difference. Everyone has a calling. Don't rush it. When the time is right, all of the pieces will come together and you will do whatever it is you are meant to do.

As you build your personal empire, remember there will always be challenges and bumps along the way. On a personal note, life experience has taught me to be a more selective empath and to be cognizant of those who may try to exploit this gift. Be true to yourself and never let another person try to change who you are. Your ingredients are on the shelf, but only through life's lessons can you prepare the recipe for your destiny. Shake them up, sift them, and make them your own!

Now, at 29, running an office, being responsible for a national company and creating my Gadfly Academy, I can reflect and appreciate all the hiccups in my life. They didn't deter me. They shaped me into the confident, proud 6-foot woman I am today. When I take the podium or walk into a boardroom seeking funding for my school, I own who I am. I'm comfortable with all eyes on me. And guess what? I even rock a heel.